PROGRESS

WITH

GCSE

STRUCTURED QUESTIONS

BIOLOGY

KEITH HIRST

Series editor:
COLIN McCARTY

Hodder & Stoughton

A MEMBER OF THE HODDER HEADLINE GROUP

Orders: please contact Bookpoint Ltd, 39 Milton Park, Abingdon, Oxon OX14 4TD. Telephone: (44) 01235 400414, Fax: (44) 01235 400454. Lines are open from 9.00 - 6.00, Monday to Saturday, with a 24 hour message answering service. Email address: orders@bookpoint.co.uk

British Library Cataloguing in Publication Data
A catalogue record for this title is available from The British Library

ISBN 0 340 72043 3

First published 1998
Impression number   10 9 8 7 6 5 4 3 2 1
Year   2004 2003 2002 2001 2000 1999 1998

Cover photo from Science Photo Library/P. Menzel

Typeset by Multiplex Techniques Ltd, St. Mary Cray, Kent.
Printed in Great Britain for Hodder & Stoughton Educational, a division of Hodder Headline Plc, 338 Euston Road, London NW1 3BH by Hobbs Ltd, Totton, Hampshire.

Contents

Teacher's notes

Introduction

Progress with GCSE Science is a series of three photocopiable packs of structured questions, one for Biology, one for Chemistry and one for Physics.

The structured questions in the three packs, provide complete coverage of Key Stage 4 of the National Curriculum and cover the Double and Single GCSE Science Syllabuses of each Examination Board together with the core part of the separate Science Syllabuses. These questions will help your students to progress and succeed whether the class you are teaching is taking single science, double science or all three sciences at GCSE.

Part of any successful learning requires students to check their progress to confirm what they know of the topic they are studying, to practise answering questions focused on the topic and to find out where their knowledge and understanding is partial or weak so that appropriate action may be taken.

Each pack in this series has been written to help teachers in a number of ways.

- The pack is designed in nine chapters which match the majority of teaching patterns. However, the contents may be customised to suit your own specific requirements, because separate sheets may be individually copied and then used in any order.
- Each chapter gives students practice at answering well constructed questions written by a Chief Examiner.
- Answers to all the questions are provided for you to use when marking, or which may be given to students to illustrate where and how marks are awarded.
- Each chapter starts with two annotated examples of structured questions with a student's answers included and commented upon by a Chief Examiner. These comments are extremely helpful to students as they illustrate how to answer questions properly, and where marks are gained or lost.
- The questions are all entirely new, being written especially for the pack, and have never appeared on any examination paper as far as the examiner is aware.
- The questions are written in an overall style which reflects the structured nature of all GCSE terminal papers and will provide excellent practice for these examinations.

- All the various styles of structured questions are included to ensure that students meet and become familiar with what is required at GCSE. In particular there is ample opportunity for students to practise answers in the form of extended writing, which is now an important element of all GCSE terminal papers.
- Each pack will help to solve a perennial problem..... 'What do I give them for homework?'

The design of GCSE: some background information

Irrespective of whether students take all three separate sciences, double science or single science the GCSE papers are offered in two ways:

a Foundation Tier covering grades C, D, E, F, G;
a Higher Tier covering grades A*, A, B, C, D.

Grades C and D can be obtained by taking either tier of entry.

The questions written to test grades C and D will generally be the same on either tier of paper. This is called the **standard** level of demand.

When the examination papers are constructed, questions are written to provide the correct number of marks to fit the following design:

- Foundation grade only questions (E, F and G) carry about 55% of the total marks on the foundation paper;
- Standard demand grade questions (C and D) carry about 45% of the total marks on both the foundation and higher papers;
- Higher grade only questions (A*, A and B) carry about 55% of the total marks on the higher paper.

To make sure that the papers are fairly balanced in terms of difficulty and that all boards make the same demands of candidates, all GCSE Chief and Principal Examiners work to the same code of practice. The Qualifications and Curriculum Authority (QCA) has been involved in developing this code of practice with representatives from the Examinations Boards over a number of years, in particular, as the latest set of syllabuses have been developed.

The Double and Single Science Syllabuses of each examination board are very similar in content but each board has designed its presentation differently. Keith Hirst the author of this pack, has studied all the Syllabuses and the National Curriculum for Key Stage 4, and brought together the topics in ways that will match most teaching schemes. This has been done to try to ensure that questions are there:

- to support teachers;
- to help students recognise both what they do and do not know at all stages in their learning;
- to encourage students to acquire good examination practice and techniques from the very start, so that they may be best prepared when it comes to the actual GCSE examinations.

The importance of structured questions

The terminal examination of every GCSE (both modular and linear) is composed of sets of structured questions. It is therefore important that students meet and practise answering these types of question at all stages in their GCSE course. This is particularly so with Modular Science courses which only employ multiple choice questions as end of module tests. Here students may miss opportunities to practise the structured question style of testing until too late in the course to help them become familiar with its demands.

It has become quite evident that many students fail to gain more than one of the available marks on questions which carry two, three or more marks. One cause of this may be that they are unaware of the need to give full answers rather than just 'one liners'. By using these questions regularly at all stages of the GCSE course, and understanding the marking scheme requirements, students should become much more familiar with what is required to earn all of the available marks. It is important that they do not miss opportunities to gain credit for their knowledge by either casualness or brevity of answer.

A distinct weakness of multiple choice questions, which test the coverage of syllabuses very well, is that they cannot test students' communication skills, nor do they test their ability to explore an idea fully or argue out a reason or explanation. The present GCSE examinations are placing a greater emphasis on this aspect of communicating learning and understanding, so it is important that students are fully prepared to handle questions which require more in-depth answers. The questions in this series have been designed to help students answer structured questions and thereby both improve their learning and understanding of science and develop their skills at answering questions fully to gain all the available marks.

Each question in this pack has been written by an experienced GCSE Chief Examiner for Biology and all of them have then been carefully edited by a Chief Examiner for Modular Science. The writing and editing has been undertaken using the common guidelines all Chief and Principal Examiners are working within when they prepare the actual papers. This ensures that the different parts of these structured questions carry similar mark allocations to those found on GCSE papers.

Besides writing the papers and marking schemes for the Examination Boards, Chief and Principal Examiners are in charge of the marking process. They also are members of the awarding committee which makes the decisions about the overall number of marks needed to obtain each grade. As such, these questions have been developed by people who know what is required and can only be of considerable help to students who wish to succeed.

The questions in this series of packs have been brought together in nine chapters which cover the major topics in GCSE Biology. Each chapter covers all the different aspects of the topic with questions of varying degrees of difficulty, in general provided in progressive order of difficulty within a chapter. Some will be ideal for students when they first meet the topic; others will be more suitable when much of the topic has been covered; some may be saved for revision purposes towards the end of the course. A detailed breakdown of the level of demand of every part of each question is given at the beginning of each chapter, relating the demand to the different tiers of papers at GCSE. This is available to help you choose the appropriate questions for your students.

These structured questions, like those in the actual GCSE examinations, are designed to stretch students. They will:

- test their ability to recall facts;
- ensure they use their scientific knowledge and build answers which explain the specific point that is being asked for;
- ask students to apply their knowledge and understanding to new or unfamiliar situations.

The more your students answer questions and read the mark schemes, the more they will learn to read the question carefully and make sure that the answer matches what is required. Equally, the more questions they do, the better practised they become at giving full and complete answers. This is where the exemplar material at the beginning of each chapter should complement your work as a teacher by reinforcing good practice and illustrating how marks may easily be lost by poor examination technique.

If your students can do all the questions, getting most of the marks, then there will be very little in the GCSE examination which will baffle them. You and they can feel confident about obtaining a top grade. Equally, less strong students who do not always succeed will benefit enormously by the practice they get when answering the questions and examining the mark schemes.

The structure of the pack and its key features

Format of pack

In this pack there are nine chapters. Each chapter has a number of important features:

- A teacher summary sheet. This contains a complete list of all the questions and their parts, showing the level of demand of each part and the skills tested. It also provides a useful contents page for you.
- A student summary sheet. This provides a checklist of syllabus coverage and also provides students with a valuable progress chart and the opportunity for self evaluation.
- At the beginning of each chapter are two worked examples. They have annotations accompanying them, written by a Chief Examiner.
- The structured questions give complete coverage of the topic.
- Each question has a brief, but appropriate, title for ease of cross reference.

In addition, there are teachers' notes and students' handouts, and at the end of the pack there are clear mark schemes for all the structured questions in each chapter which can be used by the teacher or given out to students (cutting as shown so answer sheets go with appropriate question sheets).

The teacher summary sheet

The contents list gives the title and content of each question, information about the level of demand of each part and which skill is being tested. The following is an example taken from the biology pack where F is Foundation level, S is Standard level and H is Higher level.

QUESTION	TITLE & CONTENT	LEVEL	SKILLS TESTED
1	**Measuring pulse rate**		
(a)	Grouping pulse rate	F	Data handling
(b)	Constructing a bar chart of pulse rates	F	Graph construction
(c)	Differences in pulse rates	S	Understanding

Levels of demand of questions

Each chapter in the pack has questions which have been designed to match the demands of GCSE. They will be either a Foundation Tier question or a Higher Tier question. In general the Foundation Tier questions come first in each chapter. Collecting together the topics in this way has allowed questions to be written around the types of contexts which will regularly appear on the actual papers in GCSE. The particular demand level of each part of a question, foundation, standard or higher, is shown in the teachers' summary sheet at the beginning of each chapter (see above).

Students' checklist

At the beginning of each chapter is a summary sheet of key points in the chapter. These have been established by the author checking the contents of each Examination Board's Syllabus as well as referring to the National Curriculum for Key Stage 4.

Alongside each point is a self evaluation checklist for students to use, either at the end of a topic or when they are revising for their GCSE examination.

Worked examples

There are two example questions with answers to start each chapter. These show the sorts of answers which candidates make, accompanied by a Chief Examiner's comments on these answers. Some of the answers are completely correct, others are only partly correct and sometimes there are wrong answers. It is important that students read the comments carefully because they explain how to make sure the students obtain all the marks available and do not lose marks by silly slips, casualness or poor examination technique.

Spelling and punctuation in these answers are usually correct. However, it is a major concern of examiners that many candidates' answers are very poorly presented in terms of spelling, sentence construction and clarity of meaning. The Chief Examiner's comments will often focus on this last point.

Students taking examinations need to remember that merely implying that they know an answer is not good enough; a nod and a wink cannot be understood by someone miles away a week after the examination has taken place. Unless answers are written clearly and unambiguously there is always a chance of the marker misinterpreting what has been written, reading it in the wrong way and giving no credit.

The first worked example is almost always a mixture of foundation and standard demand parts and would be expected to be found on a Foundation Tier paper. The second worked example usually starts with standard demand parts, but contains a lot of higher demand material. It would only be found on a Higher Tier paper and will often contain an example of a longer answer which requires the student to describe or explain something through extended writing.

Extended writing questions

Questions which require a number of sentences for a full answer are found on both Foundation and Higher Tier GCSE papers and each paper is designed with about 25% of the marks allocated for these types of answers.

Extended writing questions require more than a word or phrase as an answer, but probably not more than a few sentences. However these sentences must fully address the question, link cause and effect and show a flow of logic. This is the area where many students fail to gain marks because they do not give sufficient detail in their answers. How to approach extended writing is fully covered in the student handouts (see page ix).

AN INTRODUCTION TO STRUCTURED QUESTIONS

Your GCSE examination papers test a balance of three main skills through structured questions. These are questions which have a number of parts and are based around a particular topic. Some parts will require just one word for an answer, others will require you to write in some detail. The information which follows will help you know how to answer each part of a structured question.

The three main skills are:

- **To recall** or remember facts or information.
    - *e.g. What is the symbol for sodium?*
- **To understand** or use facts and information and your knowledge to explain an answer.
    - *e.g. Why does the amount of carbon dioxide around a plant increase at night?*
- **To apply** or take information and your knowledge and use it in a new situation.
    - *e.g. When they fall through the air, why is the terminal velocity of a mouse lower than that of a man?*

Remembering is usually thought to be easier than understanding, and application is generally the most difficult skill. However if you cannot remember a piece of knowledge in the first place you will not be able to show your other skills. Science is based on facts and you need to know **names, functions, reactions, properties** and **relationships** if you want to succeed. If you have a wide, secure knowledge base then examination questions will be much easier for you.

Good science gives facts and explains them. Good answers give information with reasons or explanations. Poor answers give only a hint of a fact or a vague generalization.

SELF EVALUATION

During your GCSE course you may be given a checklist which will enable you to note down the work you have covered. It may also give you an opportunity to assess how well you feel you understand a part of a topic. Be honest with yourself, and if there is an area you do not feel secure about then go over it again. Be willing to ask your teacher for help.

Answering structured questions and checking your answers is one way of revising a topic and assessing your knowledge and understanding.

Remember everyone gets thing wrong. When you get a question wrong you should be able to learn from your error and make sure it does not happen a second time. Wise people learn from their mistakes. Very clever people learn to make mistakes only when it does not matter!

Use the evaluation scales as follows:

1 I have to learn this material as I am not as yet getting questions correct.

2 (between 1 and 3)

3 I am fairly confident of this and get the easy questions correct.

4 (between 3 and 5)

5 I know this and can answer everything on it.

 Progress with GCSE Structured Questions: Biology

Types of structured question: WHAT THEY TEST AND HOW TO ANSWER THEM

SHORT ANSWER QUESTIONS

Straightforward questions on recall usually start with **what** or **which** or **give**. Often one word, a phrase or a short sentence is all that is required.

You need to be more careful if the question starts with **how** or **why** as these may sometimes be straightforward, but often require a link to be made between a cause and an effect to show that you understand the science. With how and why questions you should always check the number of marks available or the number of lines to write on, as these will be very helpful clues to the depth of answer required.

Some questions require you to match one piece of information with another, such as linking the names of organs in the body to their functions. These are an easy type of recall question. Another style of question which is considered to be quite easy is the cloze question (sentence completion). Usually you are given a number of words to choose from to complete the sentences in a short passage. This method is often used to test if you know definitions or the names of processes.

Another area of recall is labelling diagrams, or completing diagrams of apparatus. The latter is where many students lose marks for sloppy work. You must be neat, use a ruler wherever possible and make sure that the apparatus will work as you have drawn it. For example, all joints must be 'gas tight' and the level of any liquid must be horizontal and touch both sides of the container. Excellent work will show a meniscus here.

EXTENDED WRITING QUESTIONS

A rough and ready rule for the length of answer required can be worked out from the mark allocation. It is as follows.
One mark (1) will require at the most a sentence, but could be just one word;
Two marks (2) show there are two separate marking points. This could be two reasons, two facts, or a fact and an explanation or reason. This is the shortest form of extended writing.
Three marks (3) or more, will require a number of sentences to be written. A good answer will contain facts, together with reasons and explanations which are logically linked.

Questions which require a number of sentences for a full answer are found on both Foundation and Higher Tier papers. They account for about 25% of the marks available on the paper.

Extended writing questions require more than a word or phrase as an answer but it need only be a few sentences. However the few sentences must:

■ be appropriate and fully address the question;
■ be sensibly argued and related to each other, not just offer a couple of unrelated comments;
■ use good, clear English with correct grammar and spelling;
■ use scientific terminology where appropriate;
■ show a flow of logic when a sequence of events or ideas is needed.

Most extended writing questions carry three marks and sometimes four or more marks. They usually start with the command word **describe**, **explain** or **suggest**. Marks can usually be gained for:

■ giving a number of specific facts;
■ writing a correct sequence of points or logic;
■ making links between cause and effect.

Another useful clue is that **suggest** usually means the question is about a topic which is original and is unlikely to have been covered in lessons. You have to use your knowledge to give sensible suggestions or reasons when answering the question. Clear arguments are important; so is a sensible guess.

CALCULATION QUESTIONS

Parts of questions which require calculations usually carry three marks in total:

- one mark is given for the formula or evidence to show that you know the formula, eg. putting the numbers down in the correct way;
- one mark for doing the calculation;
- one mark for the correct unit, particularly if it is one of the more complicated units.

If you get the answer right you get the marks even if you show no working. However, it is always best to **show your working** as you can get marks if you use the right method even if your final answer is wrong.

On Higher Tier papers you are sometimes required to use two equations to work out the answer to a problem. Often the first one is given but you need to know the second one.

Every GCSE Science syllabus has the same number of required equations, which you must know, they are all in the physics part of the syllabus. Any other equation is most likely to be given to you, or is specific to one board's syllabus.

- Many of the required equations occur at standard level so can be present on both tiers of papers.
- If you take the Higher Tier paper you must know and be able to use all the required equations.

It is expected that you will be able to find any unknown quantity in an equation.
For example Ohm's law is often remembered as:

$$\text{volts} = \text{amps} \times \text{ohms} \text{ or } V = I \times R$$
$$voltage = current \times resistance$$

In a standard demand question you may be given the resistance and the voltage and be expected to work out the current.
You should substitute into the standard form of the equation and then solve it for the unknown. This is easier and safer than trying to sort out the equations using algebra.

Command words and what they mean

Most parts of a structured question start with a key word which requires a specific sort of answer. These are called command words.

The list below shows the sorts of answers you could give to questions which start with these key command words. To get all the marks available you should always register what the command word is. If you do not give the right sort of answer then it is unlikely that you will get any marks. When you hear your teachers telling you to 'read the question' they are asking you to make sure you are quite clear what the question is demanding.

WORDS ASSOCIATED WITH QUESTIONS ASKING YOU TO RECALL FACTS

What, Which, Give, State
These require a one word answer, a phrase or a sentence.

Choose, Complete, Label
These often require you to select an answer from a list or they may require you to recall the word and put it in the correct place.

Describe
This requires a detailed answer. It will pay to plan your answer so that you get the points you want to make in a sensible order.
It may be modified to become 'describe how' or 'describe why'.

Draw
Circuits and apparatus need to be drawn neatly and carefully. Gas must not be able to get out of the 'joints' and electricity needs to be able to flow along the 'wires' and not have to jump gaps. Sometimes you may be asked to sketch an apparatus. This too should be drawn as neatly as possible.

WORDS ASSOCIATED WITH QUESTIONS THAT REQUIRE UNDERSTANDING

How, Why
These two command words are difficult to pin down. They usually require an explanation to be given without specifically asking for one. Assume that they mean explain how or explain why unless it is a very straightforward question such as; 'How high is it?'

Explain, Give a reason
These commands want you to give information about the theoretical part of science. 'Explain why' is very similar to 'give a reason'. You have to write about the cause of something happening. 'Explain how' requires more than a description, you have to give an explanation for the effect.
For example:
Water is boiling in a beaker. Explain why.
It is being heated by a Bunsen burner.
Water is boiling in a beaker. Explain how.
The energy is being passed from the flame through the glass, by conduction, to the water where convection carries the energy into the water.

Progress with GCSE Structured Questions: Biology

student handout **3**
(continued)

WORDS ASSOCIATED WITH QUESTIONS THAT WANT YOU TO APPLY KNOWLEDGE AND UNDERSTANDING

Suggest, Predict
These command words are invitations to you to come up with something sensible. You should always go on and justify your answer using your knowledge. Your answer is likely to contain the word 'because'.

Compare
You must refer to both the 'things' you are comparing. Starting with 'It' is a disaster and generally means no marks can be awarded, as the examiner does not know which of the two things being compared is 'It'.

Draw or sketch a graph
A smooth curve, or straight line drawn with a ruler is required, not a hairy, wobbly caterpillar!

Calculate, Work out
Always show the equation unless it is given to you. Put the numbers in the equation as you remember it then sort out the answer. This is much easier than using algebra to manipulate an equation. Remember to give the units.

© 1998 Hodder & Stoughton Educational   *Progress with GCSE Structured Questions: Biology*

1 Human nutrition and respiration

TEACHER SUMMARY SHEET

QUESTION	TITLE AND CONTENT	LEVEL	SKILLS TESTED
1	**The food we eat**		
(a)	Food types	F	Data interpretation
(b)	Food types	F	Calculation
(c)	Protein digestion	S	Understanding
2	**The digestive system**		
(a)	Structure of digestive system	F	Recall
(b)	Functions of digestive system	S	Understanding
(c)	Adaptation of villus	S/H	Understanding
(d)	Function of glands and enzymes	H	Understanding
(e)	Function of muscular tissue in intestine	S	Understanding
3	**Digestive juices**		
(a)	Digestive juices	S	Calculation
(b)	Digestive enzyme production	S	Recall
(c)	Functions of bile	H	Understanding
(d)	Role of HCl in protection from microbes	S	Understanding
4	**Investigating protein digestion**		
(a)	Protein digestion	S/H	Graph construction
(b)	Protein digestion	S	Interpolation
(c)	Nature of enzymes	S	Understanding
(d)	Effect of pH on digestive enzymes	H	Understanding
5	**Investigating fat digestion**		
(a)	Fat digestion	S/H	Interpretation
(b)	Fat digestion	H	Interpretation
6	**The breathing system**		
(a)	Structure of the breathing system	F	Recall
(b)	Functions of the breathing system	S	Understanding
(c)	Parts of an animal cell, defence mechanisms	S	Understanding
7	**Energy needs**		
(a)	Energy needs	S	Calculation
(b)	Aerobic respiration	S	Recall
8	**Gaseous exchange**		
(a)	Gaseous exchange in alveoli	S/H	Understanding
(b)	Pressure changes during breathing cycle	H	Data interpretation
9	**Smoking and health**		
(a)	Trends in smoking habits	F/S	Data interpretation
(b)	Effect of smoking on lungs	S	Understanding
(c)	Lung cancer	S	Understanding
10	**Anaerobic respiration**		
(a)	Aerobic and anaerobic respiration	S/H	Understanding
(b)	Contribution of anaerobic respiration in exercise	H	Data interpretation

1 Human nutrition and respiration

TOPIC	COVERED	EVALUATION
	Circle the term that best describes how well you feel you have covered this topic.	On a scale of 1 – 5 how well do you feel you have understood this topic? (1 = not understood; 5 = fully understood).
The essential parts of a balanced diet	no/partly/yes	1 2 3 4 5
The organs of the digestive system	no/partly/yes	1 2 3 4 5
The functions of the organs of the digestive system	no/partly/yes	1 2 3 4 5
The composition of digestive juices	no/partly/yes	1 2 3 4 5
The optimum conditions for digestive enzymes	no/partly/yes	1 2 3 4 5
How carbohydrates are digested	no/partly/yes	1 2 3 4 5
How fats are digested	no/partly/yes	1 2 3 4 5
The role of bile in the digestion of fats	no/partly/yes	1 2 3 4 5
How proteins are digested	no/partly/yes	1 2 3 4 5
Structure of villi	no/partly/yes	1 2 3 4 5
The adaptation of villi for the absorption of soluble food	no/partly/yes	1 2 3 4 5
The role of gastric juice in preventing infection	no/partly/yes	1 2 3 4 5
The organs of the breathing system	no/partly/yes	1 2 3 4 5
Functions of the organs of the breathing system	no/partly/yes	1 2 3 4 5
The role of the ribs, muscles and diaphragm in breathing	no/partly/yes	1 2 3 4 5
The adaptations of alveoli for gaseous exchange	no/partly/yes	1 2 3 4 5
The parts of an animal cell	no/partly/yes	1 2 3 4 5
The functions of the parts of an animal cell	no/partly/yes	1 2 3 4 5
The role of the breathing system in preventing infection	no/partly/yes	1 2 3 4 5
The energy needs of living organisms	no/partly/yes	1 2 3 4 5
The chemical equation for aerobic respiration	no/partly/yes	1 2 3 4 5
The differences between aerobic and anaerobic respiration	no/partly/yes	1 2 3 4 5
The effects of smoking on health	no/partly/yes	1 2 3 4 5

WORKED EXAMPLE 1

CHIEF EXAMINER'S COMMENTS

Read the following passage

ALL FOOD IS GOOD BUT DIETS MAY BE BAD OR GOOD

Experts recommend a balanced diet, containing a mixture of carbohydrates, fats and proteins. The amount of animal fat should be kept low, to reduce the risk of heart disease. The diet should include plenty of starchy foods, such as bread and pasta, and at least one piece of fresh fruit per day. Only small quantities of alcohol should be drunk.

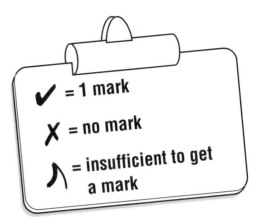

✔ = 1 mark

✗ = no mark

⅄ = insufficient to get a mark

(a) As well as carbohydrates, fats and proteins, name two other types of substance that a balanced diet should contain. (2)

1. *vegetables* ✗

2. *Fibre* ✔

(a) The question asks for substances; NOT types of food. Carbohydrates, fats and proteins are given in the passage. The other acceptable answers are 'minerals', 'vitamins' and 'water'.

(b) Suggest why 'one piece of fresh fruit' should be eaten each day. (1)

It contains vitamin C ✔ *which stops scurvy*

(b) The student wasn't sure whether 'vitamin C' would gain the mark, so she also gave 'which stops scurvy'. This is good practice to make sure you get maximum marks. But take care, as writing something contradictory shows insecure knowledge and may cancel out the mark.

(c) Explain why large quantities of alcohol should not be drunk. (2)

Because it makes you drunk ✔ ⅄

(c) The student has not explained how alcohol actually affects the body. Alcohol may damage the liver and the brain. It also slows our reactions and affects our judgements. The answer 'makes you drunk' gets only one mark. To get the second mark the student must focus on how the alcohol affects the body.

(d) Keeping the amount of animal fat in the diet low helps people to avoid heart attacks. Explain why this is so. (3)

The fats go from the stomach into the blood stream. As they flow through the heart they stick to the arteries and make them smaller ✔ *and the heart pumps not as easily causing heart problems.* ⅄

(d) The student has not fully answered the question, which was to explain how a diet low in animal fat helps to avoid heart attacks. She started off well by explaining that fats 'stick to the arteries making them smaller'; but she should have gone on to say that this 'reduces blood flow to the heart muscle' and 'might prevent enough oxygen getting to the heart muscle'. Her conclusion 'causing heart problems' is too vague and little more than a restatement of the question.

(e) A person eats a meal containing fat. Describe what happens to the fat from the time it is eaten to when it is stored under the skin. (4)

The fat settles in the stomach, goes into the blood stream ✔ *and gets pumped round the body. Some is used by the muscles and some stays in muscles under the skin.* ⅄

(e) This is a very weak answer, receiving only one mark for the idea that the food is absorbed into the blood stream. Her answer does not mention the essential points about the digestion of fats:

■ *that large fat molecules are broken down into smaller molecules;*

■ *that these smaller molecules are called fatty acids and glycerol;*

■ *that this breakdown is speeded up by enzymes called lipases;*

■ *that lipase enzymes are produced by the pancreas and by the small intestine.*

On the higher tier paper, candidates are also expected to know that bile, produced in the liver, speeds up fat digestion by emulsifying fats. This increases the surface area for enzymes to act upon. They should also know that fat which is not used in respiration is stored.

WORKED EXAMPLE 2

CHIEF EXAMINER'S COMMENTS

(a)   A student breathed out into an empty bag five times.

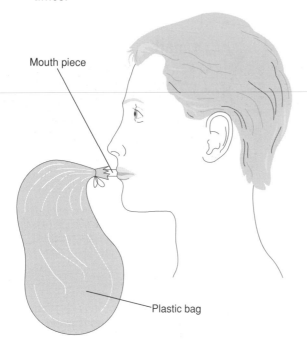

Mouth piece

Plastic bag

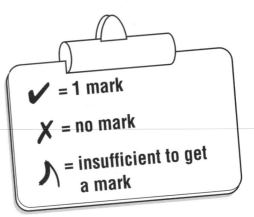

✔ = 1 mark

✗ = no mark

⌡ = insufficient to get a mark

After breathing out five times the volume of air in the bag measured 3000 cm³.
The student then did some strenuous exercise for two minutes. The volume breathed out in five breaths this time measured 9000 cm³. What does this tell you about the effect of exercise on breathing?   (1)

It tells me that we breathe faster after exercise ✗

(a) Always read the question carefully and do not jump to conclusions. This student did not notice that the student breathed into the bag the same number of times before and after exercise – so any answer which implies faster breathing is not answering the question. The increase in the **volume** of air in the bag after exercise is caused by **deeper** breathing.

(b)   (i) Name the chemical process that releases energy when it takes place in the cells of the body.   (1)

Respiration ✔

(ii) Name the substances produced by this process.   (2)

carbon dioxide ✔ *and energy* ✗

(iii) Explain why this process has to take place more rapidly during exercise.   (2)

we need to get more oxygen to the muscles because they are working harder ⌡

(b) (ii) Although energy is released during exercise it is not a substance and would not receive a mark. 'Water' is the second substance required for full marks.
(iii) Do not confuse respiration with breathing. Breathing is moving air in and out of the lungs. The circulatory system moves oxygen and carbon dioxide between lungs and organs. The student therefore received no marks for stating that there was a need to get more oxygen to the muscles. Respiration takes place inside cells and is a series of reactions in which energy is released from sugars. Exercising muscles need more energy than resting muscles so the rate of respiration is increased to supply this extra energy. The answer implies that the student has an understanding of the process but it is not written in sufficient detail to gain marks.

          Progress with GCSE Structured Questions: Biology

1 The food we eat

(a) The bar chart shows information about the actual and recommended consumption of various foods in Britain.

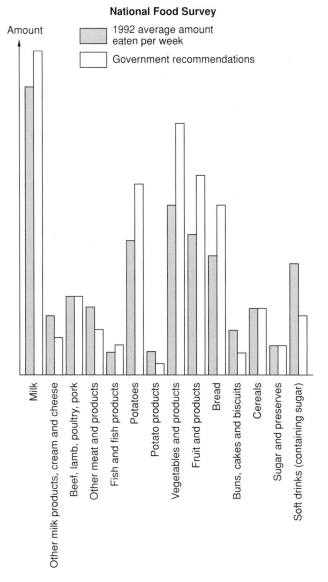

Use only foods from the chart to answer parts (i), (ii) and (iii) of the question.

(i) Name two foods that we eat too much of. (2)

(ii) Name one food that contains large amounts of carbohydrate. (1)

(iii) Name one food that contains large amounts of fat. (1)

(b) The drawing shows a chicken cheeseburger. The table shows how much protein there is in different foods.

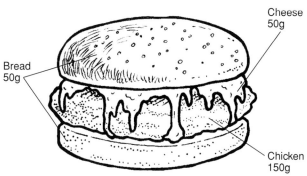

Food	Amount of protein in 100 g of food
Bread	8.8
Baked beans	5.1
Chips	3.8
Chicken	26.5
Cheese	26.0

Calculate how much protein there is in the chicken cheeseburger. Show your working. (2)

(c) Describe what happens to proteins as they pass through the digestive system. (4)

2   The digestive system

The drawing shows the digestive system.

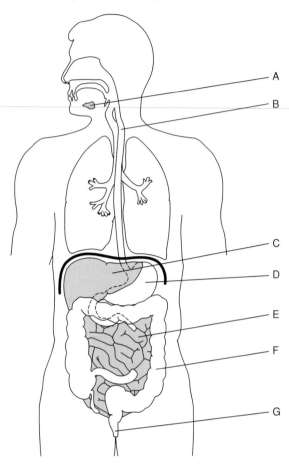

The drawing shows a section of the wall of the small intestine.

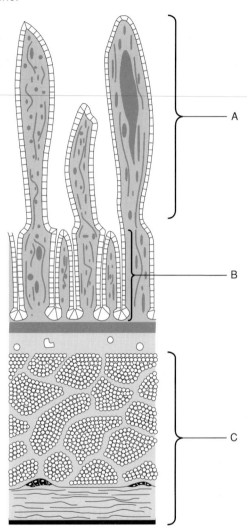

(a)   Name the parts labelled **B**, **C**, **D**, **E** and **F**.   (5)

(b)   What are the functions of the parts labelled **A**, **F** and **G**?   (3)

(c)   The structure labelled **A** is a villus.

   (i)   What is the function of the villi in the small intestine?   (1)
   (ii)   Describe how a villus is adapted for carrying out its function.   (3)

(d)   The structure labelled **B** is a gland.

   (i)   Name **three** different digestive enzymes, which are produced by glands in the small intestine.   (3)
   (ii)   Explain why the fluid produced by this gland should be alkaline.   (3)

(e)   (i)   The layers labelled **C** consist of muscular tissue. What is 'tissue'?   (1)
   (ii)   Describe the function of the muscle tissue of the small intestine.   (2)

3 Digestive juices

The diagram shows the amounts of water entering and leaving the digestive system in one day

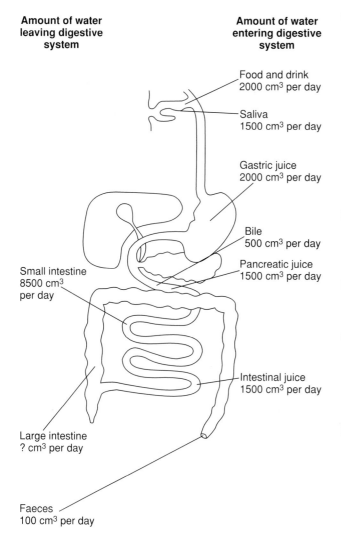

Amount of water leaving digestive system

Amount of water entering digestive system

Food and drink 2000 cm³ per day

Saliva 1500 cm³ per day

Gastric juice 2000 cm³ per day

Bile 500 cm³ per day

Pancreatic juice 1500 cm³ per day

Small intestine 8500 cm³ per day

Intestinal juice 1500 cm³ per day

Large intestine ? cm³ per day

Faeces 100 cm³ per day

(a) Calculate how much water is absorbed in one day by the large intestine. Show your working. (2)

(b) In which of the digestive juices named on the diagram are the following enzymes found:

(i) carbohydrase, (1)
(ii) protease, (1)
(iii) lipase? (1)

(c) Describe and explain the functions of bile in digestion. (3)

(d) Explain how gastric juice is able to protect the body from infection. (2)

4 Investigating protein digestion

Egg white is a protein. A student measured the time taken for an enzyme to digest similar small amounts of egg white at different temperatures. His results are shown in the table.

Temperature (°C)	Time taken to digest egg white (minutes)
0	30
10	15
20	7
30	3
40	1
50	8
60	25

(a) Plot the data on graph paper (use a scale of 2 cm = 10°C for the vertical axis and 2 cm = 5 minutes for the horizontal axis). (2)

(b) Use your graph to find how long it would take the egg white to be digested at 35°C. (1)

(c) Explain why it took so long to digest the egg white:

(i) at 10°C compared to 40°C,
(ii) at 60°C compared to 40°C. (4)

(d) The graph shows how pH affects the activity of two different proteases from the human digestive system.

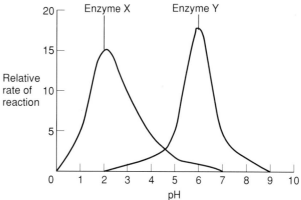

Where in the digestive system would you expect to find:

(i) enzyme **X**,
(ii) enzyme **Y**?

Explain the reason for your answer in each case. (4)

5　Investigating fat digestion

A student investigated fat digestion. She set up four tubes, **A**, **B**, **C** and **D** as shown in the diagram. To each tube she added 4 drops of an indicator. It is yellow in acidic solutions and pink in alkaline solutions. She then added just enough sodium hydrogen carbonate solution to turn the mixture pink.

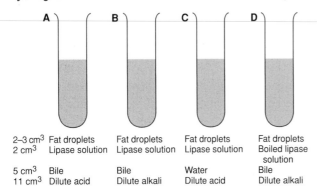

	A	B	C	D
2–3 cm³	Fat droplets	Fat droplets	Fat droplets	Fat droplets
2 cm³	Lipase solution	Lipase solution	Lipase solution	Boiled lipase solution
5 cm³	Bile	Bile	Water	Bile
11 cm³	Dilute acid	Dilute alkali	Dilute acid	Dilute alkali

Her results are shown in the table.

Tube	Time taken for indicator to turn yellow (minutes)
A	10
B	5
C	15
D	Indicator did not change colour

(a)　Explain why the indicator turned yellow in some of the tubes. (2)

(b)　Explain the results for each of the tubes **A**, **B**, **C** and **D** and comment on the relative rates of colour change. (8)

6　The breathing system

The drawing shows the organs in the human thorax.

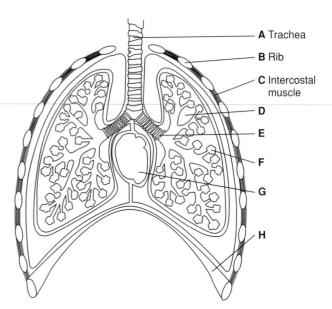

A Trachea
B Rib
C Intercostal muscle
D
E
F
G
H

(a)　Name the structures labelled **D**, **E**, **F**, **G**, and **H**. (5)

(b)　(i)　Give one function of each of the structures labelled **A**, **B** and **C**. (3)
　　　(ii)　Explain how **B**, **C** and **H** work together to cause a person to breathe in. (4)

(c)　The drawing shows the cells that line structure **E**.

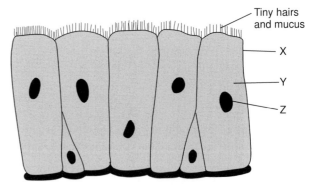

Tiny hairs and mucus
X
Y
Z

　　(i)　Copy and complete the table for the parts of the cell labelled **X**, **Y** and **Z**. (6)

Structure	Name	Function
X		
Y		
Z		

　　(ii)　Suggest how the tiny hairs and mucus help to protect the body from infection. (2)

7 Energy needs

The table shows how much energy is needed for a number of activities.

Activity	Energy needed (kJ per minute)
Dancing	25
Running	25
Sitting	5
Swimming	35
Walking	15

A student spent an activity evening with her youth group. During the evening she spent 30 minutes sitting, 10 minutes walking, 30 minutes swimming and 45 minutes dancing.

(a) Calculate how much energy she needed for the activity evening. Show your working. (2)

(b) (i) Name the process, in the student's muscles, that released energy. (1)

(ii) Copy and complete the word equation for this process. (2)

glucose + ... → water + ...

8 Gaseous exchange

(a) The drawing shows a group of alveoli together with their air and blood supply.

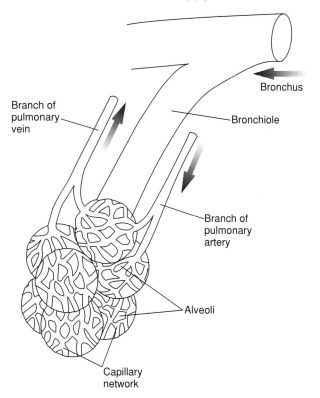

Use information from the drawing to help you explain how the lung is adapted for the efficient exchange of gases. (4)

(b) The graph shows how the pressure in the alveoli of a healthy student changes during one breathing cycle.

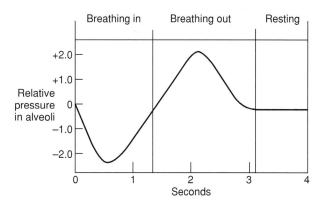

(i) Explain how the fall in pressure during breathing in is brought about. (3)

(ii) Calculate the breathing rate of the student in breaths per minute. (2)

(iii) Calculate the percentage of time the student spends on breathing out. (2)

9 Smoking and health

The bar chart shows trends in the smoking habits of teenagers between 1982 and 1994.

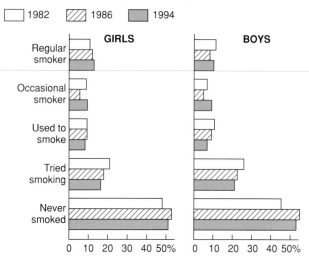

Young smokers Percentage of 11-to 15-year-old smokers

☐ 1982　▨ 1986　■ 1994

(a) (i) What percentage of girls were 'occasional smokers' in 1986? (1)

(ii) Describe the trend for the percentage of boys who 'used to smoke' between 1982 and 1994. (1)

(iii) Suggest **one** reason why the percentage of teenagers who had 'tried smoking' fell between 1982 and 1994. (1)

(iv) Describe the differences in the trends between 1982 and 1994 of girls and boys who were 'regular smokers'. (2)

(b) The diagram shows one effect of smoking on the lungs.

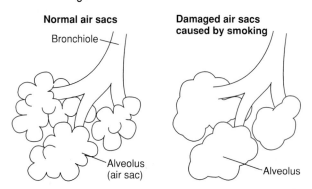

Explain how this damage to the lungs can affect gas exchange. (2)

(c) Explain why people who smoke have a greater risk of developing lung cancer than people who do not smoke. (3)

10　Anaerobic respiration

(a) Give **four** differences between aerobic respiration and anaerobic respiration. (4)

(b) The two graphs show the relative contributions of anaerobic and aerobic respiration to releasing energy for the body when a person is making maximum physical effort.

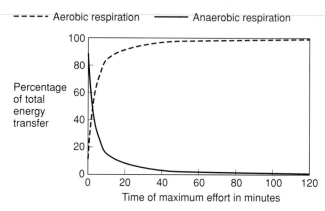

(i) What percentage of energy is transferred by anaerobic respiration at the end of a four-minute mile? (1)

(ii) Suggest the advantages to a long distance runner in receiving a high percentage of energy transfer from aerobic rather than anaerobic respiration. (4)

(iii) A 100-metre sprint athlete receives almost all the energy required from anaerobic respiration rather than from aerobic respiration. Suggest an explanation for this. (3)

2 Human circulation and defence

QUESTION	TITLE AND CONTENT	LEVEL	SKILLS TESTED
1	**Measuring pulse rates**		
(a)	Grouping pulse rates	F	Data handling
(b)	Constructing a bar chart of pulse rates	F	Graph construction
(c)	Differences in pulse rates	S	Understanding
2	**The human heart**		
(a)	Labelling heart parts	S	Recall
(b)	Functions of heart parts	S	Understanding
(c)	Foetal heart	S	Understanding
(d)	Single and double circulation	S	Understanding
3	**Human blood vessels**		
(a)	Naming types of blood vessel	S	Understanding
(b)	Structure of capillary in relation to function	S	Understanding
(c)	Role of valves in blood vessels	S	Understanding
4	**Supplying organs with blood**		
(a)	Constructing a bar chart of blood flow to organs	F	Graph construction
(b), (c)	Calculating blood flow; increase in heart beat	F/S	Calculation, understanding
(d)	Calculation; advantage of increased blood flow	S	Calculation, understanding
(e), (f)	Advantages of changes in blood flow to organs	S	Understanding
5	**Red blood cells**		
(a)	Function of red blood cells	S	Understanding
(b)	Comprehension exercise on 'blood doping'	H	Understanding
6	**White blood cells**		
(a)	Parts of white blood cell	S	Recall
(b)	Role of white cells in defence	S	Understanding
7	**Problems with vaccination**		
	Comprehension exercise on problems with vaccination	H	Understanding
8	**Blood plasma**		
(a)	Calculations on plasma components	S	Calculation
(b)	Transport role of plasma	S	Understanding
(c)	Production and function of blood protein	S	Recall
9	**Bacteria and viruses**		
(a)	Parts of bacteria and viruses	S	Recall
(b)	Infection and illness	S	Understanding
10	**The defeat of polio**		
(a)	Plotting line graph of incidence of polio	S	Graph construction
(b)	Reasons for fall in polio numbers	S/H	Understanding

2 Human circulation and defence

TOPIC	COVERED	EVALUATION
	Circle the term that best describes how well you feel you have covered this topic.	On a scale of 1 – 5 how well do you feel you have understood this topic? (1 = not understood; 5 = fully understood).
The position and functions of the parts of the heart	no/partly/yes	1 2 3 4 5
The path of blood through the heart	no/partly/yes	1 2 3 4 5
The structure and functions of arteries	no/partly/yes	1 2 3 4 5
The structure and functions of veins	no/partly/yes	1 2 3 4 5
The structure and functions of capillaries	no/partly/yes	1 2 3 4 5
The advantages of the double circulatory system	no/partly/yes	1 2 3 4 5
The structure and function of red blood cells	no/partly/yes	1 2 3 4 5
The structure and function of white blood cells	no/partly/yes	1 2 3 4 5
The function of blood platelets	no/partly/yes	1 2 3 4 5
The composition of blood plasma	no/partly/yes	1 2 3 4 5
The role of plasma in transporting materials	no/partly/yes	1 2 3 4 5
The structure of a bacterium	no/partly/yes	1 2 3 4 5
The structure of a virus	no/partly/yes	1 2 3 4 5
How microbes make us ill	no/partly/yes	1 2 3 4 5
How the body protects itself from microbes	no/partly/yes	1 2 3 4 5
How living conditions and lifestyle affect the spread of disease	no/partly/yes	1 2 3 4 5

 Progress with GCSE Structured Questions: Biology

CHAPTER 2 HUMAN CIRCULATION AND DEFENCE

WORKED EXAMPLE 1

The diagram shows part of the circulatory system.

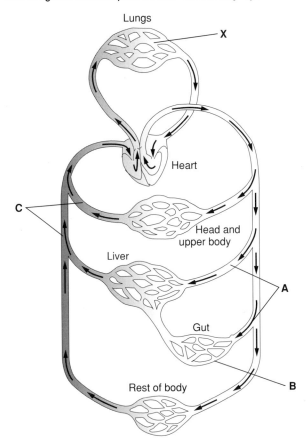

CHIEF EXAMINER'S COMMENTS

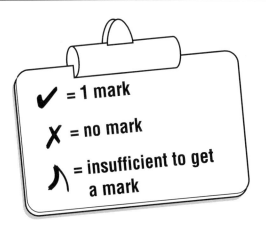

✔ = 1 mark

✗ = no mark

↲ = insufficient to get a mark

(a) Name the types of blood vessel **A**, **B** and **C**. (3)

A *Arteries* ✔

B *Capillaries* ✔

C *Vena cava* ✗

(b) Give two ways in which the composition of blood changes as it flows through the vessels labelled X. (2)

1. *It becomes oxygenated* ✔

2. *It has less carbon dioxide* ✗

(c) Blood that returns to the heart from the body then flows to the lungs. Describe the processes in the heart that cause this to happen. (5)

Blood enters the right atrium then passes through the tricuspid valve into the right ventricle. From here it goes through the pulmonary artery to the lungs. ✗

(a) Look out for key words in questions. This question asks for types of blood vessel, so naming an individual vessel such as the vena cava does not receive a mark. The correct answer for **C** would be veins.

(b) 1 This answer would be accepted, but it is much safer to use the words 'more' and 'less' when answering this type of question. A better answer would be 'Oxygen passes into the blood'.

2 This is a very common error. The examiner does not know whether the answer means there is less carbon dioxide when the blood enters the lungs or when it leaves. Always be precise e.g. 'There is less carbon dioxide in the blood which leaves the lungs.'

(c) Always read the question carefully and look for key words like 'processes'. This answer received no marks because the candidate described the **path** the blood takes rather than the **processes** that cause it to take that path. A good answer would contain five of the following points:

- Muscles in the wall of the right atrium contract;
- this forces open the tricuspid valve to allow blood to flow into the right ventricle.
- Muscles in the wall of the right ventricle contract;
- this forces the tricuspid valve to close.
- The closed tricuspid valve prevents blood returning to the atrium;
- and forces the semi-lunar valves open to allow blood to flow to the lungs.

WORKED EXAMPLE 2

CHIEF EXAMINER'S COMMENTS

✔ = 1 mark

✗ = no mark

Λ = insufficient to get a mark

Doctors are becoming alarmed at the rising number of cases of tuberculosis (TB) in Britain.
When people carrying the TB bacteria cough or sneeze TB bacteria are released into the air. Other people may then breathe them in.

(a) Which organ will be infected first when someone breathes in the TB bacteria? (1)

Lungs ✔

(a) Any part of the breathing system would have gained a mark.

(b) Explain how the TB bacteria inside the body cause disease. (2)

The bacteria eat away the natural immune system (white blood cells) in the body. ✗

(b) Using phrases such as 'bacteria eat away' creates a bad impression and shows lack of understanding.
Bacteria cause disease by multiplying rapidly and so increasing the amount of toxins (poison) in the body.

(c) Name one other group of microbes that often cause disease. (1)

virus ✔

(c) Other alternatives would have been fungi or protozoa.
Flu or measles are names of diseases, not groups, and would NOT be accepted

(d) Suggest why people who live in overcrowded areas are more likely to catch TB than people who live in less crowded areas. (2)

Those living in small areas are in physical contact and could spread TB by talking to someone and coughing. Λ Λ

(d) The word 'Suggest' means that that you will not have been taught this – so you have to work out the answer from the information given at the start of the question (people contract TB by breathing in TB bacteria) but do NOT simply repeat it.
A good answer is: 'There would be more TB bacteria in the air and therefore more chance of breathing in TB bacteria.'

(e) People infected with a small number of TB bacteria often do not develop the disease. Explain, as fully as you can, how the body defends itself against the TB bacteria. (3)

The white blood cells fight the TB and make the TB bacteria weaker and in the end there will be no bacteria left. ✗

(e) This is work that you should know, but many students spoil their answers by talking about white blood cells fighting bacteria or having battles with them.
You have to be precise about the way white cells affect bacteria:
- *they engulf (or surround) bacteria – eating bacteria would NOT be accepted;*
- *they produce antibodies to kill bacteria – simply saying white cells kill bacteria is NOT sufficient;*
- *they produce antitoxins to neutralise the toxins produced by bacteria – antitoxins do NOT kill bacteria.*

(f) Smoking can cause diseases such as lung cancer. Explain, as fully as you can, why the cancers caused by smoking are not infectious. (2)

Because it is self inflicted and repeated smoking must take place, which wouldn't happen with a non-smoker. ✗

(f) 'Because it is self inflicted' does not mean anything unless it is qualified by stating how.
This question was designed to find out if students knew that smoking causes cancer because the tobacco smoke contains harmful chemicals.
A good answer would have stated that:
- *lung cancer is caused by harmful substances in tobacco smoke, not by microbes;*
- *cancer cells remain inside the person.*

1 Measuring pulse rates

A class of students measured their pulse rates. Their results are shown in the table.

Pulse rate (beats per minute)				
53	78	50	63	51
58	47	76	60	56
72	55	74	63	68
74	70	73	67	61
62	75	49	72	74

(a) Copy and complete the table. (2)

Pulse rate (beats per minute)	Number of pupils
45–49	
50–54	
55–59	
60–64	
65–69	
70–74	
75–79	

(b) Copy the bar chart below and use the data in the table to complete it. (2)

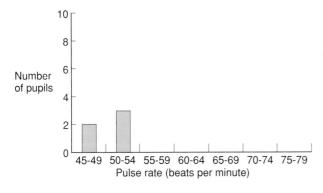

(c) Give two reasons why the pulse rates of the pupils varied. (2)

2 The human heart

The drawing shows a section through the human heart.

(a) Copy the drawing of the heart, then label:

   (i) the pulmonary artery,
   (ii) the vena cava,
   (iii) a semi-lunar valve,
   (iv) the left ventricle. (4)

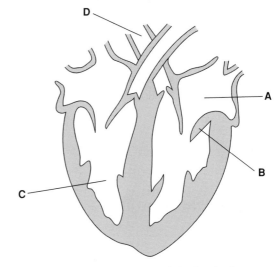

(b) (i) From which organ of the body does structure **A** receive blood? (1)
   (ii) Describe the function of structure **B** in the heart. (1)
   (iii) To which organ of the body does structure **C** pump blood? (1)
   (iv) What is the function of structure **D**? (1)
   (v) How is the blood in structure **D** different from that in structure **C**? (1)

(c) The diagram shows the heart of a baby, just before birth.

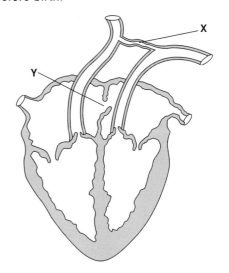

Normally, the structures labelled **X** and **Y** close shortly after birth. Explain the possible effects on the baby if these structures fail to close completely. (4)

(d) (i) Explain what is meant by a 'double circulatory system'. (2)
   (ii) Give **two** advantages of a double circulatory system over a single system. (2)

3 Human blood vessels

The drawings show three different types of human blood vessel. They are magnified by different amounts, which are indicated.

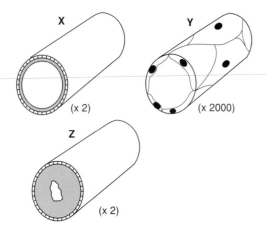

(a) Name the three types of blood vessels, **X**, **Y** and **Z**. (3)

(b) Explain how capillaries are specialised to carry out their function. (3)

(c) (i) Explain why veins often have 'watch pocket' valves. (2)
  (ii) Explain why arteries do not have valves. (2)

4 Supplying organs with blood

The table shows the volume of blood flowing through different organs, at rest and during exercise.

Organ	Blood flow (cm³ per minute)	
	Light exercise	**Maximum exercise**
Digestive system	1100	300
Kidneys	900	250
Brain	750	750
Heart muscle	350	1000
Skeletal muscles	4500	22 000
Skin	1500	600
Other	400	100

(a) Copy the bar chart and use the data from the table to complete it. (2)

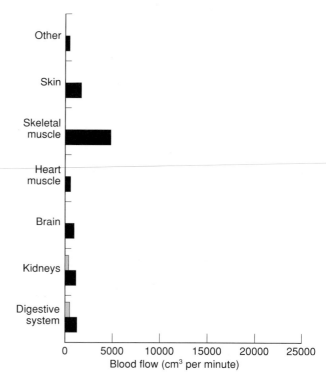

(b) Calculate the total volume of blood flowing to the organs in one minute during;

(i) light exercise, (1)
(ii) maximum exercise. (1)

(c) How is the blood flow through the body increased during exercise? (2)

(d) (i) Calculate the percentage increase in the flow of blood to the skeletal muscles when going from light exercise to maximum exercise. (2)
  (ii) Explain the advantage to the body of this increase. (4)

(e) (i) Explain the advantage to the body of the change in the volume of blood flowing to the digestive system between light exercise and maximum exercise. (2)
  (ii) Explain how this change in blood supply to the digestive system is brought about. (2)

(f) The blood supply to the brain did not change between light and maximum exercise. Suggest why. (1)

5 Red blood cells

The drawing shows a red blood cell cut in half.

(a) (i) What is the function of red blood cells? (1)
(ii) Explain how red blood cells carry out this function. (2)
(iii) Suggest how the shape of a red blood cell makes it more efficient in carrying out its function. (3)
(iv) Red blood cells live for only 120 days. Suggest **one** reason for this. (1)

(b) Read this passage.

> Red blood cell reinfusion, often called 'blood doping', came into prominence during the 1972 Olympics when a champion endurance athlete was alleged to have used this in preparation for his eventual gold medal endurance run.
> In one reinfusion technique, 900 – 1800 cm³ of an athlete's blood is withdrawn over a period of six weeks, the plasma is immediately removed and reinfused, and the packed red cells are placed in frozen storage. The stored red cells are then reinfused in the week before the race.
> The graph shows the effect of this technique on the athlete's red blood cell count.

(i) Explain how the reinfusion technique may help to improve an athlete's performance. (4)
(ii) Explain why the red blood cell count falls steadily in the weeks following reinfusion. (2)
(iii) Do you think that reinfusion is a 'fair practice'? Explain the reason for your answer. (2)

6   White blood cells

The drawing shows one type of white blood cell.

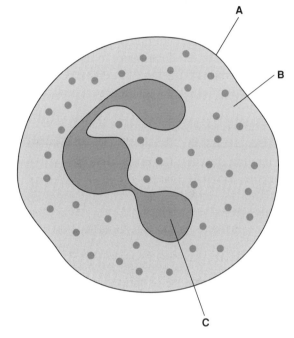

(a) (i) Name the parts labelled **A**, **B** and **C**. (3)
(ii) Describe the function of each of the parts labelled **A**, **B** and **C**. (3)

(b) Explain **three** ways in which white blood cells protect us from infection. (3)

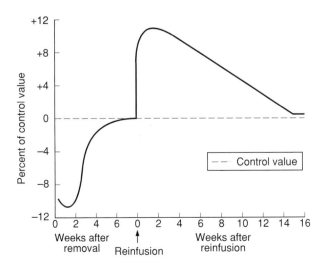

7   Problems with vaccinations

Read the following article.

CHILDREN RECEIVED VACCINE DESPITE MENINGITIS LINK

Thousands of children were given measles, mumps and rubella injections days after the Department of Health decided to stop supplying two types of vaccine because of a risk of meningitis, it emerged yesterday.

Although the decision was made last week, the department had not planned a public statement or to tell doctors not to use the two brands of the vaccine until tomorrow.

A letter to hospital pharmacists, however, was sent out last week "inadvertently" early, a department spokesman said.

As a result the decision to supply only the remaining measles, mumps and rubella vaccine, MMR II, that has not been linked to "mumps meningitis" was revealed in press and radio reports yesterday.

The MMR vaccine was introduced in 1988 and pronounced to be very safe. Three brands have been used, two containing the same "Urabe" mumps vaccine virus strain and one, MMR II, containing the 'Jeryl Lynn' strain.

The department decided to stop using the Urabe strains when detailed laboratory investigations over four years made the link with cases of meningitis.

The department stressed that the risk was very small – one in 11,000 cases – compared with one in 400 cases of meningitis when people catch mumps naturally. It also said that the meningitis following vaccination was milder than the meningitis following "wild" mumps.

Dr David Salisbury, senior medical officer at the department, said yesterday: "We had to be very certain that MMR II was as effective as the other two vaccines and that it didn't give rise to side effects before we decided to use MMR II only.

"We found only eight cases over four years. The evidence did not exactly leap out at us. I feel we have acted properly when the evidence was scientifically justified."

In a statement, Dr Kenneth Calman, the Chief Medical Officer, said yesterday that MMR II was preferable. "The risk of contracting vaccine-related meningitis is extremely rare and the benefits of immunisation, whichever vaccine was used, overwhelming."

Source: Celia Hall for *The Independent*

(i) Explain how vaccination with MMR II protects a child against measles. (4)

(ii) Use information from the passage to evaluate the use of MMR II vaccine. (4)

8 Blood plasma

The pie chart shows the proportions of solids dissolved in blood plasma.

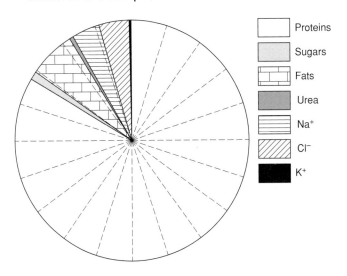

Proteins

Sugars

Fats

Urea

Na⁺

Cl⁻

K⁺

(a) (i) Estimate the proportion of proteins dissolved in blood plasma. (1)

(ii) On average there are 8.67 g of solids dissolved in 100 cm³ of blood plasma. Calculate the mass of protein dissolved in 100 cm³ of blood plasma. (1)

(b) (i) In which organ does sugar enter the blood plasma? (1)

(ii) In which organ does urea leave the blood plasma? (1)

(c) (i) In which organ are most blood proteins produced? (1)

(ii) State **one** function of large blood proteins in the circulatory system. (1)

9 Bacteria and viruses

The drawings show a virus and a bacterium.

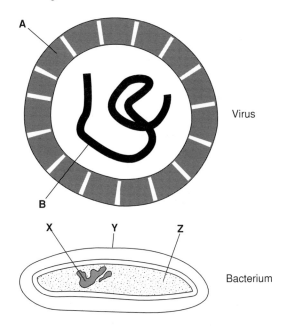

Virus

Bacterium

(a) (i) Name the structures labelled **A** and **B** on the virus. (2)

(ii) Name the structures labelled **X**, **Y** and **Z** on the bacterium. (3)

(iii) Give **two** differences in structure, other than shape, between a bacterium and a white blood cell. (2)

(b) Explain how bacterial and viral infections make us feel ill. (3)

10 The defeat of polio

Polio is caused by a virus. The table shows the number of cases of polio in Britain between 1959 and 1971.

Year	Number of cases
1959	1028
1962	271
1965	91
1968	24
1971	7

(a) Plot a graph of the data. (3)

(b) Suggest **two** explanations for the fall in the number of cases of polio between 1959 and 1971. (2)

3 Nerves and hormones

QUESTION	TITLE AND CONTENT	LEVEL	SKILLS TESTED
1	**Nerve cells**		
(a)	Types of receptors	S	Recall
(b)	Label parts of nerve cell	S	Recall
(c)	Function of myelin sheath	S	Understanding
(d)	Skin receptor	S	Understanding
(e)	Position of parts of a sensory neurone	S	Understanding
2	**The eye**		
(a)	Labelling eye parts	S	Recall
(b)	Functions of eye parts	S	Understanding
(c)	Mechanism of focusing	S/H	Understanding
3	**Reflex actions**		
(a)	Name reflex action	S	Recall
(b)	Advantages of reflex actions	S	Understanding
(c)	Transmission of impulses	S/H	Understanding
(d)	Analysis of reflex action	H	Understanding
4	**Controlling blood sugar**		
(a)	Interpolation from blood sugar graph	F	Interpolation
(b)	Role of insulin	S	Understanding
(c)	Extrapolation on blood sugar – insulin graph	S	Understanding
5	**Drinking and driving**		
(a)	Graph plotting – blood alcohol levels, interpolation	S	Graph construction
(b)	Effects of blood alcohol	S	Understanding
(c)	Long term effects of alcohol abuse	S	Understanding
6	**Diet and training**		
	Effects of diet on glycogen storage	H	Understanding
7	**Drug addiction**		
(a), (b)	Data extraction from table of addict numbers	S	Data extraction
(c)	Why some drugs are addictive	S	Understanding
(d)	Long term effects of drug abuse	S	Understanding
8	**Sex hormones**		
(a), (b)	Hormones and secondary sexual characteristics	S	Understanding
(c), (d), (e)	Data interpretation – sex hormones in the menstrual cycle	H	Understanding
(f)	Evaluating use of hormones in controlling human fertility	H	Evaluation
9	**How some fish can camouflage themselves**		
	Analysing change in skin colour response	H	Understanding

3 Nerves and hormones

TOPIC	COVERED	EVALUATION
	Circle the term that best describes how well you feel you have covered this topic.	On a scale of 1 – 5 how well do you feel you have understood this topic? (1 = not understood; 5 = fully understood).
The types of receptors and where they are found in the body	no/partly/yes	1 2 3 4 5
The positions of the parts of the eye	no/partly/yes	1 2 3 4 5
The functions of the parts of the eye	no/partly/yes	1 2 3 4 5
How the eye focuses on near and distant objects	no/partly/yes	1 2 3 4 5
How information is transmitted by the nervous system	no/partly/yes	1 2 3 4 5
The structures involved in reflex actions	no/partly/yes	1 2 3 4 5
What a hormone is	no/partly/yes	1 2 3 4 5
Where hormones are made and how they are transported	no/partly/yes	1 2 3 4 5
The cause of diabetes and its treatment	no/partly/yes	1 2 3 4 5
How hormones control blood sugar levels	no/partly/yes	1 2 3 4 5
Sex hormones controlling secondary sexual characteristics	no/partly/yes	1 2 3 4 5
The role of sex hormones in the menstrual cycle	no/partly/yes	1 2 3 4 5
The use of sex hormones in controlling human fertility	no/partly/yes	1 2 3 4 5
How solvents affect the body	no/partly/yes	1 2 3 4 5
How tobacco smoke affects the body	no/partly/yes	1 2 3 4 5
How alcohol affects the body	no/partly/yes	1 2 3 4 5
Why some drugs are addictive	no/partly/yes	1 2 3 4 5

WORKED EXAMPLE 1

CHIEF EXAMINER'S COMMENTS

The doctor is testing the child's nervous system by tapping the tendon just below the knee.
This causes a pull on cells which are sensitive to stretching.

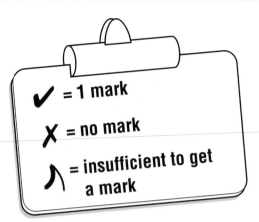

✔ = 1 mark

✗ = no mark

ʌ = insufficient to get a mark

(a) What are cells which are sensitive to stretching called? (1)

Nerve cells. ✗

(a) There are many different kinds of nerve cells. You must be precise in your answers. The type of nerve cell that is sensitive to a stimulus is a receptor.

(b) These cells send information to the spinal cord. In what form is this information sent? (2)

Impulses ✔ʌ

(b) To gain both marks you should state 'electrical impulse.'

(c) The healthy response to the stimulus is the leg straightening. What is the effector in this response? (1)

The leg muscle. ✔

(c) Although 'leg muscle' is correct, there are many muscles in the leg. 'Muscle in the thigh' would be a better answer.

(d) The straightening of the leg is one example of a reflex action. Describe one other example of a reflex action in terms of: stimulus → receptor → co-ordinator → effector → response. (4)

when something comes quickly towards the eye, we automatically blink. This is because the eye receives the stimulus ʌ *and sends a message* ✗ *to the brain which is the co-ordinator.* ✔ *The brain then sends a message to the eyelid* ʌ *telling it to close quickly. This is the response.* ✔

(d) You must answer the question set, and not think that the answer you have revised will be sufficient. This question asked for a description of a reflex action 'in terms of stimulus → receptor → co-ordinator → effector → response'; so you must use these words correctly in your answer.
A better answer would have included the following points:
■ Blinking is an example of a reflex action.
■ In this reflex action the stimulus is an object moving towards the eye.
■ The retina of the eye contains receptor cells that are sensitive to light.
■ These send electrical impulses along sensory neurones to the brain which is the co-ordinator.
■ The brain sends electrical impulses to the muscles in the eyelid which are the effectors.
■ When these muscles contract the eyelid moves.
■ This movement of the eyelid is the response.

WORKED EXAMPLE 2

CHIEF EXAMINER'S COMMENTS

Read the following passage which is from an advice book for diabetics

Hypoglycaemia or 'hypo' for short, occurs when there is too little sugar in the blood.
It is important always to carry some form of sugar with you and take it immediately you feel a 'hypo' start. A 'hypo' may start because:

- you have taken too much insulin;
- you are late for a meal, have missed a meal altogether, have eaten too little at a meal;
- you have taken a lot more exercise than usual.

The remedy is to take some glucose.

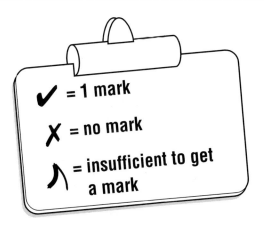

✔ = 1 mark

✗ = no mark

∫ = insufficient to get a mark

(a) Explain why diabetics need to take insulin. (2)

Diabetics need to take insulin to control their sugar levels. ✔∫

(b) Explain why there is too little sugar in the blood if too much insulin is taken. (2)

Because insulin converts sugar into glycogen. ✗ *If too much insulin is taken, all the sugar will be converted to glycogen.* ✔

(c) Explain why sugar is recommended for a 'hypo' rather than a starchy food. (3)

Because sugar is digested quicker than starch. ✗

(d) Explain how the body of a healthy person restores the blood sugar level if the level drops too low. (3)

The pancreas ✗ *converts glycogen back to sugar.* ✔

(a) *This only half answers the question. The answer should focus not only on why diabetics need to take insulin, but how it affects them. Insulin reduces blood sugar levels. The pancreas of a diabetic does not make enough insulin. With too little insulin, the blood sugar level may rise.*

(b) *A common error is to state that insulin converts sugar to glycogen. Insulin in fact stimulates the liver to convert sugar into glycogen at a faster rate. The liver then stores this glycogen. A better answer therefore is: 'Insulin stimulates the liver to convert blood sugar to glycogen at a faster rate, therefore reducing blood sugar levels.'*

(c) *This is an inappropriate answer as it does not address the question. Digestion converts insoluble compounds into soluble compounds such as glucose. Glucose is soluble, therefore it can be absorbed quickly from the gut into the blood. Starch is insoluble, so must first be broken down into glucose before it can be absorbed.*

(d) *You cannot expect to score the three available marks by writing one short sentence. You should include the following points:*
- *The pancreas secretes the hormones that control blood sugar level.*
- *Glycogen is stored in the liver and it is there that it is converted back into glucose.*
- *The hormone glucagon, secreted by the pancreas, speeds up the rate of this process.*

Make sure that you can spell glucagon and glycogen accurately. If you misspell either of them you will get no marks.

1 Nerve cells

(a) Copy and complete the table. (6)

Organ	Contains receptors sensitive to
Eye	Light
Ear	_____ and _____
Skin	_____ and _____
Tongue	_____
Nose	_____

The drawing shows a receptor and a sensory neurone (nerve cell).

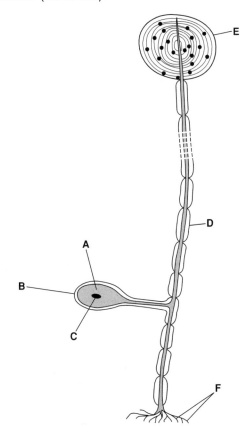

(b) The parts labelled **A**, **B** and **C** are found in most animal cells. Name them. (3)

(c) The part labelled **D** is composed mainly of fat. Suggest a function for this part. Explain the reason for your answer. (2)

(d) The part labelled **E** is the receptor. It is found in the skin on the leg. Suggest **one** stimulus it might detect. (1)

(e) In which organ of the body would you expect to find the part labelled **F**? (1)

2 The eye

The drawing shows a section through the eye.

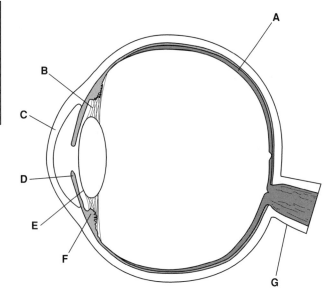

(a) Name the structures labelled **A**, **B**, **C**, **D**, **E**, **F** and **G**. (7)

(b) What is the function of each of the parts labelled **A**, **B**, **C** and **D**? (4)

(c) (i) Explain how the eye focuses light. (2)
    (ii) Explain how the eye changes from focusing on a near object to focusing on a distant object. (3)

3 Reflex actions

A student put his leg out of bed and his foot touched the cold floor. He immediately pulled his foot off the floor.

(a) What name is given to this type of response?
(1)

(b) Explain why this type of response is essential to the body. (2)

(c) Explain how information is passed from one neurone to another. (2)

The drawing shows the structures in the student's body which brought about this response.

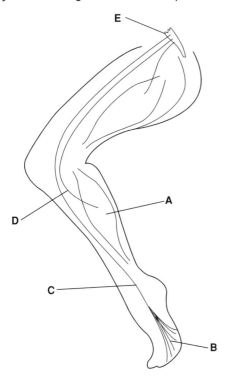

(d) Use words from the following list to name the structures labelled **A**, **B**, **C**, **D** and **E** (5)

    effector   co-ordinator   sensory neurone

      motor neurone   receptor

4 Controlling blood sugar

A healthy student drank some 'Sportsaid' – a drink containing glucose. The graph shows the changes in the levels of glucose and insulin in her blood during the hour after the drink.

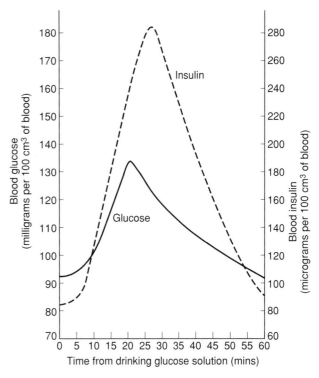

(a) (i) By how much did the blood glucose level rise after the drink? (1)
    (ii) How long after drinking the Sportsaid drink did the student's insulin level rise to its maximum level? (1)

(b) (i) Which organ produces insulin? (1)
    (ii) Explain what happens to most of the blood glucose from 20 minutes onwards. (2)

(c) (i) Sketch the graphs you would expect for blood glucose and insulin levels if the student was a diabetic and did not take any extra insulin. (2)
    (ii) Explain why the graphs are different from those of a healthy student. (2)

5   Drinking and driving

The table shows the amount of alcohol in the blood of a party-goer in the hours following a party

Time after end of party (hours)	Amount of alcohol in blood (mg per 100 cm³)
0	220
2	176
4	142
6	99

(a) (i) Plot a graph of the data using a horizontal scale of 1cm = 1 hour.   (3)

(ii) Use your graph to find how long after the party it would be before the amount of alcohol in the blood fell to 80 mg per 100 cm³ of blood – the maximum amount you may have if you are driving.   (1)

(b) Explain why it is dangerous to drive a car if there is alcohol in your blood.   (3)

(c) Give **two** permanent effects on the body of consuming excessive amounts of alcohol.   (2)

6   Diet and training

In an investigation three groups of students were given different diets for 1 week.
- Group A were given a low carbohydrate diet.
- Group B were given a normal diet.
- Group C were given a high carbohydrate diet.

At the end of the week the students were asked to pedal a bicycle machine for as long as possible. The results are shown on the graph.

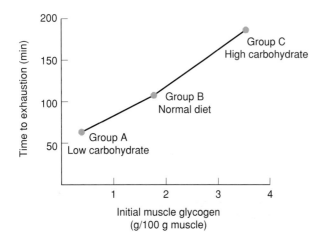

Explain why group C were able to pedal the longest. (5)

7   Drug addiction

The table shows the number of registered narcotic drug addicts in the United Kingdom between 1979 and 1984

Age (years)	Number of addicts					
	1979	1980	1981	1982	1983	1984
under 21	308	365	478	698	1135	1611
21 – 24	1054	995	1161	1536	2042	2701
25 – 29	1843	1882	2110	2569	2977	3347
30 – 34	854	1115	1538	2049	2518	2920
35 – 39	406	421	503	710	1023	1347
40 and over	322	329	367	400	540	563
females	1281	1398	1703	2220	2863	3605
males	3506	3709	4454	5742	7372	8884
Total	**4787**	**5107**	**6157**	**7962**	**10 235**	**12 489**

(a) Which age group shows the largest increase in addiction?   (1)

(b) How is the number of addicts related to;

(i) age,   (1)

(ii) sex?   (1)

(c) Explain why some drugs are addictive.   (3)

(d) Describe **two** long term effects of drug abuse. (2)

8   Sex hormones

(a)   Explain what is meant by 'secondary sexual characteristics'.   (2)

(b)   Name the hormones responsible for the development of secondary sexual characteristics in;

(i)   girls,   (1)
(ii) boys.   (1)

(c)   The graphs show the concentrations in the blood of four hormones at different times in a woman's menstrual cycle.

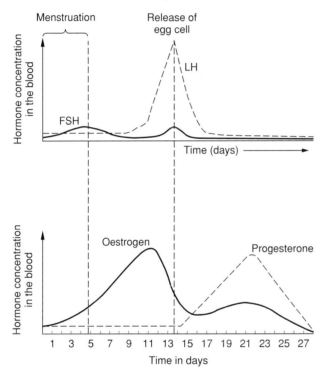

The hormone FSH is secreted by the pituitary gland at the base of the brain. It stimulates the development of immature cells into eggs in the ovary. It also stimulates the production of oestrogen.

(i)   How does FSH reach the ovary?   (1)
(ii) Use information from the graph to suggest the effect of increasing oestrogen production on the secretion of FSH.   (2)
(iii) Many types of birth-control pills contain oestrogen. Explain how oestrogen acts as a contraceptive.   (2)

(d)   The hormone LH stimulates the release of a mature egg cell in the ovary.
Use information from the graphs to suggest how LH secretion is controlled.   (1)

(e)   Progesterone is not secreted until after the egg has been released. Suggest one function for progesterone.   (1)

(f)   Evaluate an advantage and a disadvantage of the use of hormones in:

(i)   human birth control,   (6)
(ii) enhancing human fertility.   (3)

9   How some fish can camouflage themselves

Many kinds of fish can change colour to blend in with their background. They can become darker by the expansion of pigment-containing cells in the skin.

Explain the mechanisms involved in this response. You should use the following terms in your answer:

co-ordinator   effector   receptor

stimulus   response   (5)

4 Homeostasis

TEACHER SUMMARY SHEET

QUESTION	TITLE AND CONTENT	LEVEL	SKILLS TESTED
1	**Waterworks**		
(a)	Label drawing of urinary system	F	Recall
(b)	Complete table of excretory materials	F	Recall
(c)	Role of liver in excretion	S	Understanding
2	**In and out of the kidney**		
(a)	Comparison of blood entering and leaving kidney	F	Data interpretation
(b)	Mechanism of kidney including table completion	S	Calculation and understanding
3	**How the kidney works**		
(a)	Filtration and selective reabsorption	H	Understanding
(b)	Active uptake	H	Understanding
(c)	Blood osmotic pressure	H	Understanding
4	**Getting into a sweat**		
(a)	Interpolation on body temperature graph	S	Interpolation
(b)	Energy release during exercise	S	Understanding
(c)	Mechanisms for reducing body temperature	H	Understanding
5	**Hot bodies**		
(a)	Interpret patterns in skin temperature	H	Understanding
(b)	Explaining changes in skin temperature during exercise	H	Understanding
6	**Keeping cool**		
(a)	Explaining changes in brain temperature	H	Understanding
(b)	Explaining changes in skin temperature	H	Understanding

 Progress with GCSE Structured Questions: Biology

4 Homeostasis

TOPIC	COVERED	EVALUATION
	Circle the term that best describes how well you feel you have covered this topic.	On a scale of 1 – 5 how well do you feel you have understood this topic? (1 = not understood; 5 = fully understood).
The waste materials produced by the human body	no/partly/yes	1 2 3 4 5
Where these materials are produced	no/partly/yes	1 2 3 4 5
Where waste materials leave the human body	no/partly/yes	1 2 3 4 5
What homeostasis means	no/partly/yes	1 2 3 4 5
How the liver deals with excess amino acids	no/partly/yes	1 2 3 4 5
Why we sometimes sweat	no/partly/yes	1 2 3 4 5
What materials are filtered out in the kidneys	no/partly/yes	1 2 3 4 5
What materials are reabsorbed in the kidneys	no/partly/yes	1 2 3 4 5
What materials are present in urine	no/partly/yes	1 2 3 4 5
How the composition of urine is controlled	no/partly/yes	1 2 3 4 5
How blood vessels in the skin can help to keep the body warm	no/partly/yes	1 2 3 4 5
How blood vessels in the skin can help to cool the body	no/partly/yes	1 2 3 4 5
How sweating cools the body	no/partly/yes	1 2 3 4 5
How shivering can warm up the body	no/partly/yes	1 2 3 4 5
How the brain controls body temperature	no/partly/yes	1 2 3 4 5

WORKED EXAMPLE 1

The diagram shows the mean daily input and output of water for an adult.

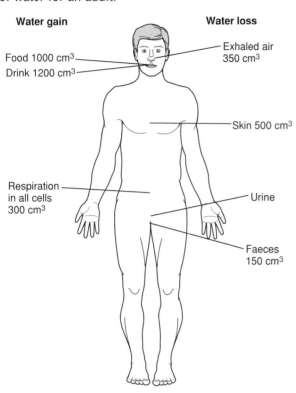

Water gain

Food 1000 cm³
Drink 1200 cm³
Respiration in all cells 300 cm³

Water loss

Exhaled air 350 cm³
Skin 500 cm³
Urine
Faeces 150 cm³

CHIEF EXAMINER'S COMMENTS

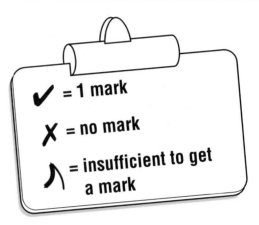

✔ = 1 mark

✗ = no mark

∫ = insufficient to get a mark

(a) Respiration is a source of water. Name the other substance produced by respiration. (1)

energy ✗

(b) The kidneys keep the water content of the body constant by controlling the volume of water passed out in the urine.

(i) Use the data in the diagram to calculate the mean daily output of water in the urine. Show your working. (2)

1000 + 1200 + 300 = 2500

350 + 500 + 150 = 900 ✗

2500 − 900 = 1600

Answer 1600 cm³ ✔✗

(ii) Describe how the amount of water in blood is controlled by the kidneys. (3)

The kidneys are able to detect the level of water in the body. If there is too much the excess water will be removed from the body in the urine. If there is too little the kidneys will not allow a lot to be excreted. ∫∫∫

(a) *Energy is not a substance, nor is it produced. Energy is **transferred** or **released** in respiration. Carbon dioxide is the correct answer.*

(b) **(i)** *Always show all your working and give the correct units. There is an arithmetical error in the water loss part of the calculation, but the answer shows the correct method and therefore gains one mark.*

(ii) *This answer is weak as it does little more than repeat the question. There are three main points which gain marks:*
1   The blood is filtered in the glomerulus and most of the water passes into the kidney tubule.
2   As the filtrate flows through the tubule, water is reabsorbed into the surrounding blood vessels.
3   Reabsorption occurs in sufficient quantities to keep the concentration of water in the blood constant.

CHAPTER 4 HOMEOSTASIS

WORKED EXAMPLE 2

(a) It was a warm day on a field trip. One of the students decided to paddle in the cold water of a stream to collect specimens. When she came out of the water the skin on her legs looked very pale and she began to shiver.
Explain how each of the changes helped her to keep a constant body temperature.

(i) Changes in her skin. (4)

Her skin went pale because her blood vessels went deeper into the skin. ✗ This meant that less heat was lost to the outside air by radiation ✔ so the blood kept warm.

(ii) Shivering. (3)

Shivering keeps you warm because heat is released when your muscles contract. ✔ This warms up the blood and the heat goes to the rest of the body. ∧∧

(b) Explain why we often produce less urine on a hot day than on a cold day. (4)

On a hot day we sweat a lot, ✔ so there is not as much water left in the body to come out as urine. ∧∧∧

CHIEF EXAMINER'S COMMENTS

✔ = 1 mark

✗ = no mark

∧ = insufficient to get a mark

(a) *(i)* One of the most common mistakes when describing the role of blood vessels in temperature control is to say that they move down (or up) in the skin – they don't. In vasoconstriction the blood supply to the surface capillaries is reduced by constriction of the arterioles that supply them. The rest of the answer was quite good – most heat is transferred from the skin by radiation since air is a poor conductor.

(ii) Shivering was correctly described as muscle contractions, but to gain full marks you must mention the process that transfers the energy – respiration. Sugars are oxidised in the muscles to release energy, some of this can be transferred to the blood passing through the muscles.

(b) We do lose more sweat on a hot day, but you must always explain that sweat is produced to reduce body temperature. Also there was no reference to the role of the kidney. If more water is lost from the body through sweating the kidney responds by reabsorbing more water into the blood, resulting in less water in the urine.

1 Waterworks

(a) The drawing shows the urinary and reproductive systems of a woman.

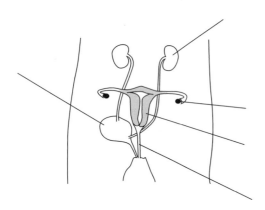

Copy the diagram and label a kidney, a ureter, the bladder and the urethra. (4)

(b) Copy and complete the table. (4)

Excretory Product	Produced in	Excreted by
Carbon dioxide	All cells	
Urea		
Excess water		
Excess salts		

(c) The flow chart shows what happens to amino acids in the liver.

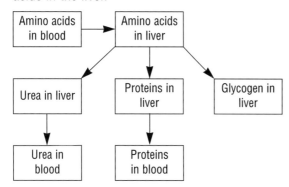

(i) In which organ do most amino acids enter the blood? (1)

(ii) Name the process by which amino acids are converted into urea. (1)

(iii) Describe what happens to the urea from the time it leaves the liver until it is excreted by the body. (5)

(iv) Glycogen is also formed from amino acids. Explain what glycogen is used for in the body. (2)

2 In and out of the kidney

(a) The table shows the concentrations of three substances in the blood and urine of a pupil.

	Concentration of sugar (g/l)	Concentration of urea (g/l)	Concentration of salts (g/l)
Blood entering kidney	10	3	12
Blood leaving kidney	10	1.5	9
Urine	0	1.5	3

(i) Give **one** similarity between the blood entering the kidney and blood leaving the kidney. (1)

(ii) Give **two** differences between the blood entering the kidney and blood leaving the kidney. (2)

(b) The table shows the amounts of substances filtered, excreted and reabsorbed by the kidney in one day.

Substance	Filtered	Excreted	Reabsorbed
Water (litres/day)	180	1.5	178.5
Glucose (g/day)	180		180
Urea (g/day)	56	28	
Sodium ions (g/day)	540		536
Chloride ions (g/day)		6	625

(i) Copy and complete the table. (4)

(ii) What proportion of the filtered glucose is reabsorbed? (1)

(iii) What proportion of the filtered urea is reabsorbed? (1)

(iv) Explain why these two proportions are so different. (2)

3   How the kidney works

Two processes in the kidneys are largely responsible for urine formation – filtration and selective reabsorption.

(a) (i)   Where in the kidney does filtration occur? (1)

(ii)   What determines the kinds of molecules that are present in the filtrate? (1)

(iii) Most of the filtered glucose is reabsorbed into the blood. Where does this reabsorption of glucose occur? (1)

(b) Most of the glucose is reabsorbed against a concentration gradient.

(i)   Explain what is meant by 'against a concentration gradient'. (2)

(ii) Explain how glucose is reabsorbed against a concentration gradient. (2)

(c) Explain why most of the sodium and chloride ions that are filtered have to be reabsorbed back into the blood. (3)

4   Getting into a sweat

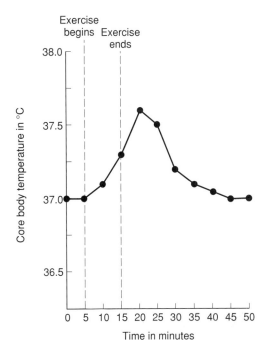

The graph shows changes in core body temperature during and after exercise.

(a) (i)   By how much did the core body temperature rise during the exercise? (1)

(ii) How long did it take for core body temperature to return to normal after exercise ended? (1)

(b) (i)   Explain why the core body temperature rose after exercise. (3)

(ii) Explain why the core body temperature continued to rise after exercise ended. (2)

(c) Describe and explain **three** processes in the body that cause core body temperature to return to normal. (6)

5 Hot bodies

Infrared detectors can be used to detect the heat radiation from the surface of the body. The drawings show heat radiation from the surface of the body before and after exercise.

Before exercise   After exercise

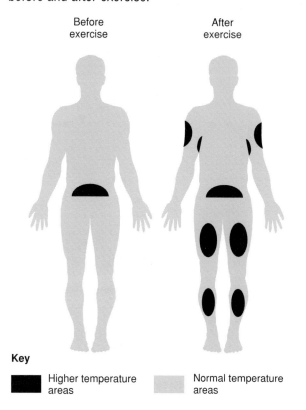

Key

■ Higher temperature areas

▨ Normal temperature areas

(a) Suggest an explanation for the pattern of heat radiation before exercise. (2)

(b) Explain the cause of the differences in the patterns of heat radiation before and after exercise. (5)

6 Keeping cool

A student was kept in a room where the temperature was maintained at 45°C. The student swallowed a piece of ice at the time indicated on the graphs.

(a) Graph 1 shows the effect of swallowing the piece of ice on brain temperature.

Graph 1

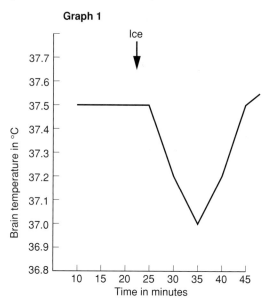

Explain the mechanisms which caused the changes in brain temperature. (3)

(b) Graph 2 shows the effect of swallowing the same piece of ice on the temperature of the surface of the skin.

Graph 2

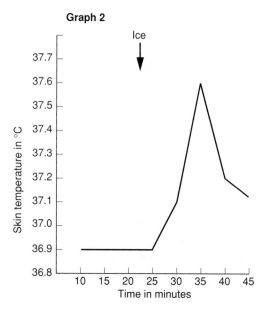

Explain the mechanisms which caused the changes in skin temperature. (5)

5 Plant physiology

QUESTION	TITLE AND CONTENT	LEVEL	SKILLS TESTED
1	**Parts of a plant**		
(a)	Labelling the parts of a plant	F	Recall
(b)	Functions of parts of a plant	F	Understanding
(c)	Shape of a leaf in relation to photosynthesis	S	Understanding
2	**What's inside a plant cell?**		
(a)	Labelling a mesophyll cell	S	Recall
(b)	Functions of the parts of a plant cell	S	Understanding
(c)	Differences between plant and animal cells	S	Understanding
(d)	Structure of a mesophyll cell in relation to function	S	Understanding
3	**Making and moving sugars**		
(a)	Function of chlorophyll	S	Understanding
(b)	Explaining results of starch test on a variegated leaf	S	Understanding
(c)	Uses of sugars in leaves	S/H	Understanding
(d)	Transport of sugars	S	Understanding
(e)	Storage of sugars	S/H	Understanding
4	**The ins and outs of water**		
(a)	Calculating rate of water uptake, the processes involved in uptake and transport of water, difference between osmosis and active uptake	S/H	Calculation, understanding
(b)	Explanation of wilting	S/H	Understanding
5	**The goings on in a bottle garden**		
(a)	Explaining changes in composition of air in a bottle over 24 hours	S/H	Understanding
(b)	Explaining why the transpiration rate in the bottle does not change	S/H	Understanding
(c)	Suggest why the stopper should be removed occasionally	S/H	Understanding
6	**Growing the most tomatoes**		
(a)	Plotting graph of optimum growing conditions	S	Graph construction
(b)	Explaining limiting factors	S/H	Understanding
(c)	Economics of heating a greenhouse	S/H	Understanding
7	**That sinking feeling**		
(a)	Word equation for photosynthesis	S	Recall
(b)	Interpreting data on floating/sinking leaf discs	H	Understanding
8	**Transpiration**		
(a)	Function of potometer	S	Understanding
(b)	Interpreting results from potometer experiment	S	Understanding
9	**Stomata**		
(a)	Function of stomata	S	Understanding
(b)	Describing and interpreting patterns of stomatal openings in potato and maize	S/H	Understanding

5 *Plant physiology*

QUESTION	TITLE AND CONTENT	LEVEL	SKILLS TESTED
10	**Mineral nutrition**		
(a)	Deficiency symptoms	S/H	Understanding
(b)	Functions of mineral ions	S/H	Understanding
(c)	Commercial plant growing	S/H	Understanding
11	**Plant responses**		
(a)	Defining tropisms	S	Understanding
(b)	Interpreting results of phototropism experiment	S	Understanding

5 Plant physiology

STUDENT CHECKLIST

TOPIC	COVERED	EVALUATION
	Circle the term that best describes how well you feel you have covered this topic.	On a scale of 1 – 5 how well do you feel you have understood this topic? (1 = not understood; 5 = fully understood).
The functions of roots, stems and leaves	no/partly/yes	1 2 3 4 5
What plants need for photosynthesis	no/partly/yes	1 2 3 4 5
The chemical equation for photosynthesis	no/partly/yes	1 2 3 4 5
What is meant by limiting factors	no/partly/yes	1 2 3 4 5
Which factors may limit the rate of photosynthesis	no/partly/yes	1 2 3 4 5
What may happen to the sugars produced during photosynthesis	no/partly/yes	1 2 3 4 5
Why plants need specific mineral ions	no/partly/yes	1 2 3 4 5
What happens if plants are deficient in these mineral ions	no/partly/yes	1 2 3 4 5
How plants respond to the stimuli of water, gravity and light	no/partly/yes	1 2 3 4 5
How plant hormones are involved in these responses	no/partly/yes	1 2 3 4 5
How plant hormones are used in agriculture and horticulture	no/partly/yes	1 2 3 4 5
Why water moves into or out of cells by osmosis	no/partly/yes	1 2 3 4 5
Why mineral salts are absorbed from the soil by active uptake	no/partly/yes	1 2 3 4 5
What is meant by transpiration	no/partly/yes	1 2 3 4 5
The external factors that affect the rate of transpiration	no/partly/yes	1 2 3 4 5
How some plants are adapted to living in dry conditions	no/partly/yes	1 2 3 4 5
The structure and role of stomata	no/partly/yes	1 2 3 4 5
The factors that affect the opening and closing of stomata	no/partly/yes	1 2 3 4 5
What is meant by turgor	no/partly/yes	1 2 3 4 5
Why turgor is important to plants	no/partly/yes	1 2 3 4 5
The function of xylem	no/partly/yes	1 2 3 4 5
The functions of phloem	no/partly/yes	1 2 3 4 5

WORKED EXAMPLE 1

CHIEF EXAMINER'S COMMENTS

The graph shows the mean light intensity at different times of the year in an oak wood.

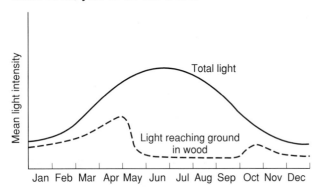

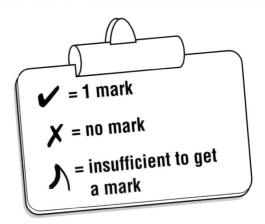

✔ = 1 mark

✗ = no mark

↗ = insufficient to get a mark

(a) (i) In which month of the year would you expect the rate of photosynthesis in the oak trees to be greatest? (1)

June/July ✗

(a) *(i)* *If the question asks for one month then give only one month in your answer. Examiners are often instructed to mark answers like this one wrong because they are not expected to choose the correct answer – that is your job.*

(ii) There are plants living on the ground in the wood. In which month would you expect their rate of growth to be fastest? (1)

April ✔

Explain your answer. (2)

The larger plants and trees will not have grown their leaves yet. As the trees have no leaves, a greater amount of light reaches the forest floor, thus increasing the rate of photosynthesis for plants on the forest floor. ✔↗

(ii) *At first sight this seems a good answer, but it does not really answer the question. Look out for the key word 'rate' in questions – if you see it, then use it in your answer. Instead of saying 'a greater amount of light' and 'increasing the rate of photosynthesis' you should say 'April is the month when these plants receive the maximum light intensity. This means that the photosynthesis will occur at the maximum rate.' You should then go on to link the rate of photosynthesis with growth rate by stating that the maximum rate photosynthesis provides the maximum amount of sugars that are needed for growth.*

(b) Name two factors, other than light intensity, that would affect the rate of photosynthesis in the oak trees. (2)

Heat ✗

Salts ✗

(b) *Never give 'heat' as a factor – always give 'temperature'. The other principal factor affecting the rate of photosynthesis is the carbon dioxide concentration in the surrounding air . 'Salts' is too vague. It would only be accepted if you gave a relevant specific answer such as 'magnesium concentration in the soil water' (which is needed for chlorophyll synthesis).*

WORKED EXAMPLE 2

Two cubes of potato were weighed. One cube was put into distilled water at 20°C, the other into distilled water at 50°C. After one hour the cubes of potato were re-weighed. The results are shown in the table.

Temperature of water (°C)	Mass of potato cube (g)	
	At start	After one hour
20	10.0	10.7
50	10.0	10.0

(a) Explain the change in mass of the potato cube kept in water at 20°C. (4)

It changed mass because of osmosis.✔ There is a strong solution inside the cube so water goes in. ⋏ This makes the cube weigh more.⋏ ⋏

(b) Explain why the potato cube kept in water at 50°C did not change mass. (3)

The high temperature killed ✗ the cells so no water could get in. ⋏ ⋏ ⋏

(c) Potato cubes placed in a solution containing potassium ions can absorb almost all the potassium ions from the solution. Explain how they are able to do this. (4)

They can do this because they have a process called active uptake ✔ which uses energy to absorb the ions.⋏ ⋏ ⋏

CHIEF EXAMINER'S COMMENTS

✔ = 1 mark

✗ = no mark

⋏ = insufficient to get a mark

(a) More marks are lost in answers to osmosis questions than in almost any other topic. The second sentence is a very weak part of the answer. 'Strong solution' is a very imprecise term and 'water' goes both in and out. You should remember that osmosis is a special case of diffusion and state that water diffuses from a region containing a high concentration of water molecules to a region with a lower concentration of water molecules. You should then explain that the concentration of water molecules inside the potato cube is lower than that in pure water because there are many substances dissolved in the water inside the potato. The answer should also have stated that the potato cells have partially-permeable membranes which allow water molecules to pass both in and out, but keep the larger molecules inside the cells.
An answer which stated that the water moves from a weak solution to dilute a strong solution would also be accepted.

(b) You rarely get marks in Biology exams for saying that things are 'killed'. The key phrase to use is 'proteins are denatured by temperatures above 45°C'. In this case it is the proteins in the membranes that are denatured. This means that the larger molecules dissolved in the water inside the potato can leave the cells, so there is no longer a lower concentration of water molecules inside the cells. Water molecules enter and leave at the same rate, so there is no change in mass.

(c) The cubes do use active uptake but you should state that this is necessary because the potassium ions are absorbed against a concentration gradient. You should also state the energy required for this process is released by respiration.

1 Parts of a plant

The drawing shows a plant.

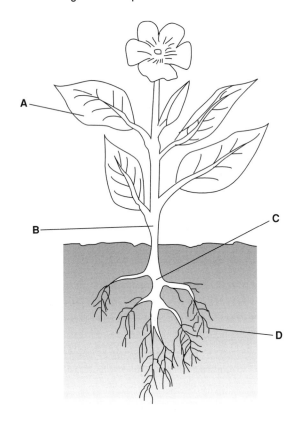

(a) Name the parts labelled **A**, **B**, **C** and **D**. (4)

(b) Give the main function of each of the parts labelled **A**, **B**, **C** and **D**. (4)

(c) Explain how the shape of part **A** helps it to carry out its function efficiently. (3)

2 What's inside a plant cell?

The drawing shows a mesophyll cell from a plant leaf.

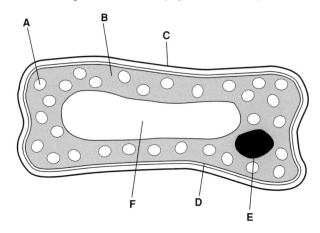

(a) Name the parts labelled **A**, **B**, **C**, **D**, **E** and **F**. (6)

(b) Give the main function of each of the parts labelled **A**, **B**, **C**, **D**, **E** and **F**. (6)

(c) Which **three** of the parts **A**, **B**, **C**, **D**, **E** and **F** are not found in animal cells? (1)

(d) (i) What is the main function of this mesophyll cell? (1)

(ii) Explain two ways in which the structure of this cell enables it to carry out its function efficiently. (4)

Progress with GCSE Structured Questions: Biology

3 Making and moving sugars

Variegated leaves are two-coloured, often green and yellow. A plant with variegated leaves was left in sunlight for several hours. Pieces of its leaves were then detached and tested for sugar. The diagram shows the results of this test.

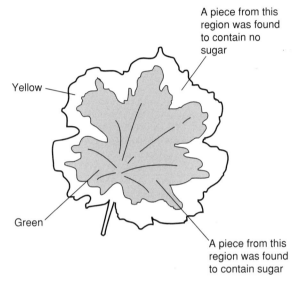

A piece from this region was found to contain no sugar

Yellow

Green

A piece from this region was found to contain sugar

(a) (i) Name the green pigment in the leaf. (1)
(ii) Give the function of this pigment. (1)

(b) Explain the results of the test. (3)

(c) Some of the sugar produced is utilised in the leaf where it is made. What is the main use of sugars within leaves? (1)

(d) Some sugars are transported out of the leaves to younger leaves and roots.

(i) Name the tissue through which sugars are transported. (1)
(ii) What are the **two** main uses of sugars in young leaves and roots? (2)

(e) Some sugars are transported to old roots. What happens to most of the sugars that are transported to older roots? (2)

4 The ins and outs of water

(a) The drawing shows the results of an experiment into the rate of water uptake by a plant.

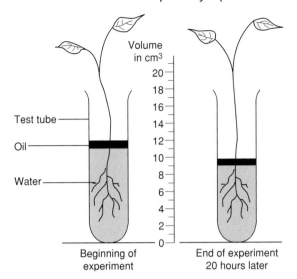

Volume in cm³

Test tube

Oil

Water

Beginning of experiment

End of experiment 20 hours later

(i) The apparatus was set up then left for 20 hours. Calculate the rate of water uptake by the plant. (2)
(ii) The water is taken in by root hairs. Name the process which causes this to happen. (1)
(iii) Name the tissue which transports water from the roots to the stem. (1)
(iv) Explain what causes water to move upwards through the stem. (3)
(v) Root hair cells also absorb mineral ions. Explain how the uptake of mineral ions by plant roots differs from the uptake of water. (3)

(b) The drawing shows a plant which has not been watered for several days.

Explain why the plant's leaves have drooped. (3)

5   The goings-on in a bottle garden

The drawing shows a bottle garden which is kept on a window ledge. The stopper is airtight.

(a)   Explain how the concentration of gases in the air in the bottle would change over a 24 hour period.   (4)

(b)   Explain why the rate of transpiration will not change over a 24 hour period.   (2)

(c)   It is recommended that the stopper is taken out occasionally. Suggest an explanation for this.   (3)

6   Growing the most tomatoes

Tomatoes are often grown in greenhouses. An investigation was carried out to find out the optimum growing conditions for tomatoes. The table shows the results of one of the experiments.

Percentage of carbon dioxide in air	Relative growth rate
0.00	0
0.02	10
0.04	15
0.06	18
0.08	20
0.10	22
0.12	23
0.14	23
0.16	23

(a)   Plot the figures and draw a graph of the results.   (3)

(b)   Explain why increasing the carbon dioxide beyond 0.12% did not further increase the rate of growth.   (2)

(c)   Commercial tomato growers often heat their greenhouses. Suggest why it is not always profitable to heat greenhouses.   (3)

7 That sinking feeling

(a) (i) Write a word equation for photosynthesis. (2)

(ii) Write a balanced chemical equation for photosynthesis. (2)

(b) A student used the following method to investigate the effect of light intensity on the rate of photosynthesis.
- She cut 50 discs from leaves of the same plant and placed them in sodium hydrogen carbonate solution in the dark. The leaves floated at first because they contained oxygen. As the discs used up the oxygen, the leaves sank.
- She then placed batches of ten sunken discs into each of five beakers containing sodium hydrogen carbonate solution. Each beaker was placed in a different light intensity. As the discs produced oxygen they rose to the surface.
- The mean time taken for each batch of discs to rise to the surface is shown on the graph.

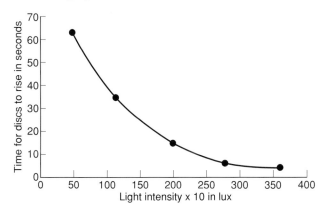

(i) At what light intensity is the rate of photosynthesis greatest? (1)

(ii) Copy the graph and sketch the curve you would expect if the discs had been placed in water rather than in sodium hydrogen carbonate solution. (2)

(iii) Explain why you have drawn the graph in this way. (2)

8 Transpiration

(a) The drawing shows a potometer.

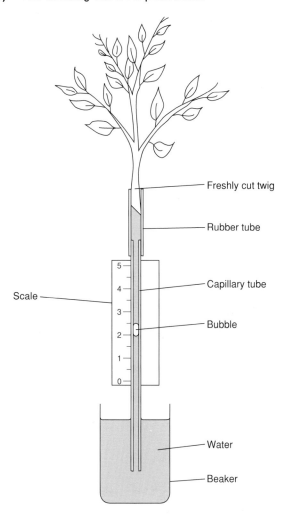

What does a potometer measure? (2)

(b) The table shows some results obtained with the potometer.

Conditions	Time taken for bubble to move 10 cm (mins)
Light, warm, windy	1
Light, cool, windy	2
Light, warm, still	5
Light, cool, still	7
Dark, warm, still	40

(i) What is meant by transpiration? (2)

(ii) What do these results indicate about the effects of wind and temperature on the rate of transpiration? (2)

(iii) Explain why the bubble moved much more slowly in the dark than in the light. (2)

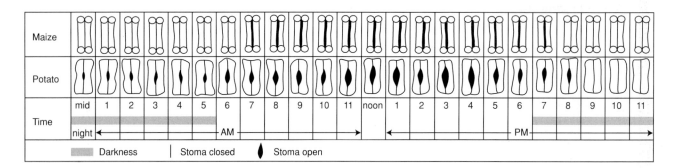

Time:

| | mid | 1 | 2 | 3 | 4 | 5 | 6 | 7 | 8 | 9 | 10 | 11 | noon | 1 | 2 | 3 | 4 | 5 | 6 | 7 | 8 | 9 | 10 | 11 |

night ← AM → ← PM →

Darkness | Stoma closed | Stoma open

9 Stomata

(a) In a leaf, what is the main function of stomata? (2)

(b) The drawing above shows the daily opening patterns of stomata in maize plants and potato plants.

    (i) Describe **two** major differences between the opening patterns of the stomata in the two plants. (2)

    (ii) Use evidence from the drawing to suggest which of the plants would grow best in a dry climate. Explain **two** reasons for your answer. (4)

10 Mineral nutrition

The diagrams below show the effects of growing plants in solutions which lack specific mineral ions.

(a) Explain;

    (i) why the plants grown without nitrogen were stunted, (2)

    (ii) why the plants with no magnesium had some yellow leaves. (1)

(b) Suggest **one** function in plants of;

    (i) phosphorus, (1)

    (ii) potassium. (1)

(c) Some crops are produced commercially by growing the plants with their roots in a solution of mineral salts. If the concentration of mineral salts in the solution is too high the plants wilts. Explain why. (3)

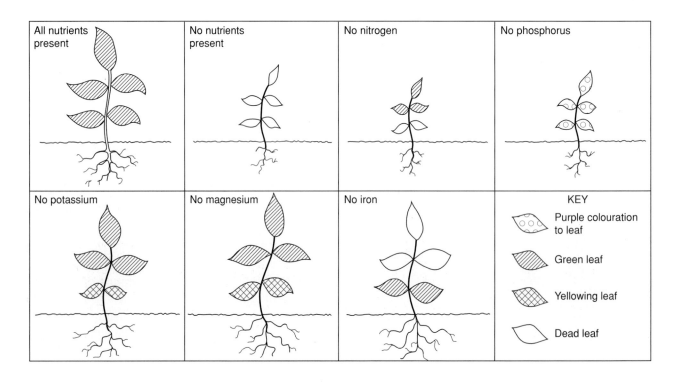

11 Plant responses

(a) State what is meant by, and give **one** advantage
to plants of;

(i) phototropism,
(ii) geotropism,
(iii) hydrotropism. (3)

(b) The drawings show an investigation into
phototropism.

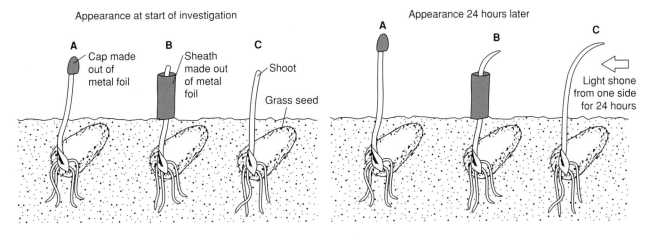

Appearance at start of investigation

A — Cap made out of metal foil
B — Sheath made out of metal foil
C — Shoot
Grass seed

Appearance 24 hours later

A
B
C
Light shone from one side for 24 hours

(i) Explain what caused shoot **C** to bend
towards the light. (3)
(ii) Explain why shoot **B** bent towards the light
but shoot **A** did not. (2)

6 Variation and evolution

QUESTION	TITLE AND CONTENT	LEVEL	SKILLS TESTED
1	**How tall wheat grows**		
(a)	Plotting bar chart of height of wheat plants	F	Graph construction
(b)	Reasons for variation in height of wheat plants	F	Understanding
2	**How tulips grow**		
(a)	Why tulips grown from bulbs have the same colour flowers	S	Understanding
(b)	Why tulips grown from seed may have different colour flowers	S	Understanding
3	**Lystosaurus**		
(a)	How fossils are formed	S	Understanding
(b)	Reasons for extinction	S	Understanding
(c)	Similarities and differences between mammals and reptiles	S	Understanding
(d)	Defining evolution	H	Understanding
(e)	Explaining how fossils provide evidence for evolution	H	Understanding
4	**Couch grass**		
(a)	Interpret diagram of mitosis	H	Understanding
(b)	Results of mitosis	H	Understanding
(c)	Meiosis in pollen production	H	Understanding
5	**Sun-beds can be dangerous**		
(a)	Cell division in skin growth	H	Understanding
(b)	Explaining differences in genetic information in sperm cells	H	Understanding
(c)	Defining mutation	H	Understanding
(d)	Explaining why sun-beds can be dangerous	H	Understanding
6	**It's not safe on the sands**		
(a)	Defining natural selection	S	Understanding
(b)	Explaining natural selection from data on banded snails	H	Understanding
7	**Mammoths**		
(a)	Selecting external features which are adaptations for life in cold climates	F/H	Understanding
(b)	Explaining evolution of mammoths in terms of natural selection	H	Understanding

6 *Variation and evolution*

TOPIC	COVERED	EVALUATION
	Circle the term that best describes how well you feel you have covered this topic.	On a scale of 1 – 5 how well do you feel you have understood this topic? (1 = not understood; 5 = fully understood).
Why young animals and plants resemble their parents	no/partly/yes	1 2 3 4 5
Why individuals of the same species show variation	no/partly/yes	1 2 3 4 5
What is meant by 'mutation'	no/partly/yes	1 2 3 4 5
Why some mutations may be harmful		
Factors that increase the frequency of mutations	no/partly/yes	1 2 3 4 5
What is meant by 'asexual reproduction' and how different organisms reproduce in this way	no/partly/yes	1 2 3 4 5
What is meant by 'sexual reproduction' and how different organisms reproduce in this way	no/partly/yes	1 2 3 4 5
What is meant by 'mitosis' and how cells divide in this way	no/partly/yes	1 2 3 4 5
What is meant by 'meiosis' and how cells divide in this way	no/partly/yes	1 2 3 4 5
Why individuals produced by asexual reproduction are genetically identical	no/partly/yes	1 2 3 4 5
Why individuals produced by sexual reproduction are genetically different	no/partly/yes	1 2 3 4 5
How fossils are formed	no/partly/yes	1 2 3 4 5
Why species may become extinct	no/partly/yes	1 2 3 4 5
What is meant by 'evolution'	no/partly/yes	1 2 3 4 5
How fossils provide evidence for evolution	no/partly/yes	1 2 3 4 5

WORKED EXAMPLE 1

Rose flowers form fruits following fertilisation. All the fruits from six rose bushes of the same species were collected and their lengths measured. The results are shown in the table below.

Length of rose fruit (mm)									
14	18	13	16	16	13	17	19	11	19
12	15	19	18	15	16	18	14	19	19
16	15	16	14	18	14	15	18	20	15
15	17	14	12	16	20	19	17	15	16
15	13	15	19	18	20	14	19	19	14

(a) Plot the data on the graph paper in the most appropriate way. Show any working in the space above the graph paper. (4)

1	2	3	7	9	7	3	6	3

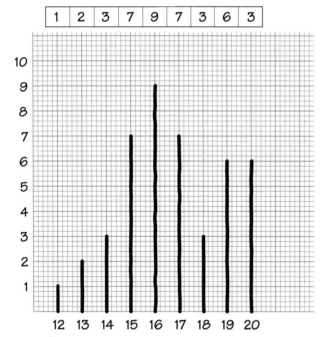

(b) The variation in the length of these rose fruits is not due to environmental factors.
Explain three possible causes for this variation in fruit length. (6)

1 Some of the bushes might have been in the shade ✗

2 Random fertilisation ✔ ∧

3 The gametes are produced by meiosis ✔ ∧

CHIEF EXAMINER'S COMMENTS

✔ = 1 mark

✗ = no mark

∧ = insufficient to get a mark

(a) Although the counting is correct, the table does not have headings. This is how you should draw the table.

Length of fruit (mm)	12	13	14	15	16	17	18	19	20
Number of fruits	1	2	3	7	9	7	3	6	3

The graph does not receive any marks because:
1 The axes are not labelled – the horizontal axis should be labelled 'Length of fruit in mm, and the vertical axis should be labelled 'Number of fruits'.
2 The bars are drawn with a felt-tip pen – it is almost impossible to start and finish exactly on the lines, so almost all graphs drawn in felt-tip receive no marks. Always draw lines with a sharp pencil with the aid of a ruler. A mistake was also made in plotting the line at 20 mm.

(b) 1 Always read the question carefully to find out what is not required. This first answer refers to shade, which might possibly produce variation – but it is an environmental factor. The question specifically states that fruit length is **not** controlled by environmental factors.
2 'Random fertilisation' is correct and receives one of the two available marks. 'Explain' normally means you have to make at least two points. It would have been better to say 'All gametes contain different genetic information. Random fertilisation means that no two fruits will have exactly the same genetic information'
3 Again, the answer does not go far enough. To gain full marks you need to give one way in which meiosis produces variation such as 'Chromosomes are arranged randomly during meiosis therefore no two gametes contain exactly the same genetic information'. A third possible cause is that the genes in a pair might be different alleles and therefore produce different characteristics.

WORKED EXAMPLE 2

The first birds evolved from reptiles. Like reptiles they had teeth. Modern birds have no teeth and the bones of the skull and beak are honeycombed with many air spaces inside the bone.

The drawings show a reconstruction of the skeleton of a fossil bird, and the skeleton of a modern pigeon.

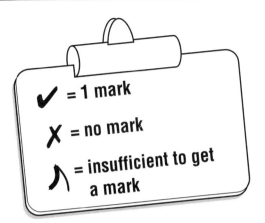

✔ = 1 mark

✗ = no mark

∧ = insufficient to get a mark

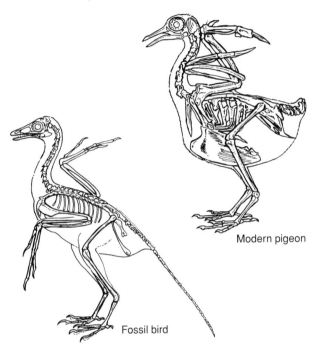

Modern pigeon

Fossil bird

(a) Describe **two** differences between the skeletons of the fossil and modern birds that can be seen in the drawings. (2)

It has thinner bones ✗

It has a long tail ✗

(a) *When you are asked for differences you must make it clear which organism you are describing. You must also be precise in your descriptions. 'It has thinner bones' does not gain marks because 'It' could refer to either organism and 'thinner bones' is too vague. 'The pigeon has a thicker thigh bone' would have been better.*
Similarly 'The fossil bird has a longer tail than the pigeon' makes clear the comparison rather than 'It has a long tail'.

(b) (i) Suggest why it is an advantage to modern birds to have air spaces inside the bones and beak. (2)

It makes them a lot lighter. ✔∧

(ii) Explain as fully as you can how birds may have evolved many air spaces inside the bones and beak as a result of natural selection. (5)

Birds with air spaces in the bones were better suited to the environment, so they survived whereas birds without air spaces in the bones died out. ✔∧∧∧∧

(b) *(i) Always look at the mark allocation – there are two marks here so you have to make two points. 'It makes them lighter so they can fly faster (or easier)' would gain both marks.*
(ii) A common mistake when answering questions on natural selection is to say what natural selection is rather than explain how it results in evolution.
- *You should always begin by stating the two main causes of variation; **1** sexual reproduction, **2** mutation.*
- *You should then explain why some variants are more likely to survive than others. In this case you could say that birds with lighter bones can fly faster and are therefore more likely to escape from predators.*
- *Finally you should state that survivors can breed and pass on their genes to their offspring.*

1   How tall wheat grows

Some pupils planted wheat seeds in a plot. When the plants had grown to maximum height the pupils measured the height of each one. The results are shown in the table.

Height of plant (cm)	Number of plants
40–49	3
50–59	5
60–69	19
70–79	25
80–89	60
90–99	75
100–109	89
110–119	30
120–129	18

(a)   Copy the axes below onto graph paper and draw a bar chart of the results.   (2)

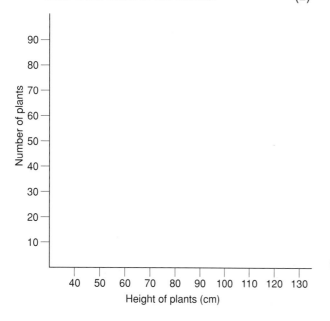

(b)   Give **three** reasons why the wheat plants did not all grow to the same height.   (3)

2   How tulips grow

The drawing shows tulip bulbs.

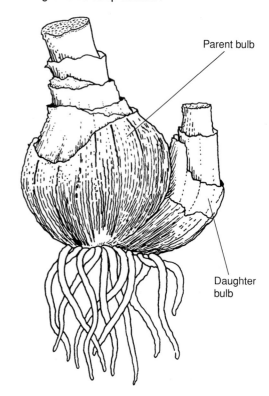

Parent bulb

Daughter bulb

(a)   The daughter bulb grows from a bud at the base of the stem of the parent bulb. It can be separated from the parent bulb and then planted. The parent and daughter bulbs produce plants with flowers of the same colour. Explain why the flowers produced by the parent and daughter bulbs are the same colour.   (3)

(b)   Tulips can also be grown from seed. The flowers of plants grown from seeds are sometimes different in colour from those of the parent tulips. Explain why.   (3)

© 1998 Hodder & Stoughton Educational   *Progress with GCSE Structured Questions: Biology*

3 Lystosaurus

The drawing shows what an extinct animal called Lystosaurus probably looked like.

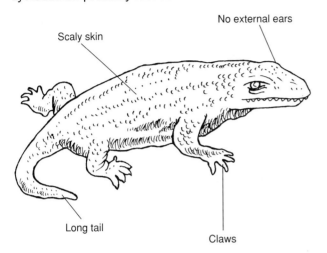

No external ears

Scaly skin

Long tail

Claws

(a) We know about Lystosaurus from its fossil remains. Describe **two** ways in which fossils may be formed. (2)

(b) Lystosaurus is extinct. Give **two** reasons why organisms may become extinct. (2)

(c) Scientists describe Lystosaurus as a 'mammal-like' reptile.

(i) Give **one** similarity between Lystosaurus and mammals. (1)

(ii) Give **one** difference between Lystosaurus and mammals. (1)

(d) Explain what is meant by 'evolution'. (2)

(e) Explain how fossils provide evidence for evolution. (2)

4 Couch grass

Couch grass is a pest in gardens because when gardeners pull up the plant, small pieces of underground stem are left in the ground. Each piece then grows into a new couch grass plant. For this to happen the cells in each remaining piece must divide many times. The diagram shows one such division.

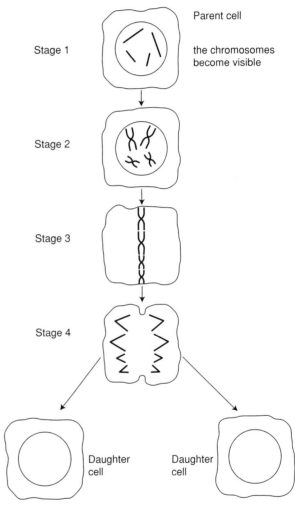

Parent cell

Stage 1 — the chromosomes become visible

Stage 2

Stage 3

Stage 4

Daughter cell

Daughter cell

(a) (i) What type of cell division is shown in the diagram? (1)

(ii) Use information from the diagram to explain your answer. (1)

(b) How does the genetic information in the two daughter cells compare;

(i) with each other, (1)

(ii) with the parent cell? (1)

(c) Give **two** ways in which the chromosomes of a pollen cell of couch grass would differ from those of the daughter cells shown in the diagram. (2)

5 Sun-beds can be dangerous

(a) A layer of cells at the base of the skin divides continually to replace the dead skin cells on the surface. Explain why the new skin cells all contain the same genetic information. (3)

(b) Cells in mature testes divide continually to produce sperm cells. Explain why no two sperm cells contain the same genetic information. (3)

(c) Explain what is meant by 'mutation'. (2)

(d) Most sun-beds have warning signs telling people the maximum time they should spend on them. The light from a sun-bed contains a high intensity of ultraviolet light. Explain why the risk of developing skin cancer is increased if the warning sign on a sun-bed is ignored. (3)

6 It's not safe on the sands

(a) Explain what is meant by 'natural selection'. (2)

(b) Cepaea is a type of snail which lives amongst grass on sand dunes. There are two forms of the snail – plain and banded.

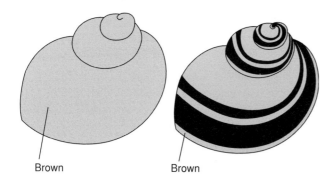

Brown   Brown

- When plain snails mate, some banded offspring may be produced.
- When banded snails mate, **all** the offspring are banded.
- Both types of snail are eaten by birds.
- Surveys of the number of snails on sand dunes usually show much higher numbers of banded snails than plain snails.

Use all the above information to suggest, in terms of natural selection, an explanation for the higher number of banded snails living amongst the grass in sand dunes. (6)

7 Mammoths

The drawings show two related species of elephant. The mammoth is now extinct.

Mammoth

Elephant

(a) Explain **two** ways in which mammoths were adapted to life in cold climates. (4)

(b) The mammoth evolved to live in very cold conditions. Explain in terms of natural selection how this might have happened. (5)

7 Inheritance

QUESTION	TITLE AND CONTENT	LEVEL	SKILLS TESTED
1	**Breeding taller plants**		
(a)	Plot a bar chart of heights of different strains	F	Graph construction
(b)	Calculating change in height	F	Calculation
(c)	Plant breeding techniques	S	Understanding
(d)	Artificial selection techniques	S	Understanding
(e)	Advantages of selective breeding	S	Understanding
2	**What makes a girl**		
(a)	Completing genetic diagram of sex determination	S	Understanding
(b)	Chance of male/female offspring	S	Understanding
3	**Breeding mice**		
(a), (b)	Construct genetic diagrams of inheritance of coat colour in mice	H	Understanding
4	**Hitch-hiker's thumb**		
(a), (b)	Interpreting pedigree of inheritance of hitch-hiker's thumb (dominant allele)	H	Understanding
5	**Cystic fibrosis**		
(a), (b)	Interpreting pedigree of inheritance of cystic fibrosis (recessive allele)	H	Understanding
6	**Huntington's chorea**		
	Interpreting pedigree of inheritance of Huntington's chorea (dominant allele)	H	Understanding
7	**Haemophilia**		
(a), (b)	Interpreting pedigree of inheritance of haemophilia (sex-linked allele)	H	Understanding
8	**DNA**		
(a)	Completing diagram of structure of DNA	H	Understanding
(b)	Explaining coding function of DNA	H	Understanding
(c)	Explaining how genetic engineering is used to produce insulin	H	Understanding
9	**New ways of growing carrots**		
(a)	Cloning	S	Understanding
(b)	Mitosis	H	Understanding
(c)	Evaluating cloning technique	H	Understanding
10	**March of the mutant tomatoes**		
	Evaluating genetic engineering techniques	H	Understanding

7 Inheritance

TOPIC	COVERED	EVALUATION
	Circle the term that best describes how well you feel you have covered this topic.	On a scale of 1 – 5 how well do you feel you have understood this topic? (1 = not understood; 5 = fully understood).
How sex is determined in humans	no/partly/yes	1 2 3 4 5
That some diseases are inherited	no/partly/yes	1 2 3 4 5
That certain characteristics are controlled by genes	no/partly/yes	1 2 3 4 5
That many genes have two forms called alleles	no/partly/yes	1 2 3 4 5
The pattern of inheritance of a disease caused by a dominant allele	no/partly/yes	1 2 3 4 5
The pattern of inheritance of a disease caused by a recessive allele	no/partly/yes	1 2 3 4 5
The pattern of inheritance of a disease caused by a sex-linked allele *(only covered in some syllabuses)*	no/partly/yes	1 2 3 4 5
How to construct genetic diagrams to explain inheritance patterns	no/partly/yes	1 2 3 4 5
That a gene is a section of DNA	no/partly/yes	1 2 3 4 5
What is meant by 'artificial selection'	no/partly/yes	1 2 3 4 5
How artificial selection can be used to produce new varieties of animals and plants	no/partly/yes	1 2 3 4 5
How cloning methods are used to produce large numbers of identical offspring	no/partly/yes	1 2 3 4 5
How genetic engineering techniques are used to transfer genetic information from one organism to another	no/partly/yes	1 2 3 4 5
The pros and cons of using genetic engineering and cloning techniques	no/partly/yes	1 2 3 4 5

WORKED EXAMPLE 1

CHIEF EXAMINER'S COMMENTS

The drawings show a wild pig and an English Large White pig. The drawings are to the same scale.

Wild pig

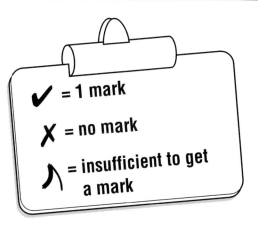

✔ = 1 mark

✗ = no mark

⌁ = insufficient to get a mark

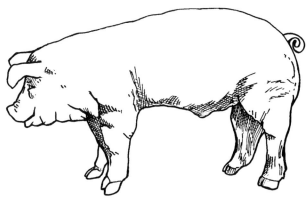

English Large White Pig

(a) The English Large White pig has been produced from the wild pig by selective breeding.

   (i) Use information from the drawings to suggest **two** characteristics which farmers selected when breeding the English Large White pig. (2)

A docile nature ✗

No tusks ✔

   (ii) Describe how farmers might have used selective breeding for one of the characteristics you have chosen. (3)

They might have chosen an animal with small tusks and mated it with another pig to see if any of the baby pigs had small tusks. ✔⌁⌁

(b) Give **two** advantages of producing new breeds of animal. (2)

You can produce an almost perfect pig e.g. strong with good meat. ⌁

You can breed healthy animals. ⌁

(a) *(i) Although 'docile nature' seems a reasonable answer you cannot see that on the drawing. You must confine your answer to features you can actually see such as tusks. Other suitable features include colour pattern and lack of hair.*

(ii) The answer started quite well by saying that an animal with small tusks was selected for mating, but didn't go far enough. The question has 3 marks so more detail is needed. It has taken hundreds of generations to produce English Large White pigs. You should go on to say that the animal with the smallest tusks in each generation was selected for mating, and that this was done for many generations.

(b) *Neither answer really answers the question which asks for advantages. Farmers are in business to make a profit, so a better first answer would be 'larger pigs have more meat on them and so can be sold for a higher price'. The second answer has the right idea but is badly worded. Farmers cannot breed healthy animals, but they can breed animals which are more resistant to disease.*

WORKED EXAMPLE 2

A particular hereditary disease is caused by a dominant allele. Sally's father has the disease, but her mother does not. There is no history of the disease in the family of Sally's husband.
Sally has just learned that she has the disease. She wonders what is the chance that her child Peter has inherited the disease.

What is the chance that Peter has inherited the disease? (1)

50% ✔

Explain why. You may use a genetic diagram if you wish. (4)

Let 'h' be the disease gene.

Peter's father

		H	h
Peter's	h	Hh	Hh
mother	h	(hh)	(hh)

✗

Therefore there is a 1 in 2 chance of Peter inheriting the disease

CHIEF EXAMINER'S COMMENTS

✔ = 1 mark

✗ = no mark

ʌ = insufficient to get a mark

*One of the commonest mistakes made in genetics is to assume that all disease alleles are recessive. The allele that causes this disease is dominant. The answer also confuses allele with gene. Most genes have two forms, a dominant allele and a recessive allele. Dominant genes are usually given a capital letter as a symbol and recessive genes a lower case letter so in this case the dominant allele could be given the symbol **H** and the recessive allele **h**.*
On the positive side, you should always use a 'checker board'.

When answering genetic problems you should always begin by giving first the genotypes of the parents, then the genotypes of their gametes.
- *Because Sally's father has the disease, but her mother does not, Sally has the genotype **Hh**.*
- *Because there is no history of the disease in Sally's husband's family, his genotype is **hh**.*
- *Sally produces two kinds of gamete – **H** and **h**.*
- *Her husband produces only one type of gamete – **h**.*
- *You should then construct a checker board.*

The simplest checker board for these gametes is:

		Father's gamete
		h
Mother's gametes	H	Hh
	h	hh

*You should then say that there is a 50% chance of Peter's genotype being **Hh**, and he therefore has a 50% chance of developing the disease.*

1 Breeding taller plants

The table shows how the height of the stems has been changed by artificially breeding wheat plants.

Variety of wheat	Year first grown	Mean height of stem (cm)
Holdfast	1935	126
Capella Despress	1953	110
Maris Huntsman	1972	106
Norman	1980	84

(a) Plot the data on a bar chart. (2)

(b) By how much did the mean height of wheat plants change between 1935 and 1972? (1)

(c) Describe how plant breeders cross two different wheat plants. (3)

(d) Describe the plant breeding process which can be used to reduce the mean height of wheat plants. (3)

(e) Suggest **two** advantages to the farmer of growing shorter wheat plants. (2)

2 What makes a girl?

(a) Copy and complete the diagram below to show how the gender of a human baby is determined. (3)

(b) (i) A couple already have two sons. They hope that their third child will be a daughter. What is the chance of this? (1)

(ii) Explain the reason for your answer. (3)

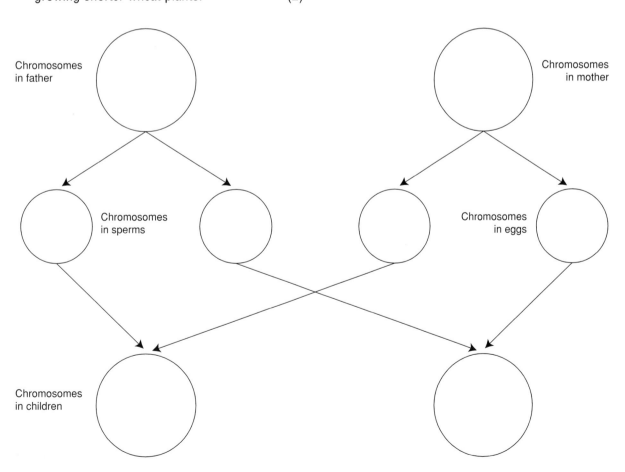

3   Breeding mice

The colour of fur in mice is controlled by a single gene. This gene has two alleles **B** and **b**.

(a)   A mouse with black fur was crossed with a mouse with white fur. The results are shown on the diagram.

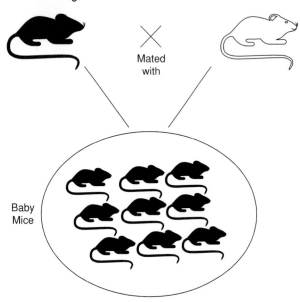

Use a genetic diagram to explain why all the baby mice had black fur.   (3)

(b)   A different mouse with black fur was crossed with a mouse with white fur. The results are shown in the diagram.

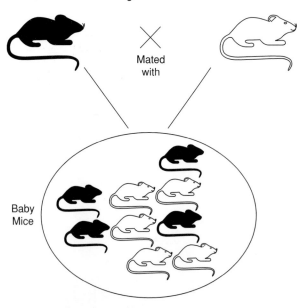

Use a genetic diagram to explain why some of the baby mice had black fur and some had white fur.   (3)

4   Hitch-hiker's thumb

Some people are born with 'hitch-hiker's thumb'.

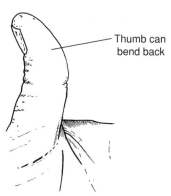

Thumb can bend back

This is caused by a dominant allele **H**. The diagram shows the inheritance of hitch-hiker's thumb in a family.

Key

☐ Male with normal thumbs   ■ Male with hitch-hiker's thumbs

○ Female with normal thumbs   ● Female with hitch-hiker's thumbs

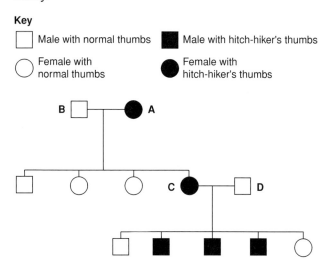

(a)   What is the genotype of grandmother **A**? Explain the reason for your answer.   (3)

(b)   Use a genetic diagram to explain why some of the children of **C** and **D** had hitch-hiker's thumb, but others did not.   (4)

5 Cystic fibrosis

The diagram shows the inheritance of cystic fibrosis.
Cystic fibrosis is caused by a recessive allele **a**.

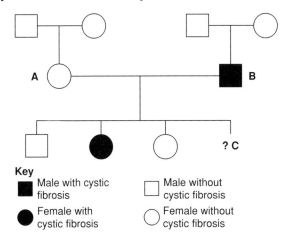

Key

■ Male with cystic fibrosis

● Female with cystic fibrosis

□ Male without cystic fibrosis

○ Female without cystic fibrosis

(a) What is the genotype of:

   (i) **A**,   (1)

   (ii) **B**?   (1)

(b) What is the chance of child **C** inheriting cystic fibrosis? Use a genetic diagram to explain the reason for your answer.   (3)

6 Huntington's chorea

The diagram shows the inheritance of Huntington's chorea in a family.

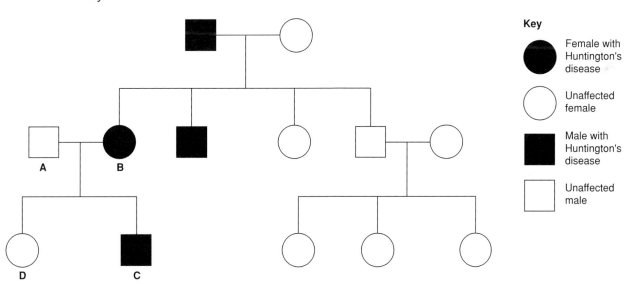

Key

● Female with Huntington's disease

○ Unaffected female

■ Male with Huntington's disease

□ Unaffected male

Use a genetic diagram to explain why one of the children of **A** and **B** inherited Huntington's chorea, but the other did not.   (5)

7 Haemophilia

The diagram shows the inheritance of haemophilia in a family.

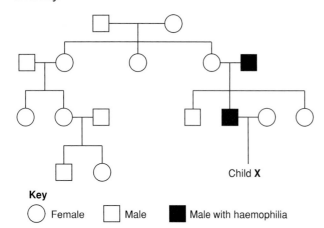

Child **X**

Key

◯ Female ☐ Male ■ Male with haemophilia

(a) What are the chances that child **X** will be a haemophiliac boy? Use a genetic diagram to explain the reason for your answer. (5)

(b) None of the females in the family has haemophilia. Explain why. (3)

8 DNA

(a) Copy and complete the drawing to show the structure of a DNA molecule. (1)

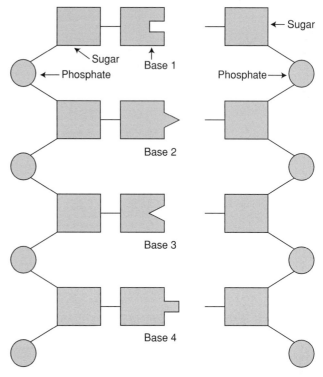

Sugar

Phosphate→

← Sugar
←Phosphate
Base 1

Base 2

Base 3

Base 4

(b) Explain how the structure of DNA determines the sequence of amino acids in a protein. (4)

(c) Insulin is a protein. Explain how genetic engineers use human cells and bacteria to make human insulin. (4)

 Progress with GCSE Structured Questions: Biology

9   New ways of growing carrots

The diagram shows a technique for producing carrot plants.

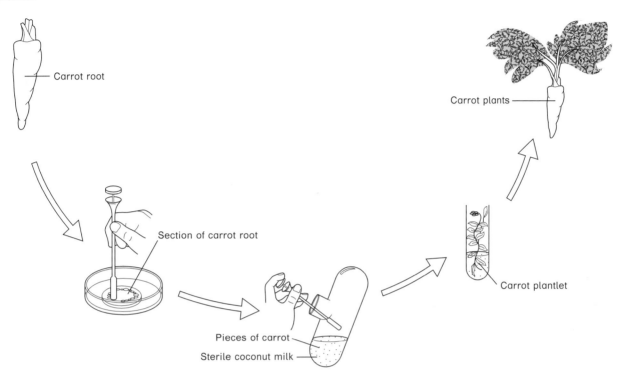

Carrot root

Section of carrot root

Pieces of carrot

Sterile coconut milk

Carrot plantlet

Carrot plants

(a)   What name is given to producing plants in this way?   (1)

(b)   What type of cell division occurs as the pieces of carrot tissue grow into plantlets?   (1)

(c)   Explain an advantage and a disadvantage of using this method to produce large quantities of a food crop.   (6)

10 March of the mutant tomatoes

Read the following article

MARCH OF THE MUTANT TOMATOES AS FRANKENFOOD HITS THE MENU

Just when you thought it was safe to go back to the dinner table, 'Frankenfoods' are heading for the menu.

Rainbow trout with human genes and tomatoes grown with traits of flounder fish are the latest products of food scientists.

It is good news for producers – the trout grow bigger and more quickly, while the tomatoes have a lower freezing point, preventing them becoming damaged.

But consumer groups fear a whole breed of these 'genetically modified organisms' (GMOs) may be introduced without proper trials.

David King, director of the pressure group Genetic Forum, said: 'The march of scientists who want to genetically alter food has very serious implications both for animal welfare and the environment.'

'You run the risk of introducing triffid-like creatures – plants which have the capacity to overtake landscapes and force out other plant life.'

Genetic Forum is to join groups including the RSPCA and World Wide Fund for Nature to debate a number of GMOs awaiting licences in the United States.

They have called for proper labelling so shoppers can decide for themselves whether they want to buy modified foods.

Two genetic compounds – certain brands of cheddar cheese and bakers' yeast, are already approved for use in British food manufacture, said Mr King.

British multi-national ICI also has a company, Zeneca Seeds, working on genetically altering food and is planning to sell tomatoes in which the ripening gene has been 'blocked' to increase shelf life.

An ICI spokesman said 'Extensive trials are carried out on all these modified foods and we are required by the Ministry of Agriculture to provide full information on all our trials.'

Growers were able to pick the new tomato when it was ripe and red instead of green and it was wrong to label such an advance 'Frankenfood', she said.

'It has very negative connotations which are not at all correct. The entire drive behind this work is to produce positive benefits to the consumer.'

ICI had helped to produce crops able to resist pests and diseases, bringing food to people who otherwise would go hungry, she added.

Source: *Daily Mail*, 24/2/93

Use information from the article, and your own knowledge and understanding, to explain the advantages and disadvantages of producing new types of food by genetic engineering. (8)

 Progress with GCSE Structured Questions: Biology

8 Adaptation, competition and environment

TEACHER SUMMARY SHEET

QUESTION	TITLE AND CONTENT	LEVEL	SKILLS TESTED
1	**Surviving in the desert**		
(a)	Adaptations of camels to desert life	F	Understanding
(b)	Adaptations of cacti to desert life	F	Understanding
2	**Surviving in the arctic**		
(a)–(e)	Adaptations of polar bears to arctic life	F	Understanding
3	**Down to the woods**		
(a), (b)	Changes in environmental conditions in woodland	F	Understanding
(c)	Competition amongst trees	S	Understanding
4	**Plumbing the depths**		
(a)	Environmental conditions in a lake	F	Understanding
(b)	Competition amongst aquatic plants	S	Understanding
(c)	Adaptations of aquatic plants	S	Understanding
5	**The moose story**		
(a)	Plotting line graph of changes in moose population	S	Graph construction
(b)	Interpreting graph of population changes	S	Understanding
(c)	Suggesting effect on population of introducing a predator	S	Understanding
6	**The dangers of DDT**		
(a)	Why insecticides are used	S	Understanding
(b)	Concentration of insecticide up food chain	S	Understanding
(c)	Evaluation of insecticide use	S	Understanding
(d)	Eutrophication	H	Understanding
7	**Dying forests**		
(a)	Interpolation from bar chart of pollution damage to trees	S	Interpolation
(b)	Relationship between age of tree and pollution damage	S	Data interpretation
(c), (d)	Acid rain formation	S	Understanding
8	**Disappearing forests**		
(a)	Reasons for deforestation	S	Understanding
(b)	Effects of deforestation on soil	S/H	Understanding
(c)	Greenhouse effect	H	Understanding
(d)	Effect of deforestation on ecosystem	S/H	Understanding

8 Adaptation, competition and environment

TOPIC	COVERED	EVALUATION
	Circle the term that best describes how well you feel you have covered this topic.	On a scale of 1 – 5 how well do you feel you have understood this topic? (1 = not understood; 5 = fully understood).
The physical factors that affect living organisms	no/partly/yes	1 2 3 4 5
How these factors vary according to time of day and time of year	no/partly/yes	1 2 3 4 5
That living organisms have features that enable them to survive in the conditions in which they live	no/partly/yes	1 2 3 4 5
The factors that affect the size of populations of living things	no/partly/yes	1 2 3 4 5
The relationships between predators and prey	no/partly/yes	1 2 3 4 5
The main pollutants of land, water and the atmosphere	no/partly/yes	1 2 3 4 5
How acid rain is formed	no/partly/yes	1 2 3 4 5
The effects of acid rain on organisms	no/partly/yes	1 2 3 4 5
The effects of fertiliser run-off on rivers and lakes	no/partly/yes	1 2 3 4 5
The effects of sewage on rivers and lakes	no/partly/yes	1 2 3 4 5
The causes and effects of the 'greenhouse effect'	no/partly/yes	1 2 3 4 5

CHAPTER 8 ADAPTATION, COMPETITION AND ENVIRONMENT

WORKED EXAMPLE 1

The drawing shows a flamingo. Flamingos live in warm shallow lakes in tropical Africa.
Flamingos feed by sieving single-celled green algae from the lake water.

CHIEF EXAMINER'S COMMENTS

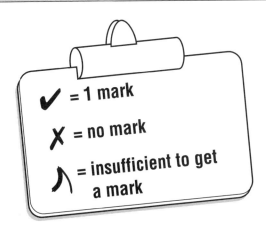

✔ = 1 mark

✗ = no mark

ʃ = insufficient to get a mark

(a) Lakes in Africa support large numbers of flamingos. There would not be enough algae in an ordinary British lake to feed large numbers of these birds.
Suggest one environmental factor which might account for the difference in the number of algae in British and African lakes. (1)

Climate. ✗

Explain how this factor causes a difference in the number of algae in the lakes. (2)

In Africa it's sunnier and this would cause algae to grow better. ✗

(b) In Africa the large numbers of flamingos in one of the lakes, Lake Nakuru, is a big attraction to tourists. The Kenyan government wants to expand a nearby industrial town. One effect will be an increase in the amount of sewage which flows into Lake Nakuru.

   (i) Explain how increasing amounts of sewage are likely to affect the organisms in the lake. (4)

The sewage is a fertiliser for the algae. They would grow very fast ✔ *and use up all the oxygen in photosynthesis.* ✗ *This would suffocate the fish* ✔ *which lived in the lake.*

   (ii) Explain the advantages and disadvantages of increasing the size of the industrial town near Lake Nakuru. (4)

The lake would be polluted ✔ *and the smell might drive tourists away.* ✔ *The area would not look as nice with factories there.* ʃʃ

(a) Never refer to 'Climate' without qualifying exactly what you mean by the word. 'Climate' could refer to Sun, wind, rain or snow. Environmental factors include temperature and light intensity, and either of these would be acceptable if included in answers such as 'it is warmer in Africa' or 'the light has a higher intensity in Africa'.
Again, 'sunnier' is far too vague – plants receive both light and heat from the Sun and you have to choose one of these. Whichever you use you have to explain how it affects the growth of algae. One of the following would be a better answer;
■ increased temperatures increase the rate of enzyme reactions that are involved in the process of growth,
■ increased light intensity increases the rate of photosynthesis, this provides more sugars for the algae to use in growth and reproduction.

(b) (i) The answer started off quite well, sewage does act as a fertiliser for algae, increasing their rate of growth. The answer also ended well, the fish would eventually suffocate. Most students make the mistake of saying that algae are mainly responsible for the fall in the oxygen concentration in the water. In fact, what happens is that the large number of algae means that many of them die because they do not receive enough light. Dead algae provide food for bacteria which multiply rapidly. It is the respiration of these bacteria which is mainly responsible for the fall in the oxygen concentration of the water in the lake.

(ii) Always give both advantages and disadvantages if you are asked to. If you only give one, in this case disadvantages, you restrict yourself to half the available marks. One advantage that might have been included is that the factory would provide employment and this would increase living standards.

WORKED EXAMPLE 2

CHIEF EXAMINER'S COMMENTS

The diagram shows some of the causes of change to the mass of carbon dioxide in the atmosphere in one year.

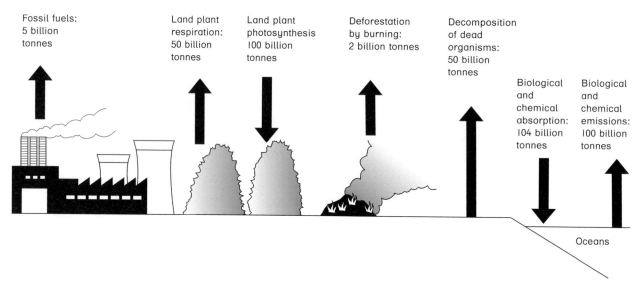

Fossil fuels:
5 billion
tonnes

Land plant respiration:
50 billion
tonnes

Land plant photosynthesis
100 billion
tonnes

Deforestation by burning:
2 billion tonnes

Decomposition of dead organisms:
50 billion tonnes

Biological and chemical absorption:
104 billion tonnes

Biological and chemical emissions:
100 billion tonnes

Oceans

(a) Calculate the net gain of carbon dioxide by the atmosphere in one year. (2)

5 + 50 + 2 + 50 + 100 ✔ *= 209* ✗

(a) *Always include you working. Although the answer is incorrect, the correct figures have been extracted from the diagram, and so the answer gains one of the two marks.*

(b) Power stations often discharge warm water into rivers.
Explain how this warm water might affect organisms which live in the river. (3)

The warm water would make life in the river grow faster. ✔ ∧ ∧

(b) *This is a description, NOT an explanation. The organisms would grow faster, because an increase in temperature increases the rate of reactions in cells. You could also have mentioned that oxygen is less soluble in warm water than in cold water, and therefore some organisms might have difficulty in obtaining enough oxygen for respiration.*

(c) The world-wide use of fossil fuels has increased rapidly during this century.
Explain how this increased use has affected the environment. (4)

There is a lot more carbon dioxide in the air and this has made holes in the ozone layer, ✗ *causing the greenhouse effect.*

(c) *Do not confuse the ozone layer and the greenhouse effect. The holes in the ozone layer are caused by the release of organic chemicals, principally CFCs.*
Never forget to say that it is the combustion of fossil fuels that increases the carbon dioxide content of the atmosphere.
It is not sufficient simply to mention the greenhouse effect – you have to explain how it causes global warming. Carbon dioxide does this by absorbing the radiant energy that is reflected from the surface of the Earth instead of allowing it to escape into space.

(d) Describe and explain the long-term effects of deforestation on the Earth's atmosphere. (4)

chopping down trees has increased the amount of carbon dioxide ✔ *in the air and decreased the amount of oxygen.* ✔ ∧ ∧

(d) *This is a weak answer because, in spite of the allocation of four marks, it only gives two facts. Never forget to relate the oxygen and carbon dioxide changes to photosynthesis. You should also refer to the reduction in the amount of water vapour in the atmosphere when trees are no longer there to transpire.*

1 Surviving in the desert

(a) The picture shows an Arabian camel.

Explain how each of the following adaptations helps the camel to survive in a hot, sandy desert:

(i) Thick, broad pads on the soles of its feet. (2)

(ii) It is able to close its nostrils and its eyes have very long eyelashes. (2)

(iii) It does not sweat unless its body temperature exceeds 40°C. (2)

(b) The drawing shows a plant which lives in hot, dry deserts.

Sharp prickles   Thick coat of
                              wax on the leaves

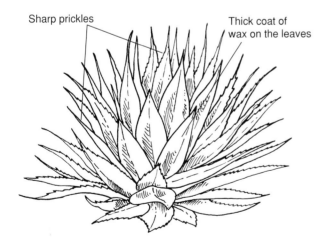

Explain how each of the following adaptations helps the plant to survive in a hot, dry desert:

(i) the thick coat of wax on the leaves, (1)
(ii) the sharp prickles. (2)

2 Surviving in the arctic

The picture shows a polar bear. It lives in the arctic amongst snow and ice.

Explain how each of the following adaptations helps the polar bear to survive amongst ice and snow:

(a) It has white fur. (2)

(b) The fur is very thick. (2)

(c) It has long hairs between the pads on its feet. (2)

(d) It has flat feet, each with five long, curved claws. (2)

(e) Its external ears are very small. (2)

3   Down to the woods

The drawing shows part of a large tropical forest.

Environmental conditions such as light intensity and temperature change considerably with the time of day and time of year. Conditions also vary within the tropical forest – conditions near the tops of the trees are very different from conditions near the bottom of the trees.

(a)   Describe how environmental conditions at the top of tree **X** change;

(i)   during a 24 hour summer's day,   (3)
(ii) during a 365 day year.   (3)

(b)   Give **three** ways in which the environmental conditions at the top of tree **Y** might be different from those at the top of tree **X** at noon on a summer's day.   (3)

(c)   Explain **two** ways in which tree **X** might affect the growth of tree **Y**.   (4)

4 Plumbing the depths

The drawing shows where some plants live at different depths in a lake.

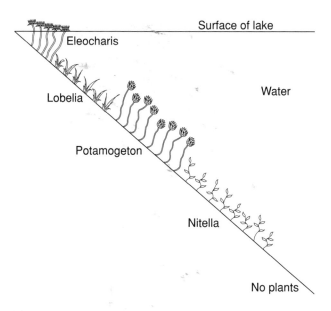

Surface of lake

Eleocharis

Water

Lobelia

Potamogeton

Nitella

No plants

(a) Give **two** reasons why no plants live in the deep water.   (2)

(b) Suggest why Nitella plants do not grow amongst the Potamogeton plants.   (2)

(c) The Eleocharis plants do not grow as tall as the Potamogeton plants, but they have a much deeper root system. Explain why.   (2)

5 The moose story

Moose are large herbivores. A herd of moose were introduced to an island in the early 1900s. There were no predators of the moose on the island. The table shows the estimated population of the moose between 1915 and 1960.

Year	Estimated size of moose population
1915	200
1917	300
1921	1000
1925	2000
1928	2500
1930	3000
1934	400
1943	170
1947	600
1950	500
1960	600

(a) Plot and draw a graph of the data in the table.   (3)

(b) Suggest explanations for;

   (i) the rise in the moose population between 1915 and 1930,   (2)
   (ii) the fall in the moose population between 1930 and 1934.   (2)

(c) Suggest how the data in the table would have been different over the period of time between 1921 and 1960 if a natural predator of the moose had been introduced in 1921.   (2)

6   The dangers of DDT

DDT is an insecticide. It is non-biodegradable. If DDT is sprayed on crops, some may leach into rivers and ponds. The drawing shows the amount of DDT in the bodies of some organisms that live in and around the pond. It is measured in ppm or parts per million.

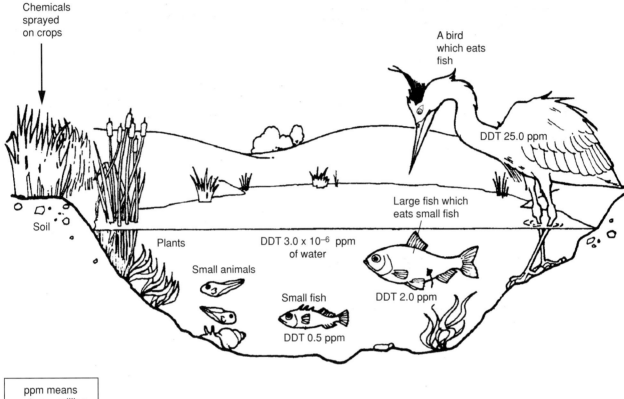

Chemicals sprayed on crops

A bird which eats fish

DDT 25.0 ppm

Large fish which eats small fish

Soil

Plants

DDT 3.0×10^{-6} ppm of water

Small animals

Small fish

DDT 2.0 ppm

DDT 0.5 ppm

ppm means parts per million

(a)   Explain why farmers spray insecticides on crops.   (2)

(b)   Use information from the question to explain why the bird has such a high concentration of DDT in its body.   (3)

(c)   (i)   DDT is now banned in this country. Explain why.   (2)

      (ii)   DDT is still used in many 'third-world' countries. Suggest why governments in some 'third-world' countries are reluctant to ban the use of DDT even though they are aware of the dangers of its use.   (3)

(d)   Besides spraying the crop with chemicals, the farmer uses artificial fertilisers. Explain what might happen to the ecosystem if fertiliser leaches into the pond.   (5)

7   Dying forests

The crown of a tree is its top branches and leaves. The graphs show the effect of pollution on the crowns of three different kinds of conifer trees.

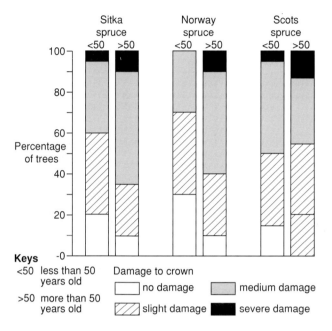

Keys
<50 less than 50 years old
>50 more than 50 years old

Damage to crown
☐ no damage   ▨ medium damage
▥ slight damage   ■ severe damage

(a) (i)   What percentage of Scots pine trees under 50 years old had slight damage to the crown?   (1)

(ii) Which trees were least affected by the pollution?   (1)

(b)   What is the relationship between the age of the trees and the amount of damage to the crown?   (2)

(c)   Most of the damage to the crowns is caused by 'acid rain'. Describe how 'acid rain' is formed.   (3)

(d)   The amount of 'acid rain' falling on forests has increased steadily for most of this century. Explain why.   (3)

8   Disappearing forests

(a)   Explain why rain forests are being cleared and burnt in many parts of the world.   (2)

(b)   Give **two** long-term effects on the soil of clearing rain forests.   (2)

(c)   Explain the long term effects on the Earth's climate of burning large amounts of rain forest.   (5)

(d)   Explain **one** ecological consequence, other than the effect on soil and climate, of clearing large amounts of rain forest.   (3)

9 Energy and nutrient transfer

QUESTION	TITLE AND CONTENT	LEVEL	SKILLS TESTED
1	**If you go into the woods**		
(a), (b), (c)	Comprehension of forest food web	F	Understanding
(d)	Effect on food chain of change in predator numbers	F	Understanding
(e)	Constructing a pyramid of numbers and a pyramid of biomass	S	Understanding
2	**The deep**		
(a), (b)	Photosynthesis, respiration and feeding in a food web	F/S	Understanding
(c)	Completing food chains	F	Understanding
(d)	Constructing a pyramid of numbers	S	Understanding
3	**What goes on in a compost heap?**		
(a)	Constructing a pyramid of numbers and a pyramid of biomass	S	Understanding
(b)	Decay process	S	Understanding
(c)	Carbon cycle description	S	Understanding
4	**Nitrogen gets around**		
(a)–(d)	Comprehension of nitrogen cycle diagram	H	Understanding
5	**Food for chickens**		
(a)	Percentage calculation for energy conversion	H	Calculation
(b)	Energy transfer in chicken	H	Understanding
6	**Round and round the aquarium**		
(a)	Carbon cycle in an aquarium	S/H	Understanding
(b)	Nitrogen cycle in an aquarium	H	Understanding

9 Energy and nutrient transfer

TOPIC	COVERED	EVALUATION
	Circle the term that best describes how well you feel you have covered this topic.	On a scale of 1 – 5 how well do you feel you have understood this topic? (1 = not understood; 5 = fully understood).
What is meant by 'producers' and 'consumers'	no/partly/yes	1 2 3 4 5
How to draw food chains	no/partly/yes	1 2 3 4 5
What is meant by 'food web'	no/partly/yes	1 2 3 4 5
How to draw pyramids of numbers	no/partly/yes	1 2 3 4 5
How to draw pyramids of biomass	no/partly/yes	1 2 3 4 5
The difference between a pyramid of numbers and a pyramid of biomass	no/partly/yes	1 2 3 4 5
The reasons why each stage in a food chain contains less materials and less energy than the previous stage	no/partly/yes	1 2 3 4 5
How the efficiency of food production can be increased	no/partly/yes	1 2 3 4 5
What is meant by decay	no/partly/yes	1 2 3 4 5
The optimum conditions for decay	no/partly/yes	1 2 3 4 5
The use of decay in sewage works and in compost heaps	no/partly/yes	1 2 3 4 5
The stages of the carbon cycle	no/partly/yes	1 2 3 4 5
The stages of the nitrogen cycle	no/partly/yes	1 2 3 4 5
That all the energy captured by green plants is eventually transferred to the environment	no/partly/yes	1 2 3 4 5

| WORKED EXAMPLE 1 | CHIEF EXAMINER'S COMMENTS |

The drawing shows a food web for a lake.

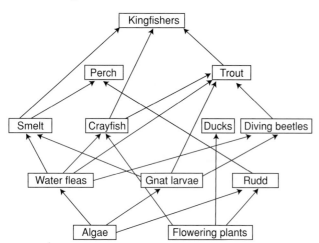

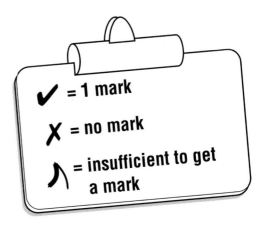

✔ = 1 mark

✗ = no mark

◡ = insufficient to get a mark

(a) Name **one** producer. (1)

flowering plant ✔

(a) Algae would have been the other correct answer.

(b) Name **one** predator of the crayfish (1)

water flea ✗

(b) Make sure that you remember the difference between predator and prey. The prey is the one that is eaten. An arrow leads from prey to predator. Prey → predator. The correct answer would have been kingfisher or trout.

(c) Complete the food chain (1)

algae _water flea_ diving beetle
trout _kingfisher_ ✔✗

(c) Although the organisms are all in the correct order, only one mark is obtained because arrows were not used to show the direction in which energy is transferred. e.g. algae → water flea.

(d) Crayfish from America were introduced into this country several years ago. They carry a disease which causes the native crayfish to die in large numbers.
Explain what might happen to the numbers of kingfishers if the crayfish in the lake become infected with disease. (2)

The kingfishers would be less ✔ *because they would have less food.* ✔

(d) Diseases are not usually passed from one species to another. A question like this tests whether you understand what happens to an organism if its prey are reduced in number – the predator also decreases in number.

(e) Algae are microscopic plants. Gnat larvae are small insects, about 5 mm in length. Smelt are small fish about 3 cm in length. The kingfisher is a bird about 20 cm in length.
Draw and label a pyramid of numbers for the food chain:
Algae → gnat larvae → smelt → kingfisher (2)

| algae |
| Gnat larvae 5mm |
| Smelt 3cm |
| Kingfishers 20 cm |

✗

(e) It is a common mistake to put the largest organism at the bottom of a pyramid of numbers. Usually, the only time you will see the largest organism at the bottom of a pyramid of numbers is when the producers are trees. Producers should always form the base of the pyramid, followed by primary consumers (herbivores) then secondary consumers (carnivores). Algae are microscopic, there must therefore be many of them if gnat larvae get all their energy from them. Similarly there must be more gnat larvae than smelt, and more smelt than kingfishers.

WORKED EXAMPLE 2

The drawing shows a food web for a small wood

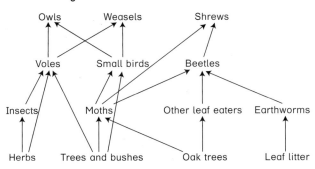

(a) Draw a pyramid of biomass for the food web.

(2)

✗

(b) Explain what eventually happens to energy from the Sun which is captured by the plants in the wood.

(6)

The plants in the wood are producers. When they capture energy they turn it into sugars. ✔ *Consumers such as insects eat the leaves of the plants.* ✔ *They use the energy from the leaves to move* ✔ *and to grow. Insects are eaten by voles. These also use the food to move and to grow. When the voles die the sugars are returned to the soil.*

(c) Leaves fall off the tree and become leaf litter. Explain how the nitrogen in the leaf litter eventually becomes part of the protein molecules in the leaf.

(5)

When the leaves fall they decompose ⅄ *into ammonia.* ⅄ *Bacteria then change the ammonia into nitrate* ⅄. *Denitrifying bacteria change the nitrate into nitrogen, but nitrifying bacteria* ✗ *turn this back into nitrate. Plants use nitrate to make proteins.* ⅄⅄

CHIEF EXAMINER'S COMMENTS

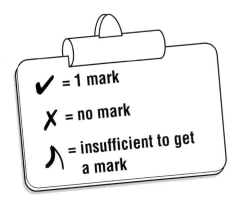

✔ = 1 mark

✗ = no mark

⅄ = insufficient to get a mark

(a) *Although the pyramid is the correct shape it receives no marks. There are four levels in the food web so there should be four bars in the pyramid. None of the bars are labelled. The label 'producers' or 'plants' would have showed the examiner that the student understood pyramids of biomass.*

(b) *This answer is little more than a description of the transfer of energy up a food chain. It misses the crucial point which is how all the energy is eventually returned to the environment – mainly as a result of respiration in plants, animals and microbes.*

The first two sentences were quite good, but mentioning photosynthesis would have made them better. At this point, always remember that plants also respire releasing energy, some of which is transferred to the environment. Similarly you should also state that animals respire and transfer some of the resulting energy to the environment. The reference to energy transfer during movement was good. You should also mention animal faeces – all animals transfer significant amounts of energy to the environment in the form of faeces.

The reference to the return of sugar to the soil when an animal dies was weak. The whole of an animal is returned to the soil and all the carbohydrates, fats and proteins can be used by the soil microbes for respiration and growth. Always remember to state that soil bacteria and fungi digest dead organisms and waste material, then use the digested food for respiration and growth. Their respiration also transfers energy to the environment.

(c) *There are common errors in the first sentence: leaves do not decompose, they decay by the action of bacteria and fungi; the result is ammonium ions, not ammonia. You should be very careful not to confuse nitrifying bacteria with nitrogen-fixing bacteria – it is nitrifying bacteria which convert ammonium ions into nitrate ions. The question does not ask about nitrogen-fixing bacteria or about denitrifying bacteria, so it is better to leave them out as there is a chance of making mistakes. You should always mention that nitrates are absorbed from the soil by plant roots, then they are converted to amino acids from which proteins can be manufactured.*

1   If you go into the woods

The diagram shows part of a food web.

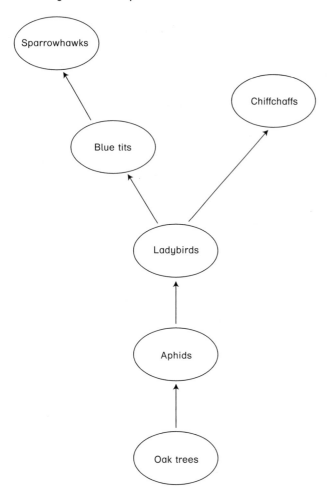

(a)   Which of the organisms is a producer?   (1)

(b)   Which animal has the lowest population?
Explain why.   (3)

(c)   Which organism has the largest biomass?
Explain why.   (2)

(d)   (i)   What effect would the death of chiffchaffs
have on the population of ladybirds?
Explain why.   (2)
(ii)   What effect would the death of chiffchaffs
have on the population of aphids?
Explain why.   (2)

(e)   (i)   Draw a pyramid of numbers for the food
chain:
oak trees → aphids → ladybirds → chiffchaffs
(2)
(ii)   Draw a pyramid of biomass for the same
food chain.   (2)

2   The deep

The diagram shows part of a food web for a pond.
Algae are microscopic single-celled organisms.

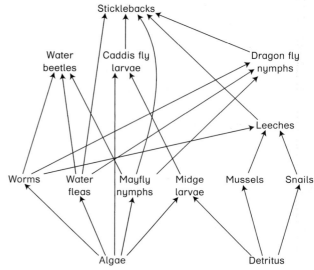

(a)   Name **one** organism (in each case) in the food
web which;

(i)   photosynthesises,   (1)
(ii)   respires,   (1)
(iii)   both photosynthesises and respires,   (1)
(iv)   eats only plants.   (1)

(b)   Name **three** animals which eat only other animals.
(3)

(c)   Complete the food chains:

(i)   …… → …… → dragonfly nymph → ……
(1)
(ii)   …… → mussels → …… → ……   (1)

(d)   Draw a pyramid of numbers for the food chain
algae → midge larvae →
caddis fly larvae → sticklebacks   (2)

3 What goes on in a compost heap?

A gardener pulled up weeds and used them to start a compost heap. The compost heap soon became colonised by large numbers of earthworms and slugs. The gardener then noticed a hedgehog rooting through the compost heap, eating the earthworms and slugs. Every so often the hedgehog stopped to scratch itself. This was because it had large numbers of fleas which fed by sucking the hedgehog's blood.

(a) (i) Construct a pyramid of numbers for the food chain:
weeds → slugs → hedgehog → fleas (2)

    (ii) Construct a pyramid of biomass for the same food chain. (2)

(b) The weeds in the compost heap soon decay.

    (i) Name a type of organism that brings about this decay. (1)

    (ii) Give **two** conditions that would speed up the rate of decay. (2)

(c) Describe the different ways in which the carbohydrates in the weeds on the compost heap may be used and what eventually happens to them. (5)

4 Nitrogen gets around

The drawing shows the nitrogen cycle.

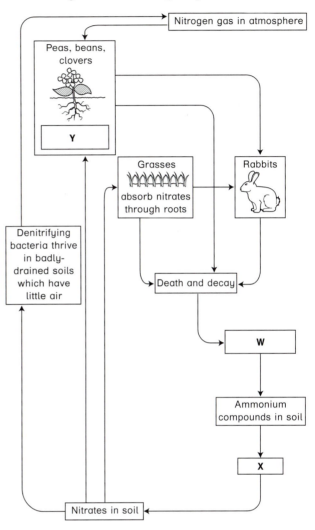

(a) Name the organisms labelled;

    (i) **W,** (1)

    (ii) **X.** (1)

(b) The organisms labelled **Y** are found in root nodules on peas, beans and clovers.

    (i) Name these organisms. (1)

    (ii) Explain why farmers sometimes grow a crop of clover then plough it into the soil. (3)

(c) Use information from the diagram to explain why farmers should try to keep their land well-drained. (3)

(d) Explain how the nitrogen in the nitrates absorbed by grass eventually becomes part of proteins in the rabbit. (5)

5   Food for chickens

The drawing shows how much of the food eaten by a chicken is converted into body tissues.

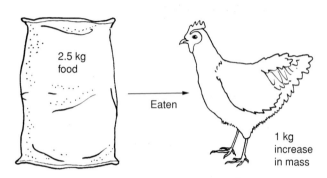

(a)   Calculate the percentage of the food that is converted into body tissues.   (2)

(b)   Explain what happens to the food that is eaten, but is not converted into body tissues.   (5)

6   Round and round the aquarium

The drawing shows an aquarium.

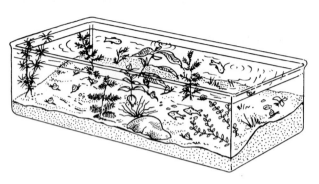

The aquarium was set up several months ago and is now 'balanced'. This means that if measured at the same time each day, the amounts of oxygen, carbon dioxide and ammonia in the water stay relatively constant.

(a)   Explain why the amounts of oxygen and carbon dioxide remain constant if measured at the same time each day.   (5)

(b)   The fish excrete ammonia rather than urea. Explain why the amount of ammonia in the water remains relatively constant.   (5)

Answers and mark schemes

1 The food we eat

(a) (i) any two of: (2)
other milk products;
other meat products;
potato products;
buns, cakes and biscuits;
soft drinks; for one mark each

(ii) any one of: (1)
potatoes;
potato products;
bread;
buns, cakes and biscuits;
cereals;
sugar and preserves;
soft drinks

(iii) any one of: (1)
milk;
milk products;
buns, cakes and biscuits

(b) bread = $\frac{8.8}{2}$ = 4.4g,
cheese = $\frac{26}{2}$ = 13.0g,
chicken = 26.5×1.5 = 39.75g,
total = 4.4 + 13.0 + 39.75 = 57.15g (2)

(c) any four of: (4)
they are broken down;
by enzymes;
called proteases;
secreted by the stomach/pancreas/small intestine;
into amino acids;
which are absorbed into the blood;
in the small intestine.

2 The digestive system

(a) B – gullet/oesophagus (1)
C – liver (1)
D – stomach (1)
E – small intestine (1)
F – large intestine (1)

(b) A – makes saliva/secretes a carbohydrase enzyme (1)
F – absorbs water from undigested food (1)
G – stores faeces (1)

(c) (i) absorbs soluble digested food into the blood (1)
(ii) its shape gives a large surface area (1)
it has a good blood supply (1)
its outer layer of cells is thin (1)

(d) (i) carbohydrase; lipase; protease, or named example
for 1 mark each (3)
(ii) fluid from stomach is acid (1)
it needs to be neutralised (1)
to provide optimum pH for intestinal enzymes (1)

(e) (i) a group of similar cells with a common function (1)
(ii) it contracts rhythmically (1)
to move food along (1)

cutting as shown allows appropriate answers
to be given out with individual questions sheets

3 Digestive juices

(a) total volume of water entering digestive system
= 9000 cm³, known volume leaving = 8600 cm³ (1)
therefore amount absorbed by large intestine
= (9000 − 8600) = 400 cm³ (1)

(b) (i) saliva, pancreatic juice and intestinal juice,
all three for 1 mark (1)
(ii) gastric juice, pancreatic juice and intestinal juice,
all three for 1 mark (1)
(iii) pancreatic juice and intestinal juice, both for
1 mark (1)

(c) any three of: (3)
alkaline
emulsifies fats
giving larger surface area for lipase to act upon
neutralises acid entering small intestine from stomach

(d) makes hydrochloric acid (1)
kills microbes (1)

4 Investigating protein digestion

(a) all plots correct for 2 marks, minus 1 mark for each
incorrect plot (2)

(b) correct reading from line drawn on graph (1)

(c) (i) molecules moving more slowly at 10 °C (1)
therefore less likely to collide and react (1)
(ii) enzymes are denatured (1)
by temperatures above 40 − 45 °C (1)

(d) (i) in the stomach (1)
because the stomach secretes hydrochloric acid
which has a low pH (1)
(ii) in the small intestine (1)
because bile/pancreatic juice/intestinal juice are
alkaline therefore have a higher pH (1)

5 Investigating fat digestion

(a) fat digested into fatty acids (1)
which changes pH to an acidic value (1)

(b) ■ tube A − rate of reaction slow because lipase does
not work well in acidic conditions (1)
but faster than C because of bile which emulsifies
fats/neutralises acid (1)
■ tube B − fastest reaction because pH optimum (1)
and bile emulsifies fats (1)
■ tube C − rate of reaction slow because acidic pH (1)
and no bile to emulsify fats (1)
■ tube D − no reaction because boiled enzyme
denatured (1)
bile does not break down fat molecules, merely
provides larger surface area of fat for lipase (1)

6 The breathing system

(a) **D** − lung (1)
E − bronchus (1)
F − alveolus (1)
G − heart (1)
H − diaphragm (1)

(b) (i) A − allows passage of air from outside to lungs (1)
B − protects heart and lungs (1)
C − moves ribcage (1)
(ii) intercostal muscles contract pulling ribs upwards (1)
diaphragm muscles contract flattening diaphragm (1)
these two changes increase the volume of the
thorax (1)
the pressure inside the thorax is less than
atmospheric pressure and air moves in (1)

(c) (i)

Structure	Name	Function
X	cell membrane (1)	controls movement of materials in and out of cell (1)
Y	cytoplasm (1)	where most chemical reactions occur (1)
Z	nucleus (1)	controls cell activities (1)

(ii) mucus traps microbes (1)
tiny hairs move mucus and microbes out of lungs (1)

7 Energy needs

(a) 30 minute sitting = 150 kJ,
10 minute walking = 150 kJ,
30 minutes swimming = 1050 kJ,
45 minutes dancing = 1025 kJ, (1)
total = 2375 kJ (1)

(b) (i) respiration (1)
(ii) glucose + oxygen $\rightarrow$ water + carbon dioxide (2)

8 Gaseous exchange

(a) alveoli spherical (1)
giving large surface area for exchange (1)
many blood capillaries give large exchange area (1)
flow of blood maintains concentration gradients (1)

(b) (i) contraction of intercostal muscles pulls ribs
upwards (1)
contraction of diaphragm muscles flattens
diaphragm (1)
these two changes increase volume of thorax (1)
(ii) 1 cycle = 4 seconds (1)
therefore 60 ÷ 4 = 15 breaths per minute (1)
(iii) (1.9 seconds × 100) ÷ 4 seconds (1)
= 47.5 % (1)

9 Smoking and health

(a) (i) 5% (1)
(ii) steady fall (1)
(iii) any reasonable reason e.g. the effect of
anti-smoking campaigns (1)
(iv) steady rise for girls (1)
fall then rise for boys (1)

(b) less surface area in damaged air sacs (1)
therefore slower rate of gas exchange (1)

(c) tobacco smoke contains harmful substances (1)
e.g. tar, not nicotine (1)
which cause mutations in lung cells (1)

10 Anaerobic respiration

(a) no oxygen used in anaerobic respiration (1)
carbon dioxide/water given out in aerobic respiration (1)
lactic acid produced in anaerobic respiration (1)
less energy released in anaerobic respiration (1)

(b) (i) 40% (1)
(ii) more energy transferred from sugars (1)
therefore greater speed possible (1)
less build up of lactic acid (1)
less likelihood of cramp (1)
(iii) energy needed quickly (1)
it cannot be supplied by aerobic respiration (1)
because insufficient time to increase rate of
oxygen supply to muscles (1)

1 Measuring pulse rates

(a) 2, 3, 3, 5, 2, 7, 3 all correct for 2 marks, minus 1
for each error (2)

(b) all bars correctly plotted gains 2 marks, minus 1
for each incorrect plot (2)

(c) any two of these differences for 1 mark each: (2)
heights;
weights;
fitness;
age;
gender.

2 The human heart

(a) each label correctly positioned for 1 mark each (4)

(b) (i) pulmonary vein (1)
(ii) prevents back flow of blood (1)
(iii) lungs (1)
(iv) takes blood to all body organs except the lungs (1)
(v) the blood in **D** has more oxygen/less
carbon dioxide (1)

(c) deoxygenated blood returning from organs (1)
bypasses lungs (1)
therefore less oxygen in circulating blood (1)
baby 'blue'/listless/short of breath (1)

(d) (i) two circulations – one from heart to lungs
and back (1)
another from heart to rest of body and back (1)
(ii) oxygenated blood going to body organs is at high
pressure (1)
no need to have blood at high pressure flowing
through lung capillaries (1)

3 Human blood vessels

(a) **X** – vein (1)
Y – capillary (1)
Z – artery (1)

(b) walls are thin (1)
small size gives collective large surface area (1)
this allows rapid passage of materials (1)

(c) (i) blood in veins is at low pressure (1)
valves prevent back flow between heart beats (1)
(ii) walls are elastic (1)
recoil means that pressure is maintained between
heart beats (1)

4 Supplying organs with blood

(a) all bars correctly plotted gains 2 marks, minus 1 for each
incorrect plot (2)

(b) (i) 9500 (1)
(ii) 25 000 (1)

(c) the heart beats faster (1)
and more strongly (1)

(d) (i) $(22\ 000 \times 100) \div 4500$ (1)
489% (or 490%) (1)
(ii) greater rate of oxygen supply to muscles (1)
greater rate of respiration possible (1)
greater rate of energy release (1)
for muscle contraction (1)

(e) (i) blood diverted from digestive system to muscles
during exercise (1)
to enable greater rate of energy release for
muscular contraction (1)
(ii) by constriction (1)
of small arteries supplying digestive organs (1)

(f) brain activity is not increased during exercise but it
needs to maintain its supply (1)

5   Red blood cells

(a) (i)   transport of oxygen   (1)
        (ii) they contain haemoglobin which combines with
              oxygen in regions of high concentration   (1)
              and releases it in regions of low concentration   (1)
        (iii) dimpled shape gives it a large surface area   (1)
              for exchanging oxygen   (1)
              and allows it to bend to pass through narrow
              capillaries   (1)
        (iv) they have no nucleus   (1)

(b) (i)   increased numbers of red cells   (1)
              increase rate of oxygen transport to muscles   (1)
              allowing increased rate of respiration   (1)
              increased energy availability to muscles   (1)
        (ii) red cells have no nucleus   (1)
              so they have a short life span   (1)
        (iii) e.g. no because confers unfair advantage   (1)
              athletic performance should depend on ability and
              training, not artificial aids   (1)

6   White blood cells

(a) (i)   **A** – cell membrane   (1)
              B – cytoplasm   (1)
              C – nucleus   (1)
        (ii) **A** – controlling passage of materials in and out
                   of cell   (1)
              B – where most chemical reactions take place   (1)
              C – controls activities of cell   (1)

(b) some white cells engulf disease microbes   (1)
        some produce antibodies which kill disease microbes   (1)
        some produce antitoxins which neutralise the toxins
        produced by microbes   (1)

7   Problems with vaccinations

(i)   less virulent virus injected   (1)
      white cells respond by producing antibodies   (1)
      which can kill any disease-producing measles
      virus which enter   (1)
      'memory cells' retain ability to produce antibodies
      quickly upon re-infection   (1)
(ii) vaccine can cause meningitis   (1)
      but MMR II less likely to cause this than MMR
      because a it contains a different virus strain   (1)
      risk of meningitis greater from catching wild mumps
      than from vaccine   (1)
      meningitis from vaccine milder than meningitis from
      catching wild mumps   (1)

8 Blood plasma

(a) (i) 5/6 or 0.8 (1)
      (ii) 8.67 × 5/6 = 7.2 g (1)

(b) (i) small intestine (1)
      (ii) kidney (1)

(c) (i) liver (1)
      (ii) blood clotting (1)

9 Bacteria and viruses

(a) (i) **A** – protein coat (1)
          B – nucleic acid/genetic material (1)
      (ii) **X** – genetic material (1)
          Y – cell wall (1)
          Z – cytoplasm (1)
      (iii) bacterium has a cell wall (1)
          white blood cell has a nucleus (1)

(b) microbes reproduce rapidly (1)
      produce toxins (1)
      viruses damage the cells they live inside (1)

10 The defeat of polio

(a) axes drawn with reasonable scale (1)
      all plots accurate (1)
      line of best fit drawn (1)
(b) increase in living standards/hygiene (1)
      vaccination campaigns (1)

1 Nerve cells

(a) sound (1)
      balance (1)
      pressure or touch (1)
      temperature (1)
      chemicals (1)
      chemicals or smell (1)

(b) **A** – cytoplasm (1)
      B – cell membrane (1)
      C – nucleus (1)

(c) insulation (1)
      so that information is not corrupted/increases
      efficiency of passage of impulses (1)

(d) pressure/temperature/touch (1)

(e) spinal cord (1)

2 The eye

(a) **A** – retina (1)
      B – suspensory ligament (1)
      C – cornea (1)
      D – iris (1)
      E – lens (1)
      F – ciliary muscle (1)
      G – optic nerve (1)

(b) **A** – contains light-sensitive cells/receptors (1)
      B – holds lens in position (1)
      C – allows light to enter eye/refracts light (1)
      D – controls amount of light entering eye (1)

(c) light is refracted (bent) first by the cornea (1)
      then by the lens (1)
      ciliary muscles relax (1)
      tension on suspensory ligaments increased (1)
      lens pulled into thinner shape/longer focal length (1)

3 Reflex actions

(a) reflex (1)

(b) protection (1)
where speed of response essential (1)

(c) by chemicals (1)
diffusing across synapse (1)

(d) **A** – effector (1)
B – receptor (1)
C – sensory neurone (1)
D – motor neurone (1)
E – co-ordinator (1)

4 Controlling blood sugar

(a) (i) 41 mg/100 cm^3 (1)
(ii) 27 minutes (1)

(b) (i) pancreas (1)
(ii) converted to glycogen (1)
in the liver/muscles (1)

(c) (i) glucose curve drawn with higher curve and more
gradual fall-off (1)
insulin curve very low (1)
(ii) insulin lower because not as much made
by pancreas (1)
glucose higher because not converted into
glycogen as fast (1)

5 Drinking and driving

(a) (i) axes drawn with reasonable scale (1)
all plots accurate (1)
line of best fit drawn (1)
(ii) reasonable extrapolation drawn (1)

(b) alcohol affects nervous system (1)
slows down reactions or induces overconfidence (1)
higher risk of accident (1)

(c) any two of: (2)
damage to liver;
damage to brain;
increases risk of heart disease

6 Diet and training

high surplus of carbohydrate in diet (1)
this converted to glycogen (1)
and stored in liver/muscles (1)
available as energy source (1)
for muscular action or respiration (1)

7 Drug addiction

(a) under 21 (1)

(b) (i) addiction rises to a peak in late 20s then falls (1)
(ii) addiction 2–3 times greater in men than in women (1)

(c) drugs affect body chemistry (1)
produce withdrawal symptoms (1)
which make it difficult to stop taking the drug (1)

(d) damage to liver (1)
damage to brain (1)

8 Sex hormones

(a) (i) a characteristic distinguishing males and females (1)
which is not present at birth (1)
(b) (i) oestrogen (1)
(ii) testosterone (1)

(c) (i) via the blood stream (1)
(ii) oestrogen depresses FSH production (1)
increase in oestrogen levels mirrored by fall in
FSH production (1)
(iii) inhibits FSH production (1)
it is FSH which stimulates eggs to mature (1)

(d) increase in oestrogen production stimulates
LH production (1)

(e) helping uterus to support fertilised egg (1)

(f) (i) either prevent unwanted pregnancy (1)
with associated health risks (1)
or plan family (1)
to suit financial ability to support children (1)
may lead to promiscuity (1)
and spread of sexual diseases (1)
(ii) can help childless couples (1)
risk of multiple pregnancies (1)
risk of babies dying in uterus or being born
prematurely (1)

9 How some fish can camouflage themselves

the stimulus is the light intensity of light reflected from the
background (1)
the receptors are light sensitive cells in the eyes (1)
the co-ordinator is the brain (1)
the effector is the pigment-containing cells (1)
the response is the expansion of the pigment-containing cells (1)

1 Waterworks

(a) labels correctly positioned for one mark each (4)

(b) lungs (1)
liver, kidney (1)
all cells/digestive system, kidney (1)
digestive system, kidney (1)

(c) (i) small intestine (1)
(ii) deamination (1)
(iii) five of: (5)
veins take it to the right side of the heart
pumped to the lungs
returns to the left side of the heart
is pumped to the kidneys
is filtered
passes to the bladder for storage
passed out in urine down urethra
(iv) storage (1)
easily converted to glucose when sugar level low (1)

2 In and out of the kidney

(a) (i) both contain the same amount of sugar (1)
(ii) the blood leaving has less urea (1)
and less salts (1)
(b) (i) 0 (1)
28 (1)
4 (1)
631 (1)
(ii) all/100% (1)
(iii) 50% (1)
(iv) glucose is needed by the body for respiration (1)
urea is a poisonous waste product (1)

 Progress with GCSE Structured Questions: Biology

3   How the kidney works

(a)   (i)   in Bowman's capsule/glomerulus   (1)
         (ii)   size – only small molecules are filtered   (1)
        (iii)   in the part of the tubule immediately after the
               capsule   (1)

(b)   (i)   it moves from a low concentration to a high
               concentration   (1)
               whereas tendency is to move in the opposite
               direction   (1)
         (ii)   energy is used   (1)
               from respiration   (1)

(c)   to keep constant proportions in the blood   (1)
        to prevent osmotic effects   (1)
        in body cells   (1)

4   Getting into a sweat

(a)   (i)   0.3 °C   (1)
         (ii)   30 minutes   (1)

(b)   (i)   increase in rate of respiration in muscles during
               exercise   (1)
               some energy transferred as heat   (1)
               to blood flowing through muscles   (1)
         (ii)   muscle still has higher temperature than blood   (1)
               therefore energy still transferred to blood   (1)

(c)   increased rate of sweating   (1)
        evaporation of sweat cools body   (1)
        blood vessels supplying skin capillaries dilate   (1)
        increased loss of energy by radiation   (1)
        panting after exercise   (1)
        air passing in and out of lungs cools blood flowing
        through lungs   (1)

5   Hot bodies

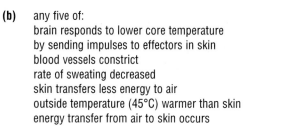

(a)   increased blood supply to digestive organs when body at
        rest   (1)
        increased rate of respiration in these organs to absorb
        soluble foods   (1)

(b)   blood supply diverted to muscle during exercise   (1)
        to increase rate of oxygen supply   (1)
        greater rate of respiration   (1)
        results in greater rate of energy release   (1)
        blood leaving these organs is warmer since energy
        transferred to it as it passes through   (1)

6   Keeping cool

(a)   ice lowers temperature of stomach   (1)
        blood cooled as it flows through stomach   (1)
        this cooled blood cools the brain   (1)

(b)   any five of: (5)
        brain responds to lower core temperature
        by sending impulses to effectors in skin
        blood vessels constrict
        rate of sweating decreased
        skin transfers less energy to air
        outside temperature (45°C) warmer than skin
        energy transfer from air to skin occurs

1 Parts of a plant

(a) **A** – leaf (1)
B – stem (1)
C – root (1)
D – root hair (1)

(b) **A** – makes glucose/photosynthesises (1)
B – supports leaves/transport (1)
C – anchorage (1)
D – absorption of water and mineral ions (1)

(c) it has a large surface area (1)
to capture the maximum amount of light energy (1)
it is thin so that gases do not have to travel far (1)

2 What's inside a plant cell?

(a) **A** – chloroplast (1)
B – cytoplasm (1)
C – cell wall (1)
D – cell membrane (1)
E – nucleus (1)
F – vacuole (1)

(b) **A** – photosynthesis (1)
B – where most chemical reactions take place (1)
C – strengthens the cell/gives it shape (1)
D – controls passage of substances into and out of cell (1)
E – controls activities of cell (1)
F – contains cell sap which helps to support cell (1)

(c) **A**, **C** and **F** (1)

(d) (i) photosynthesis (1)
(ii) it has many chloroplasts (1)
to absorb the maximum amount of light energy (1)
it has a thin cell wall (1)
to allow easy entry of carbon dioxide (1)

3 Making and moving sugars

(a) (i) chlorophyll (1)
(ii) absorbing light energy (1)

(b) only the parts which contain chlorophyll have
made sugar (1)
because only they can absorb the light energy (1)
needed for photosynthesis to make sugar (1)

(c) respiration (1)

(d) (i) phloem (1)
(ii) respiration (1)
synthesis of larger compounds (1)

(e) converted to starch (1)
for storage (1)

4 The ins and outs of water

(a) (i) $2 \text{ cm}^3 \div 20$ (1)
$= 0.1 \text{cm}^3$ per hour (1)
(ii) diffusion/osmosis (1)
(iii) xylem (1)
(iv) transpiration from leaves (1)
creates a 'pull'/tension (1)
on the water in the xylem (1)
(v) uptake of ions by active uptake (1)
which requires energy (1)
water uptake is passive (1)

(b) water vapour loss by transpiration (1)
greater than water uptake by roots (1)
cells wilt since most support is by water filling
vacuoles of cells (1)

Progress with GCSE Structured Questions: Biology

5   The goings on in a bottle garden

(a) concentration of carbon dioxide would fall and oxygen
rise during the day   (1)
because the rate of photosynthesis is greater than
the rate of respiration   (1)
concentration of carbon dioxide would rise and oxygen
fall during the night   (1)
because the rate of photosynthesis is less than the
rate of respiration   (1)

(b) because the air in the jar is saturated with
water vapour   (1)
therefore water vapour diffuses in and out of leaves
at the same rate   (1)

(c) to replenish supplies of carbon dioxide   (1)
since some becomes permanently locked into
large molecules   (1)
as plant grows   (1)

6   Growing the most tomatoes

(a) suitable scale for axes   (1)
all plots correct   (1)
suitable curve drawn   (1)

(b) some other factor now limiting the rate of
photosynthesis   (1)
e.g. light intensity/water   (1)

(c) fuel costs money   (1)
increased yield may not be enough to offset this cost   (1)
since some other factor e.g. carbon dioxide concentration
may limit the yield   (1)

7   That sinking feeling

(a) (i) carbon dioxide + water $\rightarrow$ (1)
               glucose + oxygen   (1)
        (ii) $6CO_2 + 6H_2O \rightarrow$ (1)
               $C_6H_{12}O_6 + 6H_2O$ (1)

(b) (i) 3600 lux   (1)
        (ii) curve higher up graph   (1)
             and much flatter   (1)
             less available carbon dioxide in water   (1)
             therefore rate of photosynthesis limited by
             carbon dioxide concentration rather than by
             light intensity   (1)

8   Transpiration

(a) the rate   (1)
        of water uptake   (1)

(b) (i)   the loss of water vapour   (1)
              from the shoot of a plant   (1)
        (ii) both increase the rate of transpiration   (1)
              effect of wind greater than that of increased
              temperature   (1)
        (iii) stomata close in the dark   (1)
              more difficult for water vapour to escape   (1)

9 Stomata

(a) to allow carbon dioxide to enter (1)
and oxygen to leave (1)

(b) (i) potato stomata open for longer time (1)
potato open for part of night (1)

(ii) maize because stomata only open during the day (1)
to allow carbon dioxide in for photosynthesis (1)
closed at night (1)
to conserve water (1)

10 Mineral nutrition

(a) (i) nitrogen needed to produce proteins (1)
which are needed for growth (1)

(ii) magnesium is needed for chlorophyll formation (1)

(b) (i) needed for healthy root growth (1)

(ii) needed for photosynthesis (1)

(c) water leaves plant roots (1)
by osmosis (1)
since concentration of water inside roots greater than
concentration outside roots or the converse (1)

11 Plant responses

(a) (i) enables plant leaves to receive light for
photosynthesis (1)

(ii) enables roots to anchor plants (1)

(iii) enable plant roots to obtain sufficient water for
plants (1)

(b) (i) light from right side (1)
caused hormone to accumulate on left side (1)
cells on left side grow faster than cells on
right side (1)

(ii) tip is sensitive region needs to be uncovered (1)
it is where hormone/auxin is formed (1)

  Progress with GCSE Structured Questions: Biology

1 How tall wheat grows

(a) all plots correct gains two marks, minus one for
each incorrect plot (2)

(b) any three of: (3)
some have different parents/different genes
some get more light/shaded
some get more/less mineral ions
some get more/less water

2 How tulips grow

(a) bulbs produced by asexual/vegetative reproduction (1)
only one parent involved (1)
all offspring have same genes as parent (1)

(b) seeds produced by sexual reproduction (1)
therefore contain mixture of genes (1)
from two different parents (1)

3 Lystosaurus

(a) from hard parts that do not decay or become stone (1)
where conditions for decay, e.g. oxygen, are absent (1)

(b) any two of the following for one mark each: (2)
new competitors
new predators
new diseases
change in environment, e.g. climate

(c) (i) e.g. four limbs (1)
(ii) e.g. has no external ears (1)

(d) all living organisms arose from primitive ancestors (1)
by changes which occurred over millions of years (1)

(e) the record of what was alive (1)
is preserved in fossils (1)

4 Couch grass

(a) (i) mitosis (1)
(ii) daughter cells contain same number of
chromosomes as parents (1)

(b) (i) identical (1)
(ii) identical (1)

(c) pollen cells would contain half number of
chromosomes (1)
and would have different alleles due to crossing over (1)

5 Sun-beds can be dangerous

(a) cells divide by mitosis (1)
before division a copy is made of each chromosome (1)
each daughter cell receives a complete copy of genes
of parent cell (1)

(b) sperm produced by meiosis (1)
crossing over involved (1)
which means that alleles may be different (1)

(c) a spontaneous change (1)
in genetic material (1)

(d) increase in radiation (1)
increases frequency of mutations (1)
some mutations lead to cancer (1)

6 It's not safe on the sands

(a) the survival to breed (1)
of organisms best adapted to the environment (1)

(b) banded snails camouflaged (1)
less likely to be eaten (1)
therefore survive to breed (1)
their genes passed on to next generation (1)
offspring more likely to be banded (1)
banding is a dominant gene (1)

7 Mammoths

(a) long hair (1)
for insulation (1)
small ears reduce surface area (1)
through which heat is lost (1)

(b) natural variation e.g. by mutation (1)
produced some elephants with longer hair (1)
these elephants better adapted for survival in cold
conditions (1)
therefore more likely to breed (1)
and pass on mutation to next generation (1)

1 Breeding taller plants

(a) all bars correctly plotted gains two marks, minus one
for each incorrect plot (2)

(b) 20 cm (1)

(c) take pollen from one plant (1)
place on stigma of other plant (1)
shield stigma from other pollen (1)

(d) select short plants for breeding (1)
reselect in next generation (1)
repeat for several generations (1)

(e) plants less likely to suffer wind damage/knock down (1)
less straw to dispose of (1)

2 What makes a girl

(a) parental chromosomes   XY   XX   (1)
chromosomes in sex cells   X   Y   X   X   (1)
chromosomes in children   XX   XY   (1)

(b) (i) 50:50/1:1/evens (1)
(ii) sex depends on whether egg is fertilised by
'X sperm' or 'Y sperm' (1)
these are produced in equal numbers (1)
fertilisation is random process (1)

3   Breeding mice

(a)   parental genotypes   Bb   bb   (1)
       genotype of sex cells   B   B   b   b   (1)
       genotypes of offspring   Bb   (1)

(b)   parental genotypes   Bb   bb   (1)
       genotypes in sex cells   B   b   b   b   (1)
       genotypes of offspring   Bb   bb   (1)

4   Hitch-hiker's thumb

(a)   Hh   (1)
       must have H since has the affected thumbs   (1)
       if she had been HH all her children would have had
       affected thumbs   (1)

(b)   parental genotypes   Hh   hh   (1)
       genotypes in sex cells   H   h   h   h   (1)
       genotypes of offspring   Hh   hh   (1)
       50% chance of a child having affected thumbs   (1)

5   Cystic fibrosis

(a)   (i)   Aa   (1)
       (ii)   aa   (1)

(b)   50%   (1)
       parental genotypes   Aa   aa   (1)
       genotypes in sex cells   A   a   a   a
       genotypes of offspring   Aa   aa   (1)
       50% chance of a child having aa genotype

6   Huntington's chorea

Huntington's chorea is caused by a dominant allele, H   (1)
parental genotypes   hh   Hh   (1)
genotypes in sex cells   h   h   H   h   (1)
genotypes of offspring   hh   Hh   (1)
50% chance of a child having Hh genotype   (1)

7 Haemophilia

(a) 50% (1)
haemophilia is caused by a recessive allele, h, carried only on the X chromosome (1)
parental genotypes X^hY X^HX^h (1)
genotypes in sex cells X^h Y X^H X^h (1)
genotypes of male offspring X^HY X^hY
50% chance of each male offspring having haemophilia (1)

(b) females need to have two X^h alleles to have disease (1)
one from haemophiliac father (1)
other from carrier mother (1)

8 DNA

(a) complementary bases drawn (1)

(b) chain of bases on DNA (1)
information carried as code (1)
three bases/triplet (1)
codes for insertion of a specific amino acid (1)

(c) sequence of DNA for insulin production (1)
cut from human DNA (1)
inserted into bacteria (1)
which multiply rapidly to produce insulin (1)

9 New ways of growing carrots

(a) cloning/tissue culture (1)

(b) mitosis (1)

(c) advantages
- all carrots identical (1)
- for selected characteristics (1)
- customer preference for uniformity (1)

disadvantages
- reduction in size of gene pool (1)
- leads to limited range of allele for future selection (1)
- to meet changes e.g. new strains of carrot-disease microbes (1)

10 March of the mutant tomatoes

advantages
- lower freezing points prevent damage to tomatoes (1)
- longer shelf life (1)
- cheaper food for consumers (1)
- greater profits for growers (1)

disadvantages
- insufficient trials as yet (1)
- environmental effects unknown (1)
- possible effects on humans (1)
- ethical objections (1)

1 Surviving in the desert

(a) (i) thick pads insulate it from hot sand (1)
broad feet prevent it sinking into sand (1)
(ii) these prevent sand getting into nose and eyes (1)
during sand storms (1)
(iii) this conserves water (1)
which is scarce in deserts (1)

(b) (i) reduces transpiration/water loss (1)
(ii) protection from browsing animals (1)
sharp prickles hurt animal trying to feed (1)

2 Surviving in the arctic

(a) camouflage (1)
against white background of snow (1)

(b) insulation from cold (1)
thick fur traps layer of air which is poor conductor (1)

(c) insulation (1)
prevents conduction of heat to ice (1)

(d) flat feet prevent sinking in soil/snow (1)
claws can grip ice or catch prey (1)

(e) reduced surface area (1)
leads to less heat loss to the environment (1)

3 Down to the woods

(a) (i) light during day (1)
dark during night (1)
colder during night (1)
(ii) warmest in summer (1)
days longest in summer (1)
rainfall changes with seasons (1)

(b) not as much light at Y (1)
not as warm at Y (1)
more humid at Y (1)

(c) shields it from light (1)
therefore Y slower growing (1)
competes with it for mineral salts/nitrates (1)
therefore Y slower growing (1)

4 Plumbing the depths

(a) too cold (1)
not enough light (1)
(b) they would be shaded by the taller plants (1)
there would be competition for mineral ions/nitrates (1)
(c) Potamogeton plants completely submerged (1)
therefore do not need much anchorage (1)

5 The moose story

(a) suitable scale chosen (1)
all plots correct (1)
sensible curve drawn (1)

(b) (i) few competitors (1)
no predators (1)
(ii) disease (1)
food supply fails (1)

(c) lower peak (1)
no population crash in 1930s (1)

© 1998 Hodder & Stoughton Educational *Progress with GCSE Structured Questions: Biology*

6   The dangers of DDT

(a)   to kill insects   (1)
      which damage crops   (1)

(b)   DDT non-biodegradable   (1)
      therefore concentrated at each stage in food chain   (1)
      the bird is at the top of the food chain   (1)

(c)   (i)   because it is non-biodegradable   (1)
          wild bird populations were reduced   (1)
      (ii)   DDT is cheap, they cannot afford other
          insecticides   (1)
          insect problems much worse in tropical areas   (1)
          people might starve if it was banned   (1)

(d)   rapid growth of plant life   (1)
      competition for light, some plants die   (1)
      dead plants are food for microbes which
      multiply rapidly   (1)
      microbes deplete oxygen content of water   (1)
      animals in water may suffocate   (1)

7   Dying forests

(a)   (i)   40%   (1)
      (ii)   Norway spruce under 50 years old   (1)

(b)   oldest trees   (1)
      had most damage to crowns   (1)

(c)   combustion of fossil fuels   (1)
      releases sulphur dioxide into air   (1)
      which dissolves in rain, making it acidic   (1)

(d)   increase in human population   (1)
      and living standards/cars/power stations   (1)
      have led to increase in use of fossil fuels   (1)

8   Disappearing forests

(a)   to provide more land for agriculture   (1)
      to feed increased populations   (1)

(b)   erosion   (1)
      leaching of mineral ions   (1)

(c)   increased carbon dioxide content   (1)
      from combustion   (1)
      and decreased oxygen concentration   (1)
      since less photosynthesis   (1)
      less rainfall since less transpiration   (1)

(d)   reduced numbers of species   (1)
      since habitats destroyed   (1)
      loss of alleles from gene pools of survivors   (1)

1 If you go into the woods

(a) oak trees (1)

(b) sparrowhawk (1)
since at top of food chain (1)
energy and materials lost at each step in food chain (1)

(c) oak tree (1)
since producer (1)

(d) (i) increase (1)
since fewer eaten (1)
(ii) decrease (1)
since more eaten by increased population of
ladybirds (1)

(e) (i) pyramid correct shape (narrow base with normal
pyramid on top) (1)
all organisms labelled (1)
(ii) normal pyramid shape (1)
all organisms labelled (1)

2 The deep

(a) (i) algae (1)
(ii) any organism (all respire) (1)
(iii) algae (1)
(iv) worms, water fleas or mayfly nymphs (1)

(b) any three for one mark each of beetles, caddis, leeches,
dragonfly, stickleback (3)

(c) (i) algae → worms/water fleas/mayfly nymphs →
stickleback (1)
(ii) detritus → leech → stickleback (1)

(d) normal pyramid shape (1)
all organisms labelled (1)

3 What goes on in a compost heap?

(a) (i) normal pyramid shape except wider band on top
(fleas) (1)
all organisms labelled (1)
(ii) normal pyramid shape (1)
all organisms labelled (1)

(b) (i) bacteria/fungi (1)
(ii) warmth (1)
dampness (1)

(c) digested (1)
by microbes/bacteria/fungi (1)
eaten by detritus feeders (1)
respired (1)
carbon dioxide returned to atmosphere (1)

4 Nitrogen gets around

(a) (i) putrefying bacteria (1)
(ii) nitrifying bacteria (1)

(b) (i) nitrogen-fixing bacteria (1)
(ii) nitrogen compounds in clover/bacteria (1)
enter nitrogen cycle in soil (1)
converted into nitrate for use by future
crop plants (1)

(c) nitrates will be converted to nitrogen gas (1)
by denitrifying bacteria (1)
fewer available for growth of crop plants (1)

(d) nitrates converted into protein by plants (1)
by combining them with carbohydrate (1)
grass eaten by rabbit and digested into amino acids (1)
amino acids absorbed by blood stream (1)
transported to liver cells where converted into proteins (1)

© 1998 Hodder & Stoughton Educational *Progress with GCSE Structured Questions: Biology*

5   Food for chickens

(a) $1 \times 100 \div 2.5$ (1)
   $= 40\%$ (1)

(b)   some not digested (1)
   passes out in faeces (1)
   some respired (1)
   carbon dioxide released into blood stream (1)
   into air through lungs (1)

6   Round and round the aquarium

(a)   oxygen removed from water by respiration (1)
   replaced by photosynthesis (1)
   carbon dioxide added to water by respiration (1)
   removed by photosynthesis (1)
   in balanced tank, net removals = net additions (1)

(b)   ammonia converted into nitrate (1)
   by nitrifying bacteria (1)
   absorbed by plants and converted to protein (1)
   animals eat plants (1)
   excess protein broken back down to ammonia (1)

SPOTLIGHT on fact

TEACHER'S **3**
RESOURCE BOOK **3**

Karina Law

Maureen Lewis

Gordon Askew

60057

Authors: Karina Law, Maureen Lewis, Gordon Askew
Series editor: Maureen Lewis
Design: Neil Adams, Grasshopper Design Company
Editor: Janet Swarbrick
Cover images: Oxford Scientific Films (main); Still Pictures © Gilles Martin (T);
    Ecoscene/Mark Casey (C); Corbis (B)
Illustrations: Maggie Brand
Cover design: Louise Morley

Published by HarperCollins*Publishers* Ltd
77–85 Fulham Palace Road
Hammersmith
London W6 8JB

www.Collins Education.com
Online support for schools and colleges

British Library Cataloguing in Publication Data
A catalogue record for this book is available from the British Library.

Printed in Great Britain by Martins the Printers, Berwick-upon-Tweed

You might also like to visit
www.fireandwater.com
The book lover's website

About the authors

Karina Law graduated with a BA (Hons), in Education and English, before teaching at primary schools in Surrey. She has edited a range of educational publications and is a writer of educational resources, children's fiction and poetry.

Dr **Maureen Lewis** is one of the UK's leading experts in children's reading and writing of non-fiction texts. Her research and classroom work in this area have been influential in the approach to non-fiction work in current literacy initiatives. She has had considerable experience as a primary teacher, university researcher and lecturer, educational consultant and author of both academic and classroom materials. She continues to play a leading national role in literacy teaching developments.

Gordon Askew, a former primary headteacher and English Adviser, contributes extensively to the writing of classroom guidance for literacy teaching. Gordon plays a leading national role in the development of ICT in literacy.

Contents

SPOTLIGHT
on fact

The *Spotlight on Fact* programme

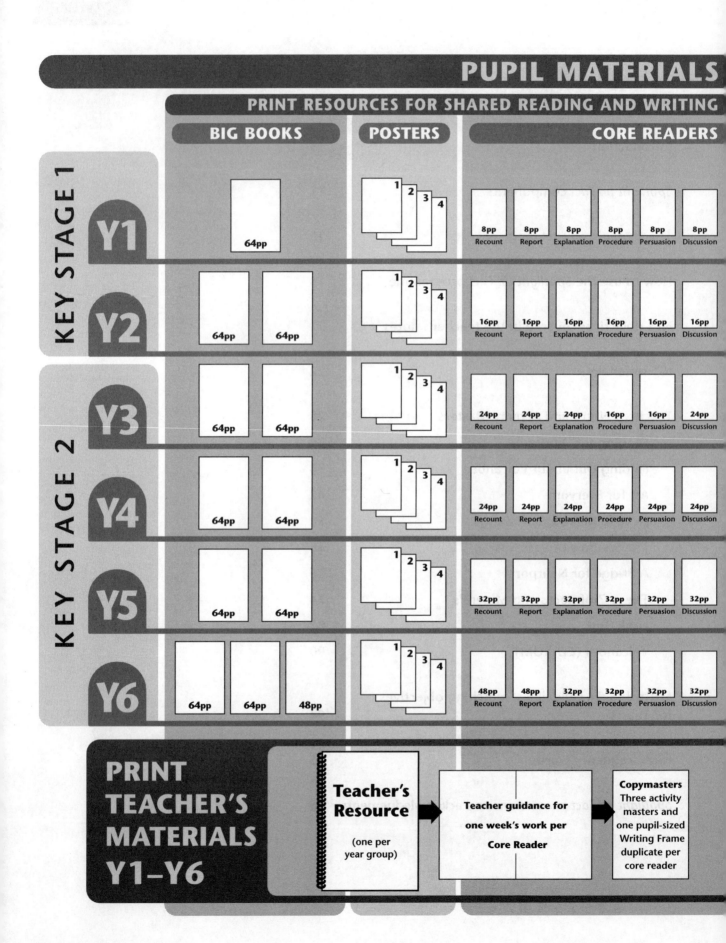

PUPIL MATERIALS

PRINT RESOURCES FOR SHARED READING AND WRITING

	BIG BOOKS	POSTERS	CORE READERS

KEY STAGE 1

Y1
- Big Books: 64pp
- Posters: 1 2 3 4
- Core Readers: 8pp Recount | 8pp Report | 8pp Explanation | 8pp Procedure | 8pp Persuasion | 8pp Discussion

Y2
- Big Books: 64pp, 64pp
- Posters: 1 2 3 4
- Core Readers: 16pp Recount | 16pp Report | 16pp Explanation | 16pp Procedure | 16pp Persuasion | 16pp Discussion

KEY STAGE 2

Y3
- Big Books: 64pp, 64pp
- Posters: 1 2 3 4
- Core Readers: 24pp Recount | 24pp Report | 24pp Explanation | 16pp Procedure | 16pp Persuasion | 24pp Discussion

Y4
- Big Books: 64pp, 64pp
- Posters: 1 2 3 4
- Core Readers: 24pp Recount | 24pp Report | 24pp Explanation | 24pp Procedure | 24pp Persuasion | 24pp Discussion

Y5
- Big Books: 64pp, 64pp
- Posters: 1 2 3 4
- Core Readers: 32pp Recount | 32pp Report | 32pp Explanation | 32pp Procedure | 32pp Persuasion | 32pp Discussion

Y6
- Big Books: 64pp, 64pp, 48pp
- Posters: 1 2 3 4
- Core Readers: 48pp Recount | 48pp Report | 32pp Explanation | 32pp Procedure | 32pp Persuasion | 32pp Discussion

PRINT TEACHER'S MATERIALS Y1–Y6

Teacher's Resource (one per year group) → **Teacher guidance for one week's work per Core Reader** → **Copymasters** Three activity masters and one pupil-sized Writing Frame duplicate per core reader

ICT RESOURCES FOR SHARED READING AND WRITING

CD-ROM *featuring* **ICT TEXT**

Teaches information gathering and processing skills in an ICT medium

plus
ELECTRONIC WRITING FRAMES

plus
ELECTRONIC BIG BOOKS

8pp	8pp
Alphabetic	Authentic

Y1: Monster Maker
Teacher and children construct a sea, snow or space monster from the options given. They make a series of choices from information provided. Children also learn basic skills about how a keyboard is used to find information on a computer.

16pp	16pp
Alphabetic	Authentic

Y2: Seaside Shop
Teacher and children go shopping on-line. Children see and learn how to use the same principles used in real on-line shopping to navigate around a store, make relevant choices and complete a purchase.

24pp	16pp
Alphabetic	Authentic

Y3: Volcanoes
Teacher and children compare information on a range of famous volcanoes using animated cross-sectional drawings, video footage and written information. Children see and learn how to skim, scan, select and reject from information given in order to produce their own informational text on volcanoes.

24pp	24pp
Alphabetic	Authentic

Y4: Bully
Teacher and children explore from a range of different types of information given, different situations where some children might get bullied at school. Children learn how to select and evaluate different types of information in order to build either a discursive or persuasive argument on the topic.

32pp	32pp
Alphabetic	Authentic

48pp	32pp
Alphabetic	Authentic

Replicas of the print Writing Frames with added electronic features that make compiling text types fun for both teacher and child. Each frame can be expanded, added to or deleted from, according to the writing purpose of a particular task. Teacher and children can share the experience of choosing from a range of typefaces and a suite of clip-art to build information written texts.

Facsimiles of all the Core Readers in "larger than life" pdf format. The electronic Core Readers can be used on a normal computer, through a projector or on an interactive whiteboard. The electronic books contain duplicate pages of each page where recommended key teaching points of text, sentence and word have been marked up in the text.

Also available on the CD-ROM

Free "print and read only" version of the Teacher's Resource Book

Introduction

Spotlight on Fact is a series of non-fiction books and related ICT materials (see pages 6–7), which provide a wide range of non-fiction texts to engage readers and provide exciting links into writing. It offers materials and teaching opportunities to enable pupils to develop as effective users of non-fiction texts who use information texts for personal pleasure, in order to learn and to function in society. Pupils will be helped to:

- read and understand a range of non-fiction text types in a variety of formats including ICT

- use a range of reading strategies such as scanning, skimming, close reading

- develop critical and thoughtful responses to texts

- use reference and study skills such as using an index, taking notes

- understand the function of textual features, e.g. headings, bullet points

- interpret a range of graphic information sources, e.g. diagrams, charts, grids

- write for a range of purposes and audiences using a range of non-fiction genres

- read and write non-fiction texts containing more formal registers and technical vocabulary

- use appropriate grammar and vocabulary within writing, depending upon the purpose of the writing and the audience for whom it is written.

Rationale for *Spotlight on Fact*

Non-fiction texts are a substantial part of the oral, written and graphic materials we encounter within any literate society. In order to learn about our fascinating world and to function effectively within society and the classroom, children need to understand how to read and write information texts. During the last few years there has been increasing awareness amongst primary teachers of the need to include non-fiction texts in English lessons as well as in other curriculum areas. The National Curriculum (NC) for England and Wales, the National Guidelines for Scotland and the National Literacy Strategy (NLS) *Framework for teaching* all stress the wide range of non-fiction texts children should encounter.

The series has been created with a number of principles in mind:

Children are motivated to read if the texts they are offered engage and enthral them.

The subjects have been chosen to interest and motivate readers. Non-fiction texts provide the opportunity to confirm what children know and take them beyond their immediate world. Such experiences can be a powerful introduction to the pleasures of reading and can extend the repertoire of more fluent readers. The books in this series have been written by experienced children's authors; contain a wide range of engrossing illustrative materials and will stimulate interest, discussion and questioning. The books are not a tightly structured reading scheme although the language levels are broadly aligned to the year group and contain many of the words from the NLS vocabulary lists.

Children should encounter a wide range of text types (including alphabetically ordered and mixed texts) in their reading and writing.

All of the six non-fiction text types identified in the *Framework for teaching* are represented in each yearly strand along with an alphabetically ordered text and an "authentic" text. This goes beyond the listed yearly focus of the NLS framework and offers teachers the flexibility to visit or revisit other text types. For, as the NLS points out, "There is a termly focus on a particular text type . . . but within each term a wide range of text types will naturally occur within English and within other curriculum areas" (Module 6, Resource Bank page 3).

Mixed texts (mixed non-fiction text types, and "faction" texts) are also included, as children will encounter such texts frequently in their lives. The series also includes an authentic text strand, which brings "real" texts from the wider world into the classroom.

Seeing the links between reading and writing supports children's literacy development.

In order to develop as thoughtful and critical readers, children need to understand that authors write in order to impact upon the reader. Recognizing how an author's choice of form, sentence structure and vocabulary helps them achieve their purpose is a crucial element in developing critical reading. Such understandings can be encouraged with young readers as well as with experienced readers.

Wide reading helps children develop a rich schema (a "feel") of how particular texts are created. This can then be drawn on when children come to write. The books in this series can provide models for children's own writing and can be used for textual analysis when appropriate. Every book contains possible stimuli for further writing and these are elaborated in the teacher's notes.

Children should learn about grammar within purposeful reading and writing contexts.

Children can explore grammatical and semantic uses within texts they are reading. This allows them to consider *why* particular aspects have been used (e.g. verb tenses) as well as *how* they are created. They can then go on to further investigation and practice as well as being asked to apply their knowledge in their own writing. The word and sentence level work given in the teacher's notes links directly to the text being read.

Literacy teaching and learning takes place in the rest of the curriculum as well as within English lessons.

By emphasizing the links between English and the rest of the curriculum, pupils are given opportunities to enhance their learning across the whole curriculum and to recognize how knowledge and skills from one area of the curriculum can be developed within another. In recently published materials on the QCA and NLS websites (www.qca.org.uk/ca/subjects/english/literacy) it is pointed out that work in English can be linked with work in other areas of the curriculum in the following ways:

- content knowledge acquired in subject area study can be brought to the Literacy Hour as the basis for informed discussion and purposeful writing;

- skills taught in the Literacy Hour (e.g. note taking, skimming and scanning, writing) can be practised and developed via purposeful use in other curriculum areas. In such cases pupils may need explicit reminders to help them make the learning links;

- skills taught in other curriculum areas (e.g. analysing evidence, reading visual information sources) can be enhanced via further focused teaching and practice in the Literacy Hour;

- subject specific vocabulary and subject specific patterns of language can be further analysed and explored within the Literacy Hour.

The books in *Spotlight on Fact* are linked to the wider curriculum in three ways. Each book:

■ has a specific curriculum focus for each book in the year strand – History, Maths, Geography, Science, ICT, The Arts and Leisure – so they can be used in other curriculum lessons as well as in English;

■ can be linked to one of QCA's curriculum schemes of work if schools are following these;

■ is linked, within the year strand, by an overarching theme: Year 1 (Scottish Level A) "Toys and Games"; Year 2 (Scottish Level A/B) "The Seaside"; Year 3 (Scottish Level C) "Active Earth"; Year 4 (Scottish Level C/D) "Living Together"; Year 5 (Scottish Level D) "Our Environment"; and Year 6 (Scottish Level D/E) "Making a Difference". Teachers who wish to use a theme to integrate their planning across the curriculum may do so and children can be encouraged to see how reading across the year strand will widen and deepen their knowledge around a subject.

*The characteristics of the **Spotlight on Fact** Core Readers*

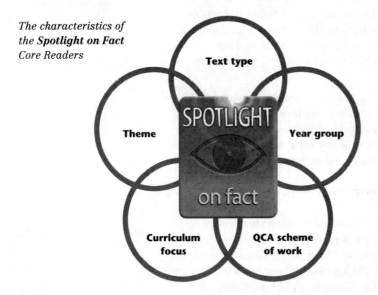

The chart on pages 16–17 shows the titles, text types, and curriculum and thematic strands for the core books in *Spotlight on Fact*.

Children are entitled to use ICT, both as a text in its own right and as a tool to support their literacy development.

ICT is an integral part of *Spotlight on Fact* and children are given opportunities to learn about ICT via the books in the series; pupils in Years 1 to 4 are given the opportunities to learn through ICT via the ICT teaching materials such as the ICT Big Books and given opportunities to learn with ICT via the computer-based texts they will read and use.

Literacy is developed through demonstration, shared experiences, guided practice, experimentation, independent work and reflection on what has been learned.

Children need to experience different levels of support as they develop as fluent readers and writers. The materials in *Spotlight on Fact* can be used successfully in a variety of contexts.

Spotlight on Fact components

Printed materials

Teacher's Resource Book

This practical handbook gives guidance on teaching each of the six text types and the alphabetic and authentic texts. All the guidance provided is in line with the recommendations of the NLS non-fiction *Writing Fliers* and the word, sentence and text level objectives from the National Literacy Strategy.

For each of the eight Core Readers in this year group there are:

- a detailed lesson plan containing a recommended week's work
- 3 Activity Masters for writing practice in extending literacy skills
- 1 pupil-sized copy of the Writing Frame for scaffolding a writing assignment.

Also provided is a detailed lesson plan containing a recommended week's work using the electronic text on the CD-ROM.

Big Book

Two *Big Books* are provided for this year group. These are designed to be the perfect non-fiction tool for whole class teaching and shared reading sessions during the Literacy Hour.

Each *Big Book* should be used in conjunction with the *Teacher's Resource Book*, which gives teaching guidance on where to use the *Big Book* to illustrate a key teaching point. Between 70 and 95 per cent of each Core Reader is duplicated. This ensures that a meaningful amount of the reader is available for whole class teaching purposes.

Each book contains large-size extracts from the Core Readers chosen specifically because they provide the teacher with opportunities to make clear key teaching objectives from the NLS non-fiction *Writing Fliers* and the word, sentence and text level objectives.

For ease of use each *Big Book* contains:

- a contents page for locating individual titles and their extracts
- the book title clearly labelled at the top of each *Big Book* page
- the page numbers of the Core Reader from which extracts are taken as well as *Big Book* page numbers for easy reference
- a miniature replica of the Core Reader's front cover at the beginning of each extract to identify it
- the cross-curricular topic, subject and text type reference on each page.

Writing Frames

A poster-sized, laminated Writing Frame (504 × 352 mm) is provided for use with each Core Reader. There are eight posters with each year's provision. These provide opportunities for the teacher, in shared writing sessions, to scaffold pupil's writing assignments.

Year 3 Writing Frames

Core readers for Year 3

Digging for Dinosaurs

Text type: Recount

Why is the Isle of Wight called "Dinosaur Island"? You'll find out when you read this exciting book about the ancient bones and fossils that have been found there.

Finding Out about Volcanoes

Text type: Report – non-chronological

Suppose that you would like to find out more about volcanoes. This book tells you about fast, easy and fun ways that you can use your computer to explore this subject. You can use ICT to find out about other subjects, too.

Art for Everyone

Text type: Explanation

People everywhere have always made art, and they have used everything from sticks to feathers, from clay to metal. Have fun reading about making art from things found in the world around us.

How to Make a Rain Gauge

Text type: Procedure

Meteorologists have many instruments to measure rainfall, which is important information in learning about the weather. You can be an amateur meteorologist by making a simple rain gauge to measure the rainfall where you live. Read this book and have fun learning how to do it.

The Shadow of Vesuvius

Text type: Persuasion plus Recount

Should the Italians be making plans to save the people of Naples when Vesuvius erupts again? Thousands of lives have been lost in the past when the volcano erupted and thousands are in danger in the future. Surely the answer to the question is "yes".

A Bridge for Nearport

Text type: Discussion plus Procedure

Bridges are used to cross rivers everywhere in the world. But there are different kinds of bridges to choose from and people have to think about which are easier or cheaper to build. Find out about different bridges from this book – and have some fun making models with the easy directions given.

The A–Z of Rocks and Minerals

Text type: Alphabetically ordered text

The Earth beneath our feet is made up of a fantastic variety of minerals and rocks. They have different colours, shapes, hardness and value, and we use them for all sorts of things.

Look Out!

Authentic text (mixed text type)

Our world can be a dangerous place, but there are many signs and notices that help keep us safe! This book tells you about some of the warning signs you might see. Always make sure you obey them!

ICT materials

Two CD-ROMs are provided for this year group. They have four main menus: the electronic Teacher's Resource Book; the electronic Big Book; 8 electronic Writing Frames; and the ICT text *Volcanoes*.

Electronic Teacher's Resource Book

This is a "print and read only" version of the printed book. It can be accessed in two ways:

- unit by unit from the electronic big book menu for use in planning lessons with the Core Readers

- in its entirety, from the main menu of the CD-ROM itself.

Electronic Big Book

The Electronic Big Book contains large-size extracts from the Core Readers chosen specifically because they provide the teacher with opportunities to make clear key teaching objectives from the NLS non-fiction *Writing Fliers* and the word, sentence and text level objectives. It is in a PDF (portable document format) which means it needs to be downloaded on Acrobat Reader. This can be put onto any computer from the Web quite easily, free of charge. The book can be used on a normal computer, through a projector or on an interactive whiteboard.

In addition to providing every page from the Core Reader for reading the text with the whole class, each page is duplicated. These duplicates may be used to illuminate key teaching points on text, sentence and word work. Each is marked up in the text with coloured highlights.

An easy to use interface provides access to the "plain" version of a chosen text, reached by pressing the purple button. Marked up duplicates are reached by clicking on the colour tags displayed on the control panel at the bottom left- and right-hand side of the screen. Each distinct type of work can be found by pressing the specific colour button associated with it on the navigation control panel: Text level – green; Sentence level – yellow; Word level – blue.

Although the software is produced as a whole class teaching tool for Shared Reading and Writing, it can easily be used by children reading on their own or in pairs.

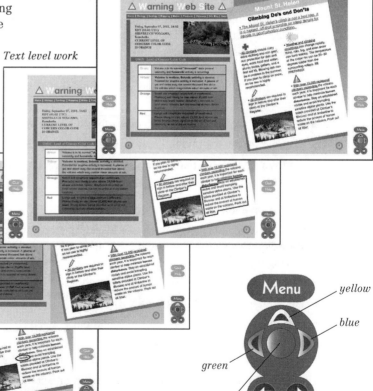

Main text

Text level work

Sentence level work

Word level work

A set of pages from the Y3 Electronic Big Book

The Electronic Big Book control panel

Menu — yellow — blue — green — purple

Electronic Writing Frames

The Writing Frames work particularly well on screen where they provide a flexible and easy to use writing tool. Text can be written, altered and styled easily. It is important that pupils should be able to adapt the structure of a Writing Frame to suit their own purposes. This can easily be achieved with an on-screen Writing Frame where none of the text prompts provided are "set in stone".

Spotlight on Fact provides eight structured Writing Frames for Year 3:

- Activity Master 3 Letter Writing
- Activity Master 8 Report Writing: Volcanoes
- Activity Master 12 Writing an Explanation
- Activity Master 15 Writing Instructions
- Activity Master 20 Skeleton Notes
- Activity Master 24 Which Bridge?
- Activity Master 27 Writing a Glossary
- Activity Master 31 Reasons for Rules.

These help children extend their literacy skills into reading and writing activities of their own choosing. Electronic Writing Frames provide a supported word processing environment for eight different writing forms. Pupils will be able to choose from four fonts in normal, bold or italic. All text can be sized to small, medium or large. It will also be possible to set the colour of the type. A choice of pictures will be provided for each writing frame. All Writing Frames can be printed out.

ICT text

The *Volcanoes* text can be used by the teacher as a whole class teaching tool as well as by pupils working in pairs or on their own.

Volcanoes simulates the sort of ICT information text often found on a CD-ROM. It presents information in multimedia format, including video, animations, slide shows and sound bites as well as the written words, pictures and diagrams you would find in a paper text.

However, unlike many other CD-ROM texts currently available, it has been specifically written to meet the reading and learning needs of Year 3 pupils, and to provide a context for teaching Y3 objectives from the *NLS Framework for Teaching*. Its written text, its subject content, and the level of ICT skill needed to use it are therefore all appropriate for use with Y3 pupils. It also provides a highly entertaining and engaging teaching tool.

Exploration of this text in shared, guided, and independent work will, in addition to fulfilling key NLS objectives, allow pupils to learn vital ICT "reading" skills:

- to **browse** an ICT text and discover what it has to offer
- to **navigate** such a text in order to seek particular information
- to **glean** and **orchestrate** information from a variety of different media sources.

How to use the software

An auto-run introduction (which can be skipped on revisiting) sets the scene, and leads into a simple point-and-click menu offering information on the following topics:

- Volcanoes of the World (geographical and scientific information)
- Volcanic Eruptions (the how and why)
- Volcanoes in History (Vesuvius and Pompeii).

Easy navigation through sub-menus, "hot links" and icons leads on to a wide variety of up-to-date information, presented in multimedia form.

Humour and user-friendliness is added by an on screen "volcano" character called Popo who helps you and the children find your way through the program.

The *Spotlight on Fact* range of texts

SPOTLIGHT
on fact

Authentic texts

Children are surrounded by non-book texts in their daily lives – from the junk mail that comes through everybody's letterbox, the road signs, advertisements and shop fronts they pass on their way to school, to the labels around the classroom and so on. The authentic text strand in *Spotlight on Fact* brings examples of these texts into the classroom so that children can make links between the information they are reading and the everyday print they encounter in their environment. Teachers should supplement the authentic text given in the series with further examples whenever possible – real catalogues, notices, signs and so on.

Y1 Authentic text

Alphabetically ordered texts

Across the series, children will encounter a wide range of alphabetically ordered text – dictionaries, encyclopedias, biographical dictionaries, gazetteers. These use alphabetical ordering up to three letters.

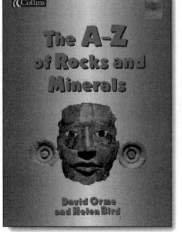

Y3 Alphabetically ordered text

Non-fiction text types

Six main non-fiction text types are included in each year strand:

- Recount
- Report
- Explanation
- Procedure
- Persuasion
- Discussion.

The text types are based on important purposes for communicating identified in the National Curriculum and the NLS framework. These are reading and writing:

- to inform, using explanations and reports
- to instruct, using instructions, procedures and directions
- to state a case, using persuasion and discussion
- to retell events, using recounts.

Y5 Recount

Y6 Report

Y1 Explanation

Y1 Procedure

Y2 Persuasion

Y4 Discussion

Mixed genres and "faction"

Some of the books have a main text type but also have other text type characteristics within them. This is both deliberate and desirable, as we would not want children to have an oversimplified view of the nature of texts. Often an author will have more than one purpose for writing a book. They may wish to recount an event and explain why it happened; they may want to give instructions for making something but then wish to evaluate it. This will naturally give rise to a mixed genre text. While it is important for children to be familiar with important text types such as recount, procedure, etc we must also help them see that texts can be complex and varied.

The *Spotlight on Fact* range of texts

Year/Scottish Level	Theme	Recount	Report	Explanation
Y1/Level A 5–6 yrs	Toys and Games	History — Toys of the Past Fifty Years	Maths — Let's Play Board Games	Science — What Makes Toys Move?
Y2/Level A/B 6–7 yrs	The Seaside	Maths — Packing for a Holiday	Science — Along the Seashore	ICT — Our Digital Holiday
Y3/Level C 7–8 yrs	Active Earth	Science — Digging for Dinosaurs	ICT — Finding Out about Volcanoes	The Arts — Art for Everyone
Y4/Level C/D 8–9 yrs	Living Together	ICT — Talking Together	The Arts — Playing Together	Geography — Why Do You Eat That?
Y5/Level D 9–10 yrs	Our Environment	The Arts — Trash to Treasure	Geography — A Home for Rubbish	History — Rubbish from the Past
Y6/Level D/E 10–11 yrs	Making a Difference	Geography — Dangerous Journeys	History — What a Hero!	Maths — Great Archimedes

The Teacher's Notes for individual books indicate when there are substantial elements of more than one text type.

"Faction" texts are those texts which, although based on fact, combine, in part, a small fictional element such as an imaginary town or a personalized diary of a traveller. Such texts can appeal to children's imagination and empathy. They are commonly encountered in both reading and in media texts such as films and television history programmes. As with all texts, we can encourage children to recognize these texts and how they work so that, as well as enjoying them, children can be critically aware of their status.

Procedure	Persuasion	Discussion	Alphabetic	Authentic
ICT	The Arts	Geography		
Telling Prog	Toys and Games in Art	Toys around the World	Toys and Games from A to Z	Choosing Toys
The Arts	Geography	History		
Take Good Holiday Photos	Places to Visit by The Sea	Holidays Then and Now	Which Holiday?	Going on Holiday
Geography	History	Maths		
How to Make a Rain Gauge	The Shadow of Vesuvius	A Bridge for Nearport	The A–Z of Rocks and Minerals	Look Out!
History	Maths	Science		
Building Together	Money Yesterday, Today and Tomorrow	Living Together Tomorrow	Dictionary of World Sports	Our Multilingual World
Maths	Science	ICT		
Make Your Own Paper	Get Rid of that Rubbish!	Can ICT Help Our World?	Recycled Materials of the World	You Decide!
Science	ICT	The Arts		
Famous Scientific Procedures	ICT: Get a Computer, Get a Life?	Comic Book Heroes	Biographical Dictionary of Recent Times	Sources for Biographies

How to use the *Spotlight on Fact* programme – reading into writing

Reading

The Core Readers are designed to be used as shared reading texts, although they can also be used for independent reading and guided reading if you choose to do so.

Shared reading

In shared reading, the teacher works with the whole class and all the children can see a copy of the text – either a *Big Book*, an ICT-based version (for Years 1 to 4) or an individual copy of the pupil's Core Reader. Shared reading enables children of all abilities to engage with the text as the less fluent reader is scaffolded by the shared nature of the reading experience and the more fluent readers can be engaged by the content, by focused interventions and by interactive teaching strategies. The initial reading of the text should focus on engagement, comprehension and response and should not be interrupted by too many "teaching interjections". Subsequent readings can then focus on explicit reading strategies, textual analysis and word and sentence features as appropriate. Suggestions for these are given in the Teacher's Notes for each individual book.

Guided reading

Guided reading takes place with a previously unseen text, which is selected to give a degree of challenge to the reader. The children should be able to read much of the text unaided. If you wish to use the pupil Core Reader books with a small group for guided reading this should be undertaken before the children have encountered the text as a shared reading text. Each child has their own copy of the text. Guided reading usually follows the sequence of introduction to the text, strategy check, independent reading, return to the text, response to the text and next steps (follow up).

Independent reading including supported reading

The pupil Core Reader books and the ICT versions can be used as independent reading texts. For inexperienced readers, independent rereading of a book previously encountered in shared reading can be a supportive experience. With fluent readers, a text, which has been partially read in shared reading, can be continued in independent reading.

Independent reading includes independent individual reading and independent group reading.

Writing

Writing activities are explicitly based on the books children have read. This enables you to teach non-fiction writing skills in a meaningful context. If you are able to link the work to ongoing work in the rest of the curriculum further purposeful contexts will arise. The Teacher's Notes show how the reading and contextualized word and sentence level work undertaken in the first few sessions with the book are then used as models for a writing task. Usually two writing tasks are suggested. You should use your knowledge of your pupils to decide whether:

■ you undertake one or both of these suggestions;

■ a session continues over more than one day. You may decide that a particular writing task might take your pupils longer than the time allowed in your independent work slot and thus you would wish to return to it on subsequent days rather than leave the writing uncompleted. It is important that children have the satisfaction of concluding a complete piece of writing. If you are linking the work in English to work in the rest of the curriculum, work started in English could also be continued in other subjects. For example, the writing a glossary activity suggested as the writing task for *A–Z of Rocks and Minerals* could also be worked on as part of Science work: "Rocks and soil" or "Characteristics of materials".

Shared writing

Shared writing is a powerful teaching strategy. It is the major way writing is taught in the NLS. Suggestions for shared writing are given in the notes for individual books. Shared writing includes teacher demonstration, teacher scribing and supported composition. But not all three aspects have to be present in every writing experience.

Teacher demonstration

In teacher demonstration, the teacher writes in front of the children (you are not taking suggestions from them at this point). As you write, you articulate how the text is written and the kind of decisions you are taking as you write.

Teacher scribing

In teacher scribing, the teacher takes on the role of secretary, writing for the children while they compose and contribute all or some of the text. However, as well as scribing for the class you will explain why you are taking some suggestions rather than others and will encourage children to reflect on the quality and appropriateness of their contributions.

Supported composition

In supported composition, the teacher will ask the children to write while they are still gathered together as a class. These occasions take place in the course of shared writing and children write parts of the text, possibly in pairs, e.g. on dry wipe whiteboards. They are "supported" both by the continued presence of the adult and also by other support such as talking to a partner, having a model to copy and so on.

Guided writing

In guided writing, the teacher undertakes the shared writing sequence, or part of it, with a small group who need to address specific objectives. You can use guided writing times to teach children to compose, edit and revise their writing independently. The Teacher's Notes give pointers to the focus you might give to a guided writing session if you were to undertake one within the outlined session.

Independent writing

Independent writing follows a shared text experience. Children continue at an appropriate level to complete, extend, or modify, work started in the shared task. They might also start a new piece based on the model offered in shared work or drawing on their experiences over several shared reading and writing sessions.

Teacher assessment

The suggested teaching sessions for each book offer opportunities to assess examples of children's:

- reading and comprehension skills
- writing and compositional skills
- knowledge of a particular text type
- use of grammar, punctuation and spelling
- use and understanding of linguistic terminology.

The shared and guided reading and writing sessions provide a context for ongoing formative assessment. You will also be able to analyse the written outcomes of sessions to assess:

- what children can do with support and independently
- what errors and misconceptions they have made
- what further teaching and experiences they need.

NLS objectives covered in the Teacher's Notes for Year 3

SPOTLIGHT
on fact

The Teacher's Notes for each book cover objectives from all three terms. This is to offer teachers maximum flexibility as to when they use the books. The teaching suggestions made in the notes on individual books are not exhaustive; teachers will also have their own creative ideas on how to use the books and may therefore include further objectives.

The chart below shows the NLS objectives covered in the Teacher's Notes for Year 3 (Scottish Level C). See page 94 for links to the Scottish Guidelines.

NLS objectives covered in the Teacher's Notes

Year 3/Level C Core Readers and CD-ROM	Term 1			Term 2			Term 3		
	Text level	Sentence level	Word level	Text level	Sentence level	Word level	Text level	Sentence level	Word level
Core Reader 1 Digging for Dinosaurs	T17	S3 S5	W13 W16 W17 W18 W19	T17		W17 W19 W20 W21 W23	T22 T23		W12 W13
Core Reader 2 Finding Out about Volcanoes	T17 T18 T19 T20 T21 T22	S6 S9		T17	S8	W15	T17 T18 T25 T26		W11
Core Reader 3 Art for Everyone	T17 T18 T21	S6 S9		T17	S4 S5 S6 S7	W11		S5 S7	
Core Reader 4 How to Make a Rain Gauge	T17 T21	S9 S11 S12	W13	T17	S10	W19	T26	S6	W14
Core Reader 5 The Shadow of Vesuvius	T17 T21 T22	S3 S4 S5	W13	T17		W12 W13 W14	T21 T22 T25	S5	W12
Core Reader 6 A Bridge for Nearport	T17 T20 T21	S6	W10 W11 W12	T12 T14 T15 T16 T17	S2 S3	W24	T21 T25 T26		
Core Reader 7 The A–Z of Rocks and Minerals	T20 T21	S9	W13 W15	T17		W17 W19 W20 W21 W23	T19 T24		W8 W12
Core Reader 8 Look Out!	T17 T22	S3 S5 S9	W13	T12 T16 T17	S8	W11	T21		W12
CD-ROM Volcanoes	T20 T22	S9	W13	T15 T16		W17	T17 T21		W12

ICT rationale

Over recent years ICT has very rapidly become an essential element of reading and writing, both for children and in the adult world. There is every reason to believe that its significance will continue to increase.

ICT is already a ubiquitous medium for communication, often utilizing text in its broadest sense. It is also a very engaging and exciting medium. It has developed, and is continuing to develop, a "literacy" of its own. Reading or writing an ICT text involves many of the same skills as communication on paper, but it also involves some new and significantly different ones – for example those of navigating through non-linear and multimedia information sources.

In addition to the widespread use of computer word processing, many people now commonly engage with text via:

■ CD-ROMs

■ the Internet

■ electronic books

■ computer and video games

■ e-mail

■ mobile phone "texting"

■ television text services.

Children are frequently just as familiar, and in some instances more familiar, with these media. To ignore ICT when teaching literacy in the classroom is becoming as impossible as it is undesirable. If we are to teach children the literacy skills they need to thrive and flourish in the present and future, then these must include the skills of accessing and creating texts through ICT.

Of course, it is unlikely that in the foreseeable future, ICT will completely replace books and other paper texts, or that the skills of ICT literacy will replace traditional literacy skills. Rightly so. Many of us still prefer to curl up with a good book rather than with a laptop. However, when seeking certain types of information, we are perhaps more likely to use a CD-ROM than a twenty-volume encyclopedia. When communicating with someone on the other side of the world (or even the other side of the street) we will often be more likely to send an e-mail than a conventional letter.

ICT has also become a significant medium for storing and retrieving information. It is therefore an essential strand running through every stage of *Spotlight on Fact*. All elements of this ICT component are fully in line with the requirements of the National Curriculum (NC) for England and Wales, the National Guidelines for Scotland and the NLS *Framework for teaching*. Whether teachers are already comfortable with classroom ICT use, or lack confidence or expertise in this field, *Spotlight on Fact* provides all the materials needed to fully integrate ICT into the teaching of literacy through non-fiction, in accessible, ready-to-use forms. Drawing on these, teachers will be able to meet all the recommendations of the NLS guidance on *ICT in the Literacy Hour* in respect of non-fiction. To this end, the ICT component of *Spotlight on Fact* comprises the following three major elements, each with a significant, but slightly different contribution to make:

Books with ICT as their subject matter

As well as providing appropriate and engaging examples of the various text types, these titles (one for each year group) give teachers and their pupils the opportunity to explore many issues relating to ICT and literacy. For example,

the Year 3 (Scottish Level C) text *Finding Out about Volcanoes* examines the potential of ICT information sources, while the Year 4 (Scottish Level C/D) text *Talking Together* prompts work involving both text messages and e-mail.

Electronic Big Books and Writing Frames

These are electronic versions of some of the books and other paper materials, which facilitate the use of ICT as a teaching tool. They mean that these texts can, on appropriate occasions, be accessed via computer:

- on standard monitors for individual pupil or group access
- on large monitors for larger group teaching
- through data projection onto screen or interactive whiteboard for whole class or group teaching
- on some or all monitors when a class is working in a computer suite.

ICT can thus be used:

- to present texts for shared and guided reading, discussion and analysis
- to draw word and sentence level teaching from a text and facilitate exploration of this
- to demonstrate in shared and guided writing.

The considerable advantages of such ICT use include:

- high levels of pupil engagement and motivation
- the facility for teacher and pupils to manipulate text easily and quickly on screen, e.g. in word and sentence level teaching and in shared and guided writing
- rapid, easy storage and retrieval of texts (including work in progress).

Perhaps even more important, however, is that exploitation of these electronic versions will demonstrate ICT in practice, familiarize pupils with its use, and lead them to both expect and accept that on-screen texts are an integral element of literacy.

ICT texts

For Years 1 to 4 (Scottish Levels A to C/D), these are simulations of "real-life" ICT texts. That is they involve elements which are:

- interactive (requiring active as well as passive reader response)
- non-linear (not necessarily read in a set sequence from beginning to end)
- multimedia (involving video and/or animation and sound as well as words and pictures).

These texts are presented in electronic form alone, as they simply could not exist on paper due to their interactive nature. However, whereas many actual texts from Internet web sites are too sophisticated in both content and language to use as teaching material with younger children (as well as being difficult and time consuming for teachers to find), these ***Spotlight on Fact*** ICT texts are purpose-designed to meet the teaching and learning needs and match the reading ability of each age group. They, thus, provide controlled, age-appropriate exploration of such commonly encountered formats as:

- multimedia CD-ROMs
- Internet web sites, e.g. shopping sites
- application "wizards" (texts which lead the user through a process of choices to achieve a given end)
- interactive simulations.

As well as providing highly motivating opportunities to pursue ongoing literacy teaching objectives, they also give the vital context for teaching specific ICT literacy skills such as those of:

- interacting with an electronic text to determine outcomes
- navigating a non-linear text
- orchestrating information from multimedia sources
- finding specific information from a complex ICT text
- "mining down" for more detailed information.

Years 5 and 6 (Scottish Levels D and D/E) pupils should be using the Internet itself to explore such ICT texts.

Teacher's Notes and Activity Masters

SPOTLIGHT

on fact

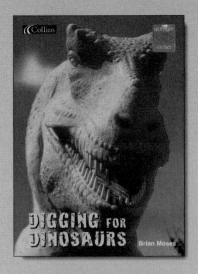

TITLE Digging for Dinosaurs

AUTHOR Brian Moses

TEXT TYPE FOCUS Recount

CURRICULUM FOCUS Science

Links to QCA schemes of work

Science 3D: Rocks and soils

Optional additional resources

Samples of fossils

Other sources of information about dinosaurs, e.g. non-fiction books, CD ROMs

Map of Britain

Children's atlas

Electronic Big Book text

Button colour	Focus
Purple	**Whole text**
Green	**Text level:** style and structure of non-fiction writing: recount
Yellow	**Sentence level:** verbs
Blue	**Word level:** synonyms

Digging for Dinosaurs

Brian Moses

NLS teaching objectives Year 3

Depending on the term you choose to use this book, the following objectives would be the focus. Pupils should be taught:

Term 1

Text level

17 *to notice differences in the style and structure of non-fiction writing;*

Sentence level

3 *the function of verbs in sentences;*

5 *to use the term* verb *appropriately;*

Word level

13 *to collect new words from reading and work in other subjects and create ways of categorizing and logging them, e.g. personal dictionaries, glossaries;*

16 *to understand the purpose and organization of the thesaurus, and to make use of it to find synonyms;*

17 *to generate synonyms for high frequency words;*

18 *to use the term* synonym;

19 *common vocabulary for introducing and concluding dialogue, e.g.* said, replied, asked.

Term 2

Text level

17 *to make clear notes;*

Word level

17 *to continue the collection of new words from reading and work in other subjects, and make use of them in reading and writing;*

19 *to use dictionaries to learn or check the spellings and definitions of words;*

20 *to write their own definitions of words, developing precision and accuracy in expression;*

21 *to use the term* definition;

23 *to organize words or information alphabetically, using the first two letters.*

Term 3

Text level

22 *to experiment with recounting the same event in a variety of ways, e.g. in the form of a short story, a letter, a news report;*

23 *to organize letters into simple paragraphs;*

Word level

12 *to continue the collection of new words from reading and work in other subjects, and make use of them in reading and writing;*

13 *to collect synonyms which will be useful in writing dialogue, exploring the effects on meaning.*

Using the Big Books/ICT Big Books: Shared reading

When you read a book, or sections from a book, always allow time for pupils to respond to the text and share their understanding and responses before moving on to analyse text and linguistic features.

Session 1

Text level

- Introduce **Digging for Dinosaurs**, focusing on the front cover. Ask the children to read the title to you. Who is the author? What does the front cover reveal about the contents and nature of the book?

- Read the contents list on page 1 of the Core Reader together. What extra information does this give about the book? Look at the first heading: *Dinosaur Island*. Where in the world do the children think this island might be? Turn to pages 2 and 3 (*Big Book 3a* pages 2 and 3) to read about Dinosaur Island and ask someone to point out the Isle of Wight on the map of Britain. Can they locate it on additional maps of Britain in your classroom or a children's atlas? How many children have been to the Isle of Wight? Did they spot any dinosaurs while they were there?

- Read the information on pages 4 and 5 (*Big Book 3a* pages 4 and 5) together. If you have fossils, pass them around and talk about how they were formed.

- Read page 6 (*Big Book 3a* page 6). How many children have visited a museum, such as the National History Museum, and seen dinosaur bones and models?

Word/Sentence level

- Write the word *dinosaur* on the board. Explain that the word comes from two Greek words: *deinos* (*fearful*) and *sauros* (*lizard*).

- Ask the class to think of different types of dinosaur and list their names on the board, e.g. *Brachiosaurus*, *Stegosaurus*, *Triceratops*, *Tyrannosaurus*, *Diplodocus*. Identify the number of syllables in each name and talk about spelling patterns and similarities, e.g. *saurus* (*lizard*).

Group/Independent task

- Ask children, in pairs, to begin compiling a Dinosaur Glossary using the list of dinosaur names you made together. Remind them to list the dinosaur names alphabetically and encourage them to write a sentence about each using dictionaries, encyclopedias, non-fiction books and IT resources. Provide children who have literacy difficulties with

pre-written labels. Alternatively, use the cut and paste tools on a computer to sequence the names.

Plenary

- Invite a child to read aloud one of their dinosaur sentences for the rest of the class to try to guess its name. Whoever guesses the dinosaur name correctly may be next to read one of their sentences.

Session 2

Text level

- Look again at a map of Britain and ask a child to point out the Isle of Wight.

- Read pages 7 to 9 (*Big Book 3a* pages 7 to 9). Ask the children to imagine how Steve Hutt and Mick Green must have felt after making their exciting discovery.

- Draw attention to the features of the recount genre. For example, the opening sentence on page 7 (*Big Book 3a* page 7) provides orientation and sets the scene: *In February 1992 . . . bones*. Pinpoint the main events, e.g. *Over the next few days, more ribs were discovered* (page 8). Look for examples of reorientation, or closing statements, e.g. *This had to be the remains of a dinosaur* (page 8). Further features of recount writing are highlighted in the Electronic Big Book.

- Draw the children's attention to the glossary in the Core Reader. How are the words in it identified in the text?

- Read pages 10 to 13 (*Big Book 3a* pages 10 to 13). Why was so much care taken when unearthing and transporting the dinosaur bones?

Word/Sentence level

- Turn to page 7 (*Big Book 3a* page 7) and draw attention to the word *looking* in the first line. Can the children find a word with a similar meaning? (*searching*)

- Locate the word *found* on page 8 (*Big Book 3a* page 8). Who can find a word with a similar meaning? (*discovered*)

- Introduce the term *synonym*, explaining that it refers to words with the same or similar meaning. Look for other synonyms on pages 9 to 11 (*Big Book 3a* pages 9 [*huge/massive*], 10 [*bones/vertebrae*] and 11 [*stopped/ended*]). Further examples are highlighted in the Electronic Big Book. Point out that good writers avoid repeating words unnecessarily and often consult a thesaurus to find alternative words. Discuss how some synonyms work equally well in the same context, e.g. *huge/massive*. However, others have slightly different meanings, e.g. *vertebrae* is

more precise than *bones*; *prehistoric* might be more accurate than *ancient* or *old*.

Group/Independent task

AM Distribute copies of **Activity Master 1** and ask children to find synonyms for the words listed, using a children's thesaurus.

Plenary

■ Find out which synonyms the children used to complete **Activity Master 1**.

■ List all the words they found as alternatives to *said* on the board. Challenge them to think of more and add them to your list. Practise reading the list together, performing each word appropriately, e.g. *whispered*, *shouted*, *asked*. Discuss how some of these words would only be appropriate in particular contexts. Ask children to type up the list on a computer and print it out to be displayed and used in the children's writing.

Session 3

Text level

■ Reflect upon the section of *Digging for Dinosaurs* that you have read so far.

■ Read the Core Reader from page 14 to the end of the book. Compare the structure of this book, which recounts a process of discovery, with other non-fiction books that include a wider range of information for the reader to select from. Identify the key events and their order. Model how to note the key events on a simple timeline.

Word/Sentence level

■ Ask the class to define a verb (a word, or group of words, that names an action or state of being).

■ Turn to page 7 (*Big Book 3a* page 7) and ask the children to locate some interesting verbs in the text, e.g. *looking, searching, slithered, scraped*. Read some sentences without the verbs to show they are essential to meaning. Write the verbs on a large sheet of paper, for the children to add to. Search through the text of the Core Reader for more verbs, e.g. *found, think, discovered* (page 8). Further examples are highlighted in the Electronic Big Book.

■ Extend children's understanding of these verbs by discussing the different tenses. Take one example of a verb, e.g. *searching*, and use it in a sentence to show past, present and future tenses, e.g. Steve *was searching* for fossils; Steve *is searching* for fossils; Steve *will search* for fossils.

Group/Independent task

AM **Activity Master 2** requires children to locate a verb in each sentence and change it for another with the same, or similar, meaning. Encourage them to use

thesauruses to find suitable replacement verbs. (Some verbs, e.g. *ate*, will need to be changed to the present tense in order to locate them in a thesaurus.)

Plenary

■ Find out which synonyms children used to replace the verbs on **Activity Master 2**. Discuss whether the words they have selected are similar in meaning or whether they have altered the meaning of the sentence.

Linking reading and writing: Shared writing

Session 4: focus 1 (Letter writing)

Text level

AM The writing frame on **Activity Master 3** is a template for a letter. Ask the class to imagine they are Steve Hutt. Who might he want to write to, to inform of his discovery? (e.g. parent, friend, colleague) What would he tell them?

■ Complete the writing frame together drawing on the notes you made in Session 3. Don't forget to make up an address, modelling where on the page it should go. Discuss how the tone, greeting and closure of the letter will vary depending on who the letter is to, e.g.

Dear Tony

I have some wonderful news! Last week I was out looking for fossils along the cliff as usual. It was a particularly wet day and the cliffs were slippery. **The next thing I knew** I slipped and landed on a ridge where I found a white piece of bone sticking out of the mud. **I think I have uncovered** the remains of a dinosaur! **This discovery is particularly exciting because** I think I have found a Sauropod. It could turn out to be Britain's biggest dinosaur find, ever! **I look forward to showing you** some of the bones when you next visit the Isle of Wight. We might even open a museum here to display the bones we found.

Yours excitedly
Steve

Word/Sentence level

■ Use the letter you have written together to reinforce your work on synonyms. Ask children to make alternative suggestions for words such as *wonderful* (*great, fabulous, terrific*), *found* (*discovered, unearthed*). Discuss the merits of each suggestion and agree upon the best word for the given context.

■ How many verbs can the children find in the letter?

**Differentiated guided/independent writing tasks
[lowest expectation first]**

- **AM** Using the writing frame on **Activity Master 3**, help the children to complete a letter from Steve and address it to a friend, relative or colleague.

- **AM** Ask the children to imagine that they have made a very important discovery, such as unearthing Roman ruins, finding a shipwreck, discovering a new type of insect. They may use the writing frame on **Activity Master 3** to write a letter reporting their discovery to a friend, relative or colleague.

- Draw on current work in other curriculum areas or direct the children to research an important historical event or discovery, e.g. Neil Armstrong landing on the moon, Christopher Columbus arriving in America. Ask them to pretend to be the person they have researched and write an imaginary letter. Encourage them to structure their own letter, using the shared writing as a model.

Pointers for guided writing

- Show children using the writing frame on **Activity Master 3** how to adapt the sentence openers to suit their own purposes.

- Encourage children to explore synonyms, using a thesaurus, for overused or uninspiring words.

- Help more able children to organize their letters into simple paragraphs.

Plenary

- Invite children to read their letters to a partner. Ask some of them to report to the whole class on the content of their partner's letter, reflecting on the most interesting features and reading out the most effective lines. (Session 5 could be used to develop and extend work on letter writing, if necessary.)

Session 5: focus 2 (News report)

Text level

- Ideally, begin this unit of work by showing the children a genuine example of a news report about an important event or discovery, such as the raising of the Mary Rose or the discovery of a local site of archaeological interest. (News items of major historical significance could be downloaded from the Internet.) Discuss the linguistic features of the report and note the way in which it is structured. Talk about the heading and look at the presentational devices.

- Ask the class to help you write a news report about Steve Hutt's discovery, starting with an appropriate, eye-catching heading. Include one or two quotes, perhaps by Steve or another colleague, or by a visitor to the museum. Provide information, at the

end of the report, for people who may want to go and see the dinosaur bones on the Isle of Wight for themselves.

Word/Sentence level

- Review the news item you have written together, assessing whether it adheres to the conventions of report writing and is interesting but concise.

- Use the report to reinforce your work on synonyms. Ask children to make alternative suggestions for words such as *found* (*discovered, unearthed*). Discuss the merits of each suggestion and agree upon the best word for the given context, bearing in mind that the purpose of the writing is to inform.

**Differentiated guided/independent writing tasks
[lowest expectation first]**

- **AM** Help the children to write their own news report about Steve Hutt's discovery, using the shared writing as a model. **Activity Master 4** may be used to present the news item on once the children have had an opportunity to discuss and redraft their writing.

- **AM** Ask the children to work in pairs. Ask one child to assume the role of Steve Hutt while the other child interviews him about his discovery (taking notes of the responses given). The children may then work together to write a report, including a few direct quotations from the interview. They may use **Activity Master 4** to present the news report once they have discussed and redrafted their writing.

- Direct the children to research an important historical event or discovery, e.g. Neil Armstrong landing on the moon, Christopher Columbus arriving in America. Ask them to write a factual news report, drawing on the evidence of their research.

Pointers for guided writing

- Encourage children to explore synonyms, using a thesaurus, for overused or uninspiring words.

- Refer back to genuine news reports to reinforce the main features of the genre.

- Remind children of the importance of presentation.

Plenary

- Give children an opportunity to read aloud their news reports in the style of a news broadcaster. Provide props, such as over-sized spectacles and a "television screen" (large box with a cut-out window). Ask the rest of the class – the audience – to evaluate whether the writing conforms to the style of a news report. (More time will be needed outside the Literacy Hour to complete the independent writing tasks.)

1 Synonyms

Digging for Dinosaurs

Use a thesaurus to replace these words from the book with the same, or similar, meanings.

looking _____   _____

found _____   _____

stopped _____   _____

huge _____   _____

little _____   _____

good _____   _____

bad _____   _____

scary _____   _____

sad _____   _____

said _____   _____

2 Digging for Verbs

Digging for Dinosaurs

Circle the verb in each sentence.

Use a thesaurus to find more interesting verbs that could be used instead.

1. Dinosaurs once lived on the Isle of Wight.

2. Steve looked for fossils of dinosaur bones.

3. He found the bones of a brachiosaur.

4. Brachiosaurs ate leaves from treetops.

5. Visitors see the bones at the Dinosaur Farm Museum.

6. They speak to the experts about the bones.

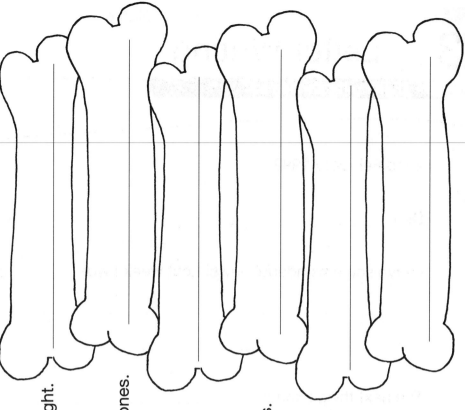

3 Letter Writing

Digging for Dinosaurs

22nd February 1992

Dear _____

I have some wonderful news! Last week I was _____

_____

_____

The next thing I knew _____

_____

_____

I think I have uncovered _____

_____

_____

This discovery is particularly exciting because _____

_____

_____

I look forward to showing you _____

_____

_____

Yours _____

Steve

4 News Report

Digging for Dinosaurs

Daily News

_____

_____

_____

_____

_____

_____

_____

_____

_____

_____

_____

_____

_____

_____

_____

_____

_____

School Fundraising Fun: page 5	**Penrith Pensioner Foils Burglary: page 8**	**Weekend Weather: page 17**

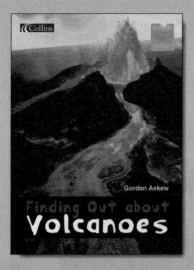

TITLE Finding Out about Volcanoes

AUTHOR Gordon Askew

TEXT TYPE FOCUS Non-chronological report

CURRICULUM FOCUS ICT

Links to QCA schemes of work

ICT: 2C Finding information

Optional additional resources

A variety of information sources about volcanoes including: books specifically about volcanoes, general books about "Our Earth", encyclopedias, CD-ROMs exploring the theme of "Active Earth", CD-ROM children's encyclopedias

CD-ROM Spotlight on Fact – *Volcanoes*

Electronic Big Book text

Button colour	Focus
Purple	**Whole text**
Green	**Text level:** differences in the style and structure of non-fiction writing: classification and description
Yellow	**Sentence level:** devices for presenting texts: speech bubbles, enlarged or italicized print, captions and headings, inset text
Blue	**Word level:** the use of the apostrophe to spell shortened forms of words

Finding Out about Volcanoes

Gordon Askew

NLS teaching objectives Year 3

Depending on the term you choose to use this book, the following objectives would be the focus. Pupils should be taught:

Term 1

Text level

17 *to notice differences in the style and structure of non-fiction writing;*

18 *to locate information using contents, index, headings, sub-headings, page numbers, bibliographies;*

19 *to compare the way information is presented, e.g. by comparing a variety of information texts including IT-based sources;*

20 *to read information passages and identify main points or gist of text;*

21 *to make a simple record of information from texts read;*

22 *to write simple non-chronological reports from known information, using notes made to organise and present ideas;*

Sentence level

6 *to secure knowledge of question marks in reading, understand their purpose and use appropriately in own writing;*

9 *to notice and investigate a range of other devices for presenting texts, e.g. speech bubbles, enlarged or italicized print, captions and headings, inset text; explore purposes and collect examples.*

Term 2

Text level

17 *to make clear notes;*

Sentence level

8 *other uses of capitalization from reading;*

Word level

15 *to use the apostrophe to spell shortened forms of words, e.g.* don't, can't.

Term 3

Text level

17 *to "scan" indexes, directories and IT sources etc. to locate information quickly and accurately;*

18 *to locate books by classification in class or school libraries;*

25 *to revise and extend work on note-making from previous term;*

26 *to summarize in writing the content of a passage or text;*

Word level

11 *to use the apostrophe to spell further contracted forms, e.g.* couldn't.

Volcanoes

Using the Big Books/ICT Big Books: Shared reading

When you read a book, or sections from a book, always allow time for pupils to respond to the text and share their understanding and responses before moving on to analyse text and linguistic features.

Session 1

Text level

- Introduce the shared text, **Finding Out About Volcanoes** by Gordon Askew. Read the introduction on page 2 of the Core Reader. Discuss how information technology has changed since the children's parents and grandparents were children.

- Read page 3 (*Big Book 3a* page 17) and ask the children to offer their own questions about volcanoes. List their questions on the board asking the class how questions should be punctuated. What different sources of information might the children use to find the answers to their questions? How many of these sources do they have access to in your classroom?

- Read pages 4 and 5 (*Big Book 3a* pages 18 and 19). Which of the headings are main headings and which are subheadings? What are the advantages and disadvantages of books and television?

Word/Sentence level

- Identify the questions on page 3 (*Big Book 3a* page 17). What clue helps readers identify questions quickly when scanning? (Question marks.) How many different words used to open questions can children find on page 3 (*Big Book 3a* page 17)? (*What, where, when, how, are.*) Can they think of any other examples, e.g. *why, who*?

- Talk about the different uses of capitalization. Look at the use of capital letters to begin sentences. Look at headings; note how the first letter of the key words in the headings and sub-headings is a capital letter. Look also at the book titles in the main body of text on page 4 (*Big Book 3a* page 18): *All About Volcanoes, Finding Out About Volcanoes, Our Earth*. Talk about the use of capitalization for CD-ROM (compact disc read-only memory) on page 2 of the Core Reader.

Group/Independent tasks

- **AM** Activity Master 5 asks children to think of six interesting questions of their own about volcanoes and to think where they might look to find out the answers to their questions.

- Provide children with an opportunity to visit the school library to find information books about

volcanoes using the school classification system. Where else might they find information? For example, general non-fiction books, encyclopedias, CD-ROMs. (The *Spotlight on Fact* CD-ROM for Year 3 has a multimedia and interactive text on volcanoes.)

Plenary

- Refer again to the use of capitalization for *CD-ROM* (compact disc read-only memory). How many other capitalized abbreviations can children think of? For example, *DIY, EU, ICT, IT, MP, OAP, PC* (personal computer or police constable), *PE, PTO, TV, UFO, VIP*. What do the abbreviations stand for?

Session 2

Text level

- Revisit pages 4 and 5 (*Big Book 3a* pages 18 and 19) briefly before going on to read about other sources of information on pages 6 to 10 (*Big Book 3a* pages 20 to 24). What advantages do CD-ROMs have over books?

Word/Sentence level

- Revise the use of capital letters: to begin sentences, within headings and sub-headings and for book titles in the main body of text, e.g. on page 8 (*Big Book 3a* page 22): *Discovering Volcanoes; Volcanoes of the World*. Talk about the use of capitalization for the abbreviations ICT, CD and CD-ROM.

Group/Independent tasks

- Divide the children into groups and give each group a different information source to evaluate, e.g. a book specifically about volcanoes, a more general book about "Our Earth", an encyclopedia, a CD-ROM exploring the theme of "Active Earth" such as the *Spotlight on Fact* CD-ROM, a CD-ROM children's encyclopedia. Ask each group to chart the advantages and disadvantages of each information source on a large sheet of paper.

- How many of the questions on page 3 (*Big Book 3a* page 17) or the questions they compiled during independent work in Session 1 are the children able to answer using only the information source allocated to their group?

Plenary

- Discuss the findings of each group. From which of the resources were the children able to find most answers to the questions on page 3 (*Big Book 3a* page 17)? Ask each group to display their charts and report back to the class on the advantages and disadvantages of the information sources they were allocated.

Session 3

Text level

■ Read the information about *Volcanoes on the Web* on pages 16 to 22 (*Big Book 3a* pages 25 to 31). Visit a website about volcanoes, such as *Volcano World*. Read the main menu together to discover the type of information that can be accessed.

Word/Sentence level

■ Talk about the use of speech bubbles in *Finding Out About Volcanoes*. What purpose do they serve?

■ Point out the word *that's* in the speech bubble on page 5 (*Big Book 3a* page 19). Talk about the function of the apostrophe to indicate where a letter is missing. Introduce the term *contraction* to refer to words that have been shortened or for two words that have been reduced into one. Which two words have been contracted to make *that's*?

■ Identify examples of contractions in the speech bubbles on pages 6 to 18 of the Core Reader: e.g. *what's*, *I'll*, *I'm* (examples are highlighted in the Electronic Big Book). Which two words have been contracted in each instance? Remind children that contractions are frequently used in informal speech, and are therefore appropriate in the speech bubbles within the text, but should be avoided in formal writing.

Group/Independent tasks

AM Activity Master 6 focuses on common examples of contractions.

■ Give the children an opportunity to explore a website about volcanoes, such as *Volcano World*.

Plenary

■ Talk about some of the confusions that may have arisen during the completion of **Activity Master 6**. Talk about the common confusion between *your* and *you're*. Find out where children put an apostrophe in *won't*. Discuss how this contraction differs in that there are two places where letter/s are missing: the *-ill* of *will* and the *o* of *not*. How many children sometimes say "should of" when they in fact mean *should've*, the shortened form of *should have*?

■ Read the summary, *And Now We Know* on page 23 of the Core Reader.

Linking reading and writing: Shared writing

Session 4: focus 1 (Making notes)

Text level

AM Activity Master 7 provides a table for collecting and recording information about volcanoes. Model how to make notes under the four suggested headings using a couple of different information sources. You may like to use an appropriate book from the class library, a CD-ROM (including the *Spotlight on Fact* CD-ROM for Year 3), an encyclopedia or *The Shadow of Vesuvius* by Maureen Haselhurst (another of the Year 3 *Spotlight on Facts* books).

■ Explain that the notes are to be used to write a report about volcanoes during Session 5. Point out that notes may be disjointed chunks of information; they do not need to be edited until you begin writing the report. They should be relevant, concise and accessible.

Word/Sentence level

■ Review the different ways in which you located the necessary information for note-taking using contents pages, index, headings, sub-headings, page numbers, bibliographies, screen menus.

Differentiated guided/independent writing tasks [lowest expectation first]

AM Provide children with an information source about volcanoes, appropriate to their reading level, and a copy of the note-making frame on **Activity Master 7**. Help them to identify and underline the key words and phrases before recording them in the note-making frame.

AM Give each child a copy of **Activity Master 7** and a variety of different information sources about volcanoes. (Ideally, children should have access to both an appropriate information book and an ICT resource.) Ask them to identify the key points and make notes under the four headings on **Activity Master 7**.

■ More able children could experiment with their own note-making formats for collating information about volcanoes using a number of different information sources. Provide them with an opportunity to evaluate the effectiveness of their format by comparing it with that of a friend.

Pointers for guided writing

- Help children to locate information using contents, index, headings, sub-headings, page numbers, bibliographies.

- Help children to make effective notes by identifying the key words and phrases in their reading.

- Remind children of the purpose for their note-taking: to inform their writing of a non-chronological report about volcanoes.

Plenary

- Compare the different ways that information is presented in the information texts and IT-based sources that the children have used.

Session 5: focus 2 (Writing a non-chronological report)

Text level

- Drawing on the children's knowledge about volcanoes and the notes that you made during Session 4, model how to structure a non-chronological report. Explain the purpose of a report – to describe the way something is.

- **AM** Begin your report with a general classification, e.g. *A volcano is an opening in the Earth's crust.* Further examples of classification and description are highlighted in the Electronic Big Book. Continue, using the sentence openers on **Activity Master 8**, to describe the features of volcanoes. For example:

   Volcanoes can be found in countries all over the world, including *Italy, Indonesia and the USA.* **When a volcano erupts,** *molten rock and burning gas explode through the opening from deep inside the Earth.* **Some volcanoes are active. This means** *that they often erupt.* **Others are** *dormant, erupting only occasionally.* **Another interesting fact about volcanoes is** *that the streams of lava that flow down their sides cool down and harden into solid rock. Volcanoes are a dangerous threat to people living in towns and villages built on their slopes.*

Word/Sentence level

- Review the shared writing together and consult your notes to see whether there is any additional information that could be included. For example, after listing countries where volcanoes can be found, you may like to include information you have gathered about specific volcanoes such as Vesuvius or Mount St Helens.

- If you have used any contractions, you may like to discuss whether they are appropriate in formal report writing.

- Look at the use of capital letters within the writing, e.g. for the beginnings of sentences, headings, names of countries or volcanoes.

Differentiated guided/independent writing tasks [lowest expectation first]

- **AM** Help the children to complete their own non-chronological report about volcanoes, using the writing frame on **Activity Master 8**.

- **AM** Ask children to write a non-chronological report about volcanoes, using the writing frame on **Activity Master 8**. Encourage them to adapt the sentence openers to suit their own purposes.

- **AM** Ask children to write a non-chronological report about volcanoes. They may use the sentence openers on **Activity Master 8** but encourage them to choose their own format for their report, incorporating an illustration or diagram if time allows.

Pointers for guided writing

- Remind children to refer back to the notes they made for this purpose during Session 4.

- Ask children to avoid using contractions in their report writing.

- Check that children have used capitalization appropriately for sentence openings, headings, names and abbreviations.

Plenary

- Allow time for children to evaluate each other's report writing in pairs.

5 Finding Out about Volcanoes

Finding Out about Volcanoes

Think of some interesting questions about volcanoes. Write them here.

_____

_____

_____

_____

_____

_____

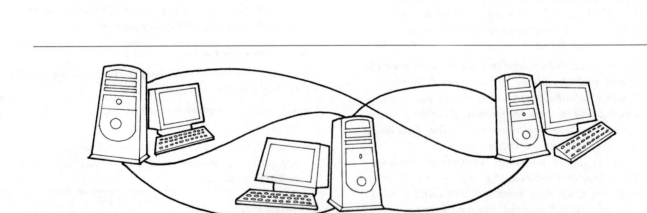

Suggest where you might look to find the answers to your questions.

_____   _____

_____   _____

_____   _____

6 Contractions

Name _____

Write the shortened forms of these words. Use an apostrophe to show where letters have been dropped.

that is   _____   what is   _____

I will   _____   I am   _____

do not   _____   cannot   _____

did not   _____   could not   _____

you are   _____   will not   _____

Use two of the shortened forms you have written to complete the sentences in the speech bubbles.

Why _____ you do your homework?

I _____ find the answers in my book.

He should've checked out my Web pages!

7 Take Note!

Finding out about Volcanoes

Note taking is an important research skill. Use this sheet to gather information about volcanoes. Take notes from different information sources including books and ICT. Use your notes later to write a report about volcanoes.

Question	Answer	Details	Source
What is a volcano?			
Where can volcanoes be found?			
Why do volcanoes erupt?			
What are 3 interesting facts about volcanoes?			

8 Report Writing: Volcanoes

Finding Out about Volcanoes

A volcano is _____

_____

_____

_____

There are volcanoes in many countries, including

_____

_____

_____

When a volcano erupts, _____

_____

_____

Some volcanoes are active. This means _____

_____

_____

Others are _____

_____

_____

Another interesting fact about volcanoes is _____

_____

_____

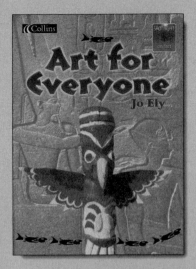

TITLE Art for Everyone

AUTHOR Jo Ely

TEXT TYPE FOCUS Explanation

CURRICULUM FOCUS The Arts

Links to QCA schemes of work

Primary Art and Design: 3B Investigating pattern

Optional additional resources

Examples of artwork from other cultures, e.g. Aboriginal, Egyptian, Native American

A globe or map of the world

Whiteboards and pens

Electronic Big Book text

Button colour	Focus
Purple	**Whole text**
Green	**Text level:** style and structure of non-fiction writing: explanation, general statements
Yellow	**Sentence level:** sentence punctuation: question marks, exclamation marks, full stops and commas
Blue	**Word level:** pluralization

Art for Everyone

Jo Ely

NLS teaching objectives
Year 3

Depending on the term you choose to use this book, the following objectives would be the focus. Pupils should be taught:

Term 1

Text level

17 *to notice differences in the style and structure of non-fiction writing;*

18 *to locate information using contents, index, headings, sub-headings, page numbers, bibliographies;*

21 *to make a simple record of information from texts read, e.g. by completing a chart of information discovered;*

Sentence level

6 *to secure knowledge of question marks and exclamation marks in reading, understand their purpose and use appropriately in own writing;*

9 *to notice and investigate a range of other devices for presenting texts, e.g. enlarged or italicized print, captions and headings, inset text.*

Term 2

Text level

17 *to make clear notes through making simple formats to capture key points;*

Sentence level

4 *to extend knowledge and understanding of pluralization;*

5 *to use the terms* singular *and* plural *appropriately;*

6 *to note where commas occur in reading and to discuss their functions in helping the reader;*

7 *to use the term* comma *appropriately in relation to reading;*

Word level

11 *to use the terms* singular *and* plural *appropriately.*

Term 3

Sentence level

5 *how sentences can be joined in more complex ways through using a widening range of conjunctions;*

7 *to become aware of the use of commas in marking grammatical boundaries within sentences.*

Using the Big Books/ICT Big Books: Shared reading

When you read a book, or sections from a book, always allow time for pupils to respond to the text and share their understanding and responses before moving on to analyse text and linguistic features.

Session 1

Text level

- Ask the children to read the title of the Core Reader: *Art for Everyone* to you. Who is the author? What does the front cover reveal about the content of the book?

- Turn to the introduction on pages 2 and 3 (*Big Book 3a* pages 32 and 33). Look firstly at the artwork. What can the children see? Read the first sentence. What sort of sentence is it? (A question.) Read to the end of page 2 (*Big Book 3a* page 32) and talk about the materials children have incorporated into their own artwork. Have they used any of the items listed?

- Read page 3 (*Big Book 3a* page 33). Reflect upon works of art that the children have made and decide whether these and examples discussed in the text were created to be useful, attractive (aesthetic), for enjoyment or as a way of expressing ideas or feelings. It could be for more than one reason.

- Turn to pages 4 and 5 (*Big Book 3a* pages 34 and 35). What does the main heading say? What about the sub-heading? Read the captions for the photographs and then read the main text.

- Read and discuss pages 6 to 9 (*Big Book 3a* pages 36 to 39). Locate Australia and Egypt on a map or globe.

Word/Sentence level

- Look at the way the comma is used to separate the items in the list of materials on page 2 (*Big Book 3a* page 32). Point out that a comma is not necessary before the word *and*. Look at the use of the comma in the shorter list of materials in the caption on page 6 (*Big Book 3a* page 36).

- Play the memory game, "I went to the shop". Ask the children to think of items with an art theme. The first child says, for example, "I went to the shop and I bought a paint brush." Write this on the board and close the statement with a full stop. The next child (facing away from the board) recalls the first child's item and adds another, for example, "I went to the shop and I bought a paint brush and a sketch pad." Erase the full stop on the board and modify the sentence accordingly. When the third child has added an item, change the sentence on the board,

including a comma, for example, *I went to the shop and I bought a paint brush, a sketch pad and some charcoal*. Continue until at least six children have taken part. Review the way you have used the comma in the list on the board.

- Look at the use of the comma in instances other than to separate items in a list, e.g. on page 3 (*Big Book 3a* page 33). Demonstrate how the comma indicates where the reader needs to pause when reading aloud.

Group/Independent task

AM Activity Master 9 provides practice in using commas to separate items in a list.

Plenary

AM Review Activity Master 9. Check that children have not separated phrases with commas, e.g. *felt-tip pens*. Remind children that a comma before a conjunction such as *and* is unnecessary.

- Repeat the memory game you played during the Word/Sentence level session. Invite a child to write the sentence on the board and modify it as the game progresses, using commas to separate the items listed.

Session 2

Text level

- Ask the class to remind you what they have already learned about Egyptian and Aboriginal art from *Art for Everyone*.

- Read and discuss pages 10, 11, 14 and 15 (*Big Book 3a* pages 40 to 43). Ask the children to reflect on why these art works were produced. Locate America and Peru on a map or globe.

Word/Sentence level

- Focus on the punctuation marks used to close sentences on the pages you have read. How many questions can the children find? What is the purpose of the question mark? Who can find an exclamation mark on page 7 (*Big Book 3a* page 37)? What is its purpose and how does it affect the way the sentence is read aloud? Look for other exclamation marks on pages 14 and 15 (*Big Book 3a* pages 42 and 43). Sentence punctuation is highlighted in the Electronic Big Book.

Group/Independent task

AM Activity Master 10 focuses on the use of punctuation marks for closing different types of sentences.

Plenary

AM Discuss the punctuation marks children used to close the sentences on **Activity Master 10**. Which

words are typically used to open a question, e.g. *what*, *why*, *where*, *who*? Point out that questions always end with a question mark. Discuss when exclamation marks are appropriate: they are used to indicate great emotion such as joy, surprise, anger or shock.

- Write on the board: *The Egyptian temple to the god Amon-Re is massive.* Read it in a straight, monotone way. Then replace the full stop with an exclamation mark and reread the sentence with more enthusiasm. Repeat for: *Some totem poles are 30 metres tall.* Ask the children to read it with a full stop and then with an exclamation mark ending.

Session 3

Text level

- Read and discuss pages 16 to 23 (*Big Book 3a* pages 44 to 51).

- Discuss the ways that different cultures use art to celebrate a person's importance. (Refer to pages 14 and 15 (*Big Book 3a* pages 42 and 43) to note the Native American headdresses and totem poles.) Discuss the significance that Egyptians, Native Americans and Chimu people attached to certain works of art. Compare this with the sand pictures that Aboriginal people create purely for themselves.

Word/Sentence level

- Revise the terms *singular* and *plural*. Turn to pages 20 and 21 (*Big Book 3a* pages 48 and 49) Ask the children to find plural nouns, e.g. *cavemen*, *cavewomen*, *sticks*, *bones*, *minerals*, *tunnels*, *animals*, *lions*, *woolly mammoths*. Ask them to tell you the singular of each. To which of the words do we simply add an *s* to make them plural, e.g. *stick*, *bone*, *lion*? Which are irregular? Scan the shared text for other plural nouns. Are they regular or irregular? Further examples are highlighted in the Electronic Big Book.

- Demonstrate how a dictionary can be used to check the pluralization of a word. Include a number of irregular plurals, e.g. *children*, *women*, *deer*.

Group/Independent task

AM **Activity Master 11** requires children to convert a variety of singular nouns into plurals.

Plenary

AM Review the task on **Activity Master 11**. Discuss the irregular words, *cavemen*, *sheep*, *children*, *mice* and *trousers*.

Linking reading and writing: Shared writing

Session 4: focus 1 (Information grid; making notes)

Text level

- Use the information in **Art for Everyone** to make a simple record of information by completing a blank four-column grid. Discuss how the information could most usefully be presented. Label the columns: *Country, Type of art, Material, Purpose*. Identify the areas of the world mentioned in the text, using the contents page, headings, subheadings and index. List the countries, e.g. *Africa, Australia, Peru*, in one column. Is it necessary to put the countries in any particular order, e.g. alphabetical order or the order in which they were introduced in the shared text?

- In column 2, make a brief note of the type of art created, e.g. *totem pole, mask, cave painting*. Stress that the notes are key words and not in sentences. Fill in just one or two of the cells in the grid. Leave others blank for completion as an independent task.

- Repeat with examples for columns 3 and 4 modelling how to locate the information and make notes in the grid.

Word/Sentence level

- Discuss how punctuation is less important in this format. The information needs to be a summary of key points rather than complete sentences.

- Remind children about using capital letters for the names of countries.

Differentiated guided/independent writing tasks (lowest expectation first)

- Ask the children to make a simple record of information by completing the grid for two countries. Ask them to describe different types of art in one column and write the name of the countries from which they came in the second.

- Ask the children to make a record of information by completing a grid with four columns. Ask them to describe different types of art in one column, write the name of the countries from which they came in the second, the materials used in the third and the purpose for creating the art in the fourth.

- In addition to the above work, challenge children to find out about further art works from other cultures using different information sources, e.g. other non-fiction texts, encyclopedias and IT sources.

- One group could use ICT to complete the grid.

Pointers for guided writing

■ Remind children that the information chart is a summary of information. Dissuade them from writing out extended chunks of information by helping them to isolate key words and phrases.

■ Encourage them to skim and scan to retrieve specific information to complete their information grids.

Plenary

■ Encourage children to volunteer to fill in missing information on the enlarged grid you used at the beginning of the session. Ask the others to check for accuracy and conciseness.

Session 5: focus 2 (Writing an explanation text)

Text level

■ Write the heading: *Why do people make art?* Ask the children to use their notes from the previous day to suggest reasons, such as for a specific use (e.g. a table, chair, jug), as a tribute to someone important (e.g. a temple), as an indication of someone's importance (e.g. a headdress), for creative expression or just for fun. Ask the children to also think about artwork that they themselves have created or studied.

■ **AM** Demonstrate how to write a simple explanation about why people from different cultures throughout history make art. You may like to use the writing frame on **Activity Master 12** to structure the writing. Offer the sentence starters and encourage oral rehearsal of possible endings. Select one and scribe it, e.g. **People from all over the world make art. We know this because** *of all the art treasures that they have left behind.* **Some of the oldest examples of art are** *cave paintings of animals.*

■ Draw children's attention to the generic features of an explanation text. Indicate the heading that poses a question to be answered. Locate the general statement used to introduce the topic, e.g. *People from all over the world make art.* Examples of general statements are highlighted in the Electronic Big Book. Locate the specific explanations given for particular types of art, e.g. *to show how important someone is.* However, do not complete every reason so that children are left with opportunities for independent writing.

■ After they have experimented with some starter sentences, encourage the children to discuss their ideas with a partner and scribe their own completed sentences on individual whiteboards.

■ Show how the sentence openers provided on **Activity Master 12** can be changed to suit the writer. Emphasize that the notes they have made provide the content of the writing and the structure needs to be appropriate for putting across the content effectively.

Word/Sentence level

■ When reviewing the shared writing together, pay close attention to the punctuation. Focus on the use of commas, full stops and exclamation marks.

■ Focus on the connectives used in your explanation writing, e.g. because, so that, to show that.

Differentiated guided/independent writing tasks (lowest expectation first)

■ **AM** Ask the children, in pairs, to write an explanation in answer to the question: "Why do people make art?" Provide a simplified version of the writing frame on **Activity Master 12**. For example: *People make many types of art. For example...; Sometimes people make...because...; People also make art to show...*

■ **AM** Ask the children to write an explanation in answer to the question: "Why do people make art?" Provide them with a copy of **Activity Master 12**, encouraging them to adapt it to suit their own purposes.

■ **AM** Ask the children to write a brief explanation about different types of art from a range of cultures and periods in history. They may like to use the sentence openers on **Activity Master 12** as a starting point. Encourage them to research a particular type of art, perhaps linked to another curricular area, e.g. Ancient Greek artefacts, and to incorporate this into their writing in addition to the information they have learned in *Art for Everyone*.

Pointers for guided writing

■ Show children using the writing frame on **Activity Master 12** how to adapt or leave out the sentence openers to suit their own purposes.

■ Ensure that children use connectives appropriately in their explanation writing.

■ Focus on the correct use of sentence punctuation.

Plenary

■ Invite children to read their explanation writing aloud. Encourage the rest of the class to comment on any effective or original features.

■ Ask children who undertook personal research to share any new findings about art from another culture with the rest of the class.

9 Commas in Lists

Art for Everyone

Write the missing commas in these sentences.

1. Art can be made from twigs sticks bark wood clay stone feathers sand mud metal and anything else from the world around us.

2. Cavemen and cavewomen used rock fur moss sticks and bones to paint with.

3. Aboriginal communities paint on wood bark and leather.

4. Some works of art can be useful, such as a table a chair or a jug.

5. We can use paints crayons felt-tip pens inks or pastels to make our pictures.

Imagine you have won an art competition. You may choose between three and six of the prizes shown here. Write a sentence to say which prizes you would choose. Don't forget the commas!

_____

_____

_____

10 Punctuate!

Art for Everyone

Close each sentence with a full stop, a question mark or an exclamation mark.

1. Why do Aboriginal people make sand paintings that nobody else will see

2. The Aboriginal people believe that art is for everyone

3. The Egyptian temple to the god Amon-Re is massive

4. Where would you find totem poles

5. Native Americans made sculptures to stand outside the homes of their leaders

6. Some totem poles are 30 metres tall

Write your own questions and comments as captions to go with each picture adding question marks, full stops or exclamation marks as appropriate.

_____

_____

_____

_____

_____

_____

_____

_____

11 More than One

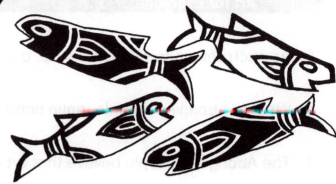

Write the plural for each singular word.

Singular noun	Plural noun
picture	
message	
child	
caveman	
sheep	
mouse	
trousers	

Write four more singular nouns from the book in the grid. Then write the plural.

Check the words you have written in a dictionary.

12 Writing an Explanation

Art for Everyone

Why do people make art?

People from all over the world make art. We know this because _____

_____

_____

Some of the oldest examples of art are _____

_____

_____

Art can be made from many different materials, such as _____

_____

_____

People sometimes make art to show _____

_____

_____

Art is also used to _____

_____

_____

Sometimes art is made _____

_____

_____

How to Make a Rain Gauge

Gareth Price

NLS teaching objectives
Year 3

Depending on the term you choose to use this book, the following objectives would be the focus. Pupils should be taught:

Term 1

Text level

17 to notice differences in the style and structure of non-fiction writing;

21 to make a simple record of information from texts read;

Sentence level

9 to notice and investigate a range of other devices for presenting texts;

11 to write in complete sentences;

12 to demarcate the end of a sentence with a full stop and the start of a new one with a capital letter;

Word level

13 to collect new words from reading and work in other subjects.

Term 2

Text level

12 to identify the different purposes of instructional texts;

13 to discuss the merits and limitations of particular instructional texts, including IT and other media;

14 how written instructions are organized;

15 to read and follow simple instructions;

16 to write instructions, using a range of organizational devices;

Sentence level

10 to understand the differences between verbs in the 1st, 2nd and 3rd person through: relating to different types of text, e.g. 2nd person for instructions;

Word level

19 to use dictionaries to learn or check the spellings and definitions of words.

Term 3

Text level

26 to summarize in writing the content of a passage or text;

Sentence level

6 to investigate through reading and writing how words and phrases can signal time sequences, e.g. first, then, after, meanwhile, from, where;

Word level

14 to explore homonyms which have the same spelling but multiple meanings and explain how the meanings can be distinguished in context.

Using the Big Books/ICT Big Books: Shared reading

When you read a book, or sections from a book, always allow time for pupils to respond to the text and share their understanding and responses before moving on to analyse text and linguistic features.

Session 1

Text level

- Introduce the shared text, **How to Make a Rain Gauge** by Gareth Price. Read the blurb on the back cover of the Core Reader.

- Read the information about rainfall figures on pages 2 and 3 (*Big Book 3a* pages 52 and 53). Find Australia on a map or globe and demonstrate how far away from Britain it is. Where is Ecuador? What problems do people face if there is too little or too much rain?

- Read and talk about pages 4 and 5 (*Big Book 3a* pages 54 and 55). Refer to the Glossary on page 16 (*Big Book 3a* page 64) for definitions of terms such as *meteorologist* and *satellites*.

- Find out how to make a simple rain gauge by reading the instructions on pages 6 and 7 (*Big Book 3a* pages 56 and 57). What is a rain gauge? What is the purpose of collecting data about rainfall? How is such information used?

- Identify the goal (statement of what is to be achieved) at the top of page 6 (*Big Book 3a* page 56). Look at the list of materials needed and discuss why it is positioned before the instructions. How many sequenced steps need to be followed to achieve the goal? How do the diagrams help to clarify the instructions?

Word/Sentence level

- Look again at the instructions on pages 6 and 7 (*Big Book 3a* pages 56 and 57). Do they need to be followed in the order in which they are set out? Note that the steps are numbered.

- Talk about the way in which instructions are worded using the imperative, for example, *Screw the top . . . Use a ruler. . . Make a mark . . .* Why is it necessary that instructions are as concise as possible? Further instruction sentences are highlighted in the Electronic Big Book.

- Introduce the term *homonyms*: words which have the same spelling but multiple meanings. Identify examples of homonyms on pages 2 to 7 (*Big Book 3a* pages 52 to 57), e.g. *rock, change, fell, rose, interest, earth, watch, face, flat, ruler, pen.* (Further examples

are highlighted in the Electronic Big Book.) Can the children define the different meanings for each? Use a dictionary to show how the different definitions of homonyms are numbered.

- Discuss how the meaning of a homonym can be distinguished in context, using examples on pages 2 to 7 (*Big Book 3a* pages 52 to 57).

Group/Independent task

AM The instructions on pages 6 and 7 (*Big Book 3a* pages 56 and 57) are printed on **Activity Master 13**. Give children, in pairs, an opportunity to read and follow the instructions to make a rain gauge. Remind children that step 5 must be carried out by an adult (this may need to be done outside of the session if you are unable to enlist the help of a classroom assistant or parent).

Plenary

- Look at one of the children's completed models and review the effectiveness of the instructions. How useful were the diagrams? Would it have been possible to make the rain gauge using the diagrams alone? Did it help to have the instructions set out in numbered steps rather than as a paragraph of text?

Session 2

Text level

- Read pages 8 and 9 (*Big Book 3a* pages 58 and 59) to find out how to use a rain gauge. Talk about the format of both the checklist for ensuring that the rain gauge has been set up correctly, and the table for organizing the data collected from it.

- Read and talk about pages 10 and 11 (*Big Book 3a* pages 60 and 61).

Word/Sentence level

- Compare the use of bullet points for the instructions on pages 8 and 9 (*Big Book 3a* pages 58 and 59) with the use of numbered steps for the instructions on pages 6 and 7 (*Big Book 3a* pages 56 and 57).

- Identify examples of homonyms on pages 8 and 9 (*Big Book 3a* pages 58 and 59), e.g. *scale, note.* Ask the class to define the different meanings for each. Use a dictionary to locate the different definitions.

Group/Independent task

- Ask children to design a table, similar to that on page 9 (*Big Book 3a* page 59), that they will be able to use to organize the data they collect from their rain gauge.

- Look at and discuss other tables, charts and checklists used in and around the classroom, e.g. register, timetable, reading records, checklist to keep track of computer use. How is each appropriate for its purpose? How many of these examples have been produced with the help of ICT?

- Give the children an opportunity to find an appropriate place to set up their rain gauges.

Session 3

Text level

- Revisit pages 10 and 11 (*Big Book 3a* pages 60 and 61). What measures can be taken to ensure that home made rain gauges work successfully?

- Read pages 12 and 13 (*Big Book 3a* pages 62 and 63). Identify the goal (statement of what is to be achieved) at the top of page 12 (*Big Book 3a* page 62). How many sequenced steps need to be followed to achieve the goal? How do the diagrams help to clarify the instructions?

Word/Sentence level

- Do the instructions need to be followed in the order in which they are set out? Note that the steps are numbered in the same way as the instructions on pages 6 and 7 (*Big Book 3a* pages 36 and 37).

- Discuss whether you could add the words *first, next, then, after that, finally* to the start of each instruction. Would you then need numbers also? Words and phrases that signal time sequences are highlighted in the Electronic Big Book.

- Discuss the way that instructions are worded using the imperative. Identify the verbs, for example, *Choose, Make, Use.*

- Discuss to whom the instructions are addressed (generic, i.e no pronoun used or 2nd person, i.e. *you* or *your*). Discuss whether this is characteristic of written instructions.

- Identify examples of homonyms on page 12 (*Big Book 3a* page 62), e.g. *well, tape, cross, draw.* Ask the class to define the different meanings for each. Use a dictionary to locate the different definitions.

Group/Independent task

- **AM** Activity Master 14 shows potential problems with home made rain gauges, similar to those illustrated on pages 10 and 11 (*Big Book 3a* pages 60 and 61). Ask children to complete the sentences summarizing how to avoid the problems illustrated.

- Give children an opportunity to compare their completed sentences with one another, either in pairs or as a whole class.

- Find time to enable the class to carry out the instructions for practical work on pages 12 and 13 (*Big Book 3a* pages 62 to 63).

Linking reading and writing: Shared writing

Session 4: focus 1 (Instruction writing: goal, resources and initial procedures)

Text level

- Drawing on the children's practical experience and the information from *How to Make a Rain Gauge*, model how to write a set of instructions.

- Begin by establishing the goal; write a statement of what is to be achieved, i.e. *to make a rain gauge.*

- Identify the materials and equipment needed, listing them in the order in which they will be needed.

- Write the first couple of instructions, in sequenced steps, for achieving the goal.

Word/Sentence level

- Talk about how best to set out the instructions. How will the separate steps be identified, e.g. using bullet points or numbers?

- Focus on your use of the imperative, e.g. *Draw a straight line.*

Differentiated guided/independent writing tasks [lowest expectation first]

- **AM** Children can begin writing their own set of instructions for making a rain gauge, using the writing frame on **Activity Master 15**. Sentence openers based on the instructions from pages 6 and 7 (*Big Book 3a* pages 56 and 57) are provided to help children structure their writing.

- **AM** Give each child a copy of **Activity Master 16**. Using the shared writing as a model, ask them to begin writing their own set of instructions for making a rain gauge. A selection of appropriate verbs from pages 6 and 7 (*Big Book 3a* pages 56 and 57) are included to help children compose each instruction using imperatives.

- Ask children to design their own instruction sheet, explaining how to make a rain gauge. Alternatively, you may prefer to extend their writing experience by

How to Make a Rain Gauge

Gareth Price

asking them to write instructions for a different procedure related to another area of the curriculum. Remind all children that more time will be allocated for the completion of their instruction writing.

Pointers for guided writing

- Remind children to begin by writing a statement of what is to be achieved. (This may be in the form of a title.)
- Check that materials and equipment needed are listed in the order in which they will be needed.

Plenary

- Have fun exploring different sentences using imperatives. Write out the following words and phrases on strips of card: *Wash*; *Eat*; *Comb*; *Pat*; *Tidy*; *your hands*; *your lunch*; *your hair*; *the dog*; *your room*. Hand the separate cards to ten different children. Ask each child holding a verb card to pair up randomly with a child holding a sentence ending. Arrange the pairs of children at the front of the class and ask them to hold up their cards for the rest of the class to read the resulting sentence, e.g. *Tidy your lunch*. Challenge the class to help rearrange the children so that the instructions all make sense.

Session 5: focus 2 (Instruction writing: sequenced steps in chronological order)

Text level

- Review the instruction writing you began during Session 4. Engage the class in completing the sequenced steps to achieve the goal identified at the start of Session 4: *to make a rain gauge*.
- Discuss the format you have used. Are there any steps that would benefit from a diagram or illustration to clarify meaning?

Word/Sentence level

- Who are the instructions written for? Discuss the way in which instruction and procedural writing is usually written for general readers rather than named individuals. In this instance, the reader could be anyone interested in researching rainfall patterns that may wish to construct a rain gauge.
- When might instructions be focused more specifically on a particular group of readers? For example, rules for a children's playground; a training manual for a pilot. Discuss how such instructions may vary, for example, rules for younger children would need to be written in simple terms with clear, large lettering. A pilot's training manual by contrast would assume previous knowledge, using specialized vocabulary,

small print and lots of diagrams. Knitting patterns and recipes may assume that the user has some experience of knitting or cookery. Instructions for construction toys, designed for children, rely heavily on diagrams with very little additional text. Show and talk about as many different types as possible.

Differentiated guided/independent writing tasks [lowest expectation first]

- **AM** Help the children to complete their own set of instructions for making a rain gauge, using the writing frame on **Activity Master 15**. Ask them to finish the instructions with a drawing of how the rain gauge should look.
- **AM** Ask children to complete their instruction writing using **Activity Master 16**, drawing a picture of the finished model in the box provided.
- Ask children who have designed their own instruction sheets to complete their instructional writing. Give those who have written instructions for a procedure other than *how to make a rain gauge* the opportunity to carry out their instructions with a partner and evaluate their effectiveness.

Pointers for guided writing

- Ensure that instructions are written in chronological order, using appropriate vocabulary, e.g. *first*, *then*, *next*, *finally*.
- Encourage children to include diagrams clarifying their written instructions, to make them more user-friendly.

Plenary

- Extend the game you played during the Plenary session on day 4, exploring different sentences using imperatives. Ask children, in pairs, to write a three-word instruction on a strip of card using the imperative, e.g. *Close the window*.
- Then ask each pair of children to cut or tear their sentence strip, removing the verb. One child retains the verb, the other retains the sentence ending. Divide the class into two groups – those holding verbs and those holding sentence endings – and ask each group to form a circle, one inside of the other.
- Ask the inside circle to move in a clockwise direction and the outside circle to move anti-clockwise until you give a signal (e.g. stop playing music, clap your hands, blow a whistle). At this point, each child in the outer ring joins with the child opposite them in the inner ring to make a new sentence. Listen as each pair in turn reads out their new sentence. Repeat to explore different combinations, creating a variety of nonsense instructions.

13 Make a Rain Gauge

How to Make a Rain Gauge

Follow the instructions carefully to make a simple rain gauge.

You will need:

A large, empty plastic bottle with straight sides
A waterproof marker pen
A ruler

1. Screw the top on the bottle.
   Stand the bottle on a flat surface.

2. Use a ruler and waterproof marker pen to
   draw a straight line from the base of your
   bottle towards the top.

3. Make a mark with the waterproof marker pen
   every centimetre along your line. Put 0 next to the
   first mark. Now put 1 by the next mark up, then 2
   by the next mark. Keep going until you reach 10.

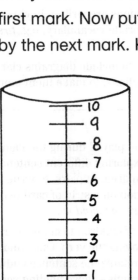

4. Draw a horizontal line around the bottle.
   It should be level because you will use this line
   to help make a clean cut in the next step.

5. Unscrew the bottle top. **Ask an adult** to
   cut carefully around the bottle along the
   horizontal line.

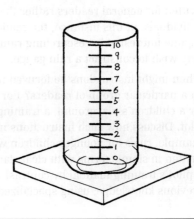

6. Your rain gauge is now finished. Make sure
   you stand it on a flat surface when in use.

14 The Good, the Bad and the Ugly

How to Make a Rain Gauge

Complete the sentences below using *How to Make a Rain Gauge*.

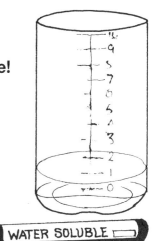

Follow these simple rules to avoid problems with your rain gauge!

Use _____

_____

_____

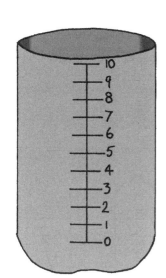

Make sure _____

_____

_____

Do not _____

_____

_____

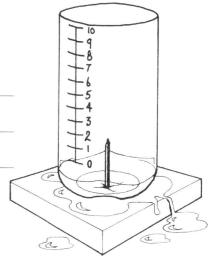

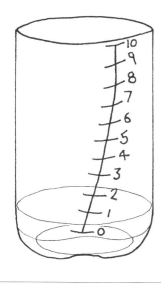

Check that _____

_____

_____

Name _____

How to make a rain gauge.

You will need.

_____

_____

_____

1. Firstly, _____

_____

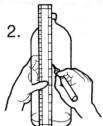

2. Next, use a ruler to _____

_____

_____

3. Make marks _____

_____

_____

_____

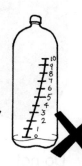

4. Draw a horizontal line around the bottle and ask an adult t

_____

_____

_____

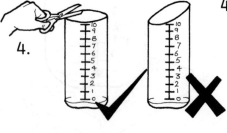

5. Your finished rain gauge should look like this:

5.

16 Writing Your Own Instructions

How to Make a Rain Gauge

How to _____

You will need:

_____

_____

_____

1. _____

_____

2. _____

_____

3. _____

_____

4. _____

_____

5. _____

_____

6. Your finished _____
   should look like this:

Useful words

use   make   draw   cut around
    stand   screw   unscrew

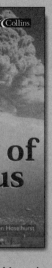

The Shadow of Vesuvius

Maureen Haselhurst

Vesuvius
selhurst

uasion (plus
–13)

istory

mes of work
ke to live here in
te how archaeology
scripts are useful

al resources
T sources on the
d natural disasters

T sources on Naples

T sources linked to
n the rest of the
Science, living

all words that can
ound words

k text

yle and structure
writing:
eiteration:
restatement of
osition
el: verbs: present

common suffixes:

NLS teaching objectives
Year 3

Depending on the term you choose to use this book, the following objectives would be the focus. Pupils should be taught:

Term 1

Text level

17 *to notice differences in the style and structure of non-fiction writing;*

21 *to make a simple record of information from texts read, e.g. by listing key words, drawing together notes from more than one source;*

22 *to use notes to organize and present ideas;*

Sentence level

3 *the function of verbs in sentences;*

4 *to use verb tenses with increasing accuracy in speaking and writing;*

5 *to use the term verb appropriately;*

Word level

13 *to collect new words from reading.*

Term 2

Text level

17 *to make clear notes;*

Word level

12 *to recognize and generate compound words and to use this knowledge to support their spelling;*

13 *to recognize and spell common suffixes and how these influence word meanings, e.g. -ly, -ful;*

14 *to use their knowledge of suffixes to generate new words from root words.*

Term 3

Text level

21 *to use IT to bring to a published form – discuss relevance of layout, font, etc. to audience;*

22 *to experiment with recounting the same event in a variety of ways, e.g. as a letter, a news report;*

25 *to revise and extend work on note taking;*

Sentence level

5 *how sentences can be joined in more complex ways through using a widening range of connectives;*

Word level

12 *to continue collection of new words.*

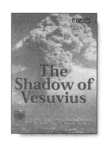

Using the Big Books/ICT Big Books: Shared reading

When you read a book, or sections from a book, always allow time for pupils to respond to the text and share their understanding and responses before moving on to analyse text and linguistic features.

Session 1

Text level

- Introduce *The Shadow of Vesuvius* by Maureen Haselhurst. Read pages 2 and 3 (*Big Book 3b* pages 2 and 3). Have any children been to Italy?

- Discuss how the opening paragraph on page 2 (*Big Book 3b* page 2) typifies the generic features of a persuasive text. Draw the children's attention to the opening statement (thesis): *The Italian government should be making an evacuation plan now for the city of Naples.* Point out the main argument: *This is because scientists warn that the volcano called Vesuvius is probably due to erupt again.* Show how the argument is elaborated upon in the next sentence.

- The argument is elaborated upon further in the second paragraph, which ends with reiteration, i.e. a summary and restatement of the opening position: *They will be in grave danger unless they can be moved away quickly in the case of an eruption.*

- Note the causal linking words, *because* and *unless*. Why are causal links used in persuasion texts?

- Begin a class list of the features/criteria of a persuasive text. Explain that this will be added to during the week so the children will be able to write their own persuasion text.

- Why does the author change subject from Vesuvius to Pompeii? Read the recount of Pompeii on page 5 (*Big Book 3b* page 5). What can Naples learn from this?

- Read about modern day Naples on page 4 (*Big Book 3b* page 4). Focus on the final paragraph. It reiterates the opening paragraph on page 2 (*Big Book 3b* page 2). What is the purpose of this restatement?

Word/Sentence level

- Show how definitions of some of the vocabulary on pages 2 to 5 (*Big Book 3b* pages 2 to 5) can be found in the glossary on page 16 of the Core Reader.

- Write the word *earthquake* on the board. What do the children notice about this word? Explain that it is a compound word made up of two smaller words: *earth* and *quake*. What does the verb *to quake* mean?

- Can the children find any other compound words on pages 3 to 5 (*Big Book 3b* pages 3 to 5), e.g. *however,*

seaside, withstand? Ask them to think of more examples. List these on the board.

Group/Independent task

AM **Activity Master 17** provides practice in identifying compound words.

Plenary

- Hand out word cards featuring small words that can be paired to make compound words. Challenge the children to pair up to make compound words as quickly as possible. Once each child has found their word partner, the compound words could be pinned or stuck onto a prepared chart. Include words that can be paired off with several other words, e.g. *fire: fighter, place, work*; or *sea: gull, horse, side, weed*.

- Ask children without a word partner at the end of the game to look at the chart of compound words and find a smaller word that could be combined with their own to make a compound word.

- Ask the children to reflect on how a knowledge of compound words can help with spelling.

Session 2

Text level

- Ask the class to remind you of the argument put forward in the introduction. What evidence have they read so far to reinforce the author's argument?

- Read and discuss pages 6 to 9 (*Big Book 3b* pages 6 to 9). Focus on the restatement of the author's opening position (reiteration) on *Big Book 3b* page 7: *It could happen again – this time to Naples, unless people can be persuaded to think about the future.*

Word/Sentence level

- Revise yesterday's teaching points by looking for more compound words on pages 6 and 7 (*Big Book 3b* pages 6 and 7), e.g. *courtyards, overlooked, however, afternoon.*

- Turn to pages 2 and 3 (*Big Book 3b* pages 2 and 3) and point out the words *probably, quickly* (page 2), *violently* and *perfectly* (page 3). What do they have in common? Talk about the function of the suffix *-ly*. Identify the root words, *probable, quick, violent* and *perfect.*

- Ask the class to scan the text on pages 4 to 9 (*Big Book 3b* pages 4 to 9) to find words with the suffixes *-ly* and *-ful*, e.g. *actually, recently, dangerously* (page 4); *beautiful* (page 5); *suddenly* (page 7); *perfectly* (page 8) and *dreadful* (page 9). (These are highlighted in the Electronic Big Book.) How do the suffixes *-ly* and *-ful* change word meanings? (They

The
Shadow of
Vesuvius

change a verb into an adjective, e.g. *helpful*, or an adjective into an adverb, e.g. *slowly*.)

- Discuss how the use of adverbs and adjectives are used to add weight to the author's argument.

- Continue to create the class list of features of a persuasive text.

Group/Independent tasks

AM Activity Master 18 focuses on the suffixes *-ly* and *-ful*.

- A group could investigate the spelling rules for adding these suffixes to words ending with vowels.

Plenary

- Practise generating new words from root words by adding the suffix *-ly* or *-ful*, e.g. *quiet/quietly*, *proud/proudly*, *hope/hopeful*, *care/careful*. Revise how suffixes *-ly* and *-ful* change word functions.

- Ask the investigation group to share their findings.

Session 3

Text level

- Read and discuss pages 10 to 13 (*Big Book 3b* pages 10 to 13). Talk about the information recorded by Pliny the Younger. What do the letters tell us about Pompeii? Can the children think of other historical figures who made records of important historical events, e.g. Samuel Pepys, Anne Frank? Draw attention to the recount nature of pages 12 and 13 (*Big Book 3b* pages 12 and 13) and note the time connectives used.

- Read pages 14 and 15 (*Big Book 3b* pages 14 and 15). Talk about the function of these pages as a summary of the persuasive argument about the danger to the people of Naples. Identify the statements on these pages that are a reiteration of the opening paragraph on page 2 (*Big Book 3b* page 2). (These are highlighted in the Electronic Big Book.)

- Note the use of the rhetoric question that the author then answers herself. Discuss why this is an effective device. Add to the list of features.

Word/Sentence level

- Help the children to identify some of the verbs on pages 12 and 13 (*Big Book 3b* pages 12 to 13), ensuring that they understand the term *verb* and are able to use it appropriately, for example, *towered*, *exploded*, *fell*, *stayed*, *survived*. Can they tell you the tense of these verbs? Remind the class that verbs in the past tense are a feature of recount writing.

- Turn to page 14 (*Big Book 3b* page 14) and ask the children to find more verbs, e.g. *understand*, *erupt*, *say*, *are*, *is*. What is the tense of these verbs?

Establish that the majority of the verbs on page 14 are in the present tense; simple present tense verbs are a feature of persuasion writing. Encourage children to identify other verbs and their tenses. Examples of present tense verbs are identified in the Electronic Big Book.

- Model rewriting one or two of the sentences on pages 12 and 13 (*Big Book 3b* pages 12 to 13) in the present tense, as though you were giving a live broadcast from the site.

Group/Independent tasks

AM Ask a group to complete **Activity Master 19** focusing on present tense verbs in the context of persuasive writing.

- Depending on ability, ask children to rewrite the information on pages 12 and 13 (*Big Book 3b* pages 12 to 13) as a "live broadcast".

Plenary

- Look for compound words on pages 11 to 15 (*Big Book 3b* pages 11 to 15), e.g. *eyewitness*, *boathouse*, *airports*.

- Ask children to read their "broadcasts" aloud with appropriate expression – you could use a microphone prop.

Linking reading and writing: Shared writing

Session 4: focus 1 (Making notes)

Text level

- Demonstrate how to make skeleton notes on the information presented in *The Shadow of Vesuvius*, using a basic bullet and elaboration skeleton (see *NLS Writing Flier 9*). Identify the author's main argument and the evidence she uses to support this.

AM Once children are familiar with this model for making notes, use the template for children to make notes on another topic. They will be using these notes to write a persuasive text using the checklist of characteristics you have created during the week. The persuasive topic can be linked to ongoing work in the rest of the curriculum or you may wish to use **Activity Master 20** to make notes about a topic that children can relate to personally: how to stay healthy. Encourage them to contribute their own ideas to help complete the skeleton notes, including at least three points under each topic. Scribe one example of this, e.g. (if you are using **Activity Master 20**)

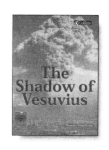

Looking after teeth:
visit the dentist regularly
avoid sugary foods
brush teeth at least twice a day.

■ Discuss which task the children found easier: writing notes using the information source or making notes using shared knowledge. Remind children that writing notes is a useful way of organizing thoughts and ideas and is an effective tool for writing.

Word/Sentence level

■ The children should look for examples of compound words included in their notes, e.g. *toothbrush*.

■ Have they used words with the suffixes *-ly* or *-ful*?

Differentiated guided/independent writing tasks [lowest expectation first]

NB: If you are using a different topic, use these ideas but substitute your own topic.

AM In pairs, children use a copy of **Activity Master 20** to organize their own knowledge about how to stay healthy. Explain that they will be using these notes to make a persuasive poster during Session 5.

AM Ask each child to complete the skeleton notes on **Activity Master 20**. Explain that they will use these notes to write a persuasive information leaflet during Session 5. Children who wish to record their notes in a different way may experiment with their own formats and review them during the Plenary.

■ Ask children to make notes on *The Shadow of Vesuvius* using a basic bullet and elaboration skeleton. They will use these notes to produce a piece of persuasive writing during Session 5.

Pointers for guided writing

■ Dissuade children from writing out extended chunks of information by helping them to isolate key words and phrases.

■ Remind children that note making is a tool for writing. Encourage them to review their own notes for their effectiveness as an aid to writing.

Plenary

■ Select children who have used differing note taking formats. Encourage them to explain their layout and compare the information they have recorded. Discuss how a format can help when they are making notes.

Session 5: focus 2 (Persuasion text)

Text level

■ Show how the notes made during Session 4 can be used to write persuasive guidance on how to stay healthy. Make an introductory statement stressing the

importance of looking after your body. Use persuasive language in the present tense, drawing children's attention to the features of persuasive writing. Support statements, e.g. *Avoid sugary food* with evidence, e.g. *Sugar causes tooth decay*. Finally, write a summary and restatement of the opening position.

■ Check your writing against the criteria list you have been developing all week.

■ Discuss different ways of presenting the writing you have produced, bearing in mind the intended audience. Do you need to break the information down under separate headings? How can you ensure that the most important points stand out?

Word/Sentence level

■ Identify the verbs you have used, e.g. *avoid*, *causes*. Which tense have you used? Have you used language that is direct and concise?

Differentiated guided/independent writing tasks [lowest expectation first]

■ In pairs, pupils reorganize their skeleton notes about how to stay healthy into a poster for other children in their class or school.

■ Ask the children to use their notes about how to stay healthy to write an information leaflet for other children in their class or school stressing the importance of looking after their bodies.

■ Ask children to use their notes on *The Shadow of Vesuvius* to produce a piece of persuasive writing. They may choose to write a letter to the Italian government or a leaflet warning the citizens of Naples of the danger posed by Vesuvius.

Pointers for guided writing

■ Give the children an opportunity to utilize IT to present their writing. Ideally, use the computer as a tool for the drafting and editing process.

■ Remind the children to refer to the criteria list.

■ Ask them to include evidence and factual information to support their arguments, e.g. *If you don't clean your teeth regularly you will get tooth decay*.

■ Help children writing leaflets or letters to review their writing to check that they have included a general statement of introduction, arguments in the form of points plus elaboration and a summary and restatement of the opening position.

Plenary

■ Invite children to share their writing with a partner. Ask them to comment on the most effective aspects of each other's writing. As an extension activity, give them an opportunity to organize a presentation using the notes and writing they have produced this week.

17 Compound Words

The Shadow of Vesuvius

Join up these words to make compound words.
One has been done for you.

broom	quake	_earthquake_
shoe	ball	_____
earth	fly	_____
dragon	port	_____
rain	lace	_____
foot	corn	_____
finger	forest	_____
air	stick	_____
under	nail	_____
pop	wear	_____

Underline the compound words in this sentence.

An eyewitness described how the villas at the seaside resort of Herculaneum could not withstand the earthquake in AD 62.

18 Suffixes: -ly, -ful

The Shadow of Vesuvius

Add -ly or -ful in each space to complete each sentence.

1. Vesuvius erupted violent_____ in AD 79.

2. It was a dread_____ disaster.

3. There have been several small earthquakes recent_____.

4. The volcano is probab_____ due to erupt again.

Write the root word for each of the following.

helpful _____   slowly _____

beautiful _____   careful _____

suddenly _____   happily _____

Choose a suffix -ly or -ful to add to these words. Write the words.

accidental _____   hope _____

power _____   skill _____

natural _____   use _____

amazing _____   perfect _____

Name _____

Complete the following sentences by choosing the correct tense for each verb.

Eat/Ate   Avoid/Avoided   Visited/Visit   Got/Get

Exercise/Exercised   Drank/Drink   Have/Had

Stay fit and healthy!

_____ lots of fresh fruit and vegetables.

_____ sugary foods.

_____ the dentist regularly.

_____ plenty of sleep.

_____ regularly.

_____ lots of water.

_____ a bath or shower every day.

Look after your body – it's the only one you'll get!

20 Skeleton Notes

The Shadow of Vesuvius

Use the following pointers to make notes about how to stay healthy.

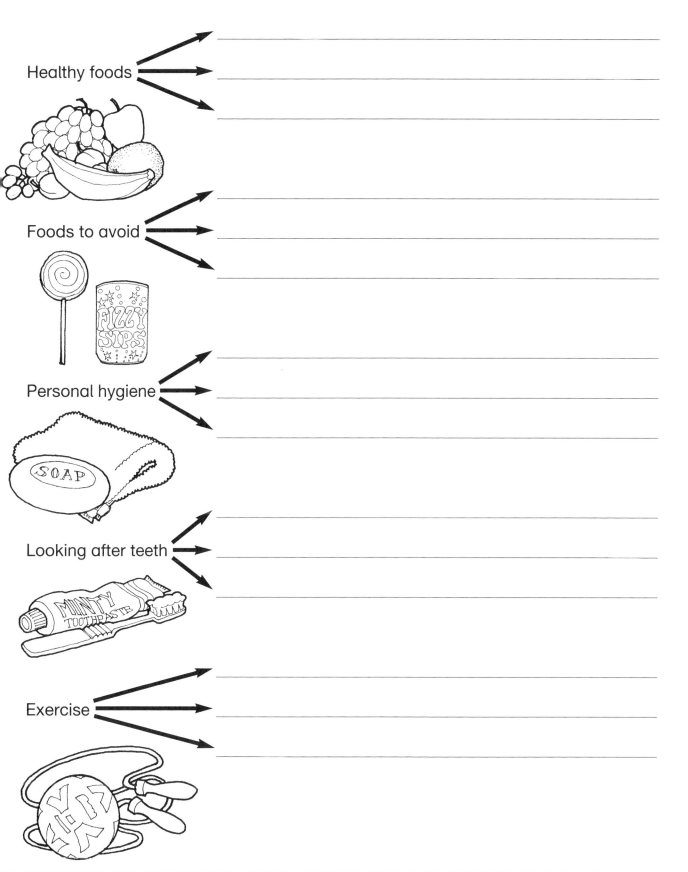

Healthy foods

Foods to avoid

Personal hygiene

Looking after teeth

Exercise

A Bridge for Nearport

Ray Swarbrick

NLS teaching objectives
Year 3

Depending on the term you choose to use this book, the following objectives would be the focus. Pupils should be taught:

Term 1

Text level

17 *to notice differences in the style and structure of non-fiction writing;*

20 *to read information passages and identify main points or gist of text, e.g. by noting key words or phrases;*

21 *to make a simple record of information from texts read, e.g. by completing a chart of information discovered, by listing key words;*

Sentence level

6 *to secure knowledge of question marks in reading, understand their purpose and use appropriately in own writing;*

Word level

10 *to recognize and spell common prefixes and how these influence word meanings, e.g. dis-;*

11 *to use their knowledge of prefixes to generate new words from root words, especially antonyms;*

12 *to use the term prefix.*

Term 2

Text level

12 *to identify the different purposes of instructional texts;*

14 *how written instructions are organized;*

15 *to read and follow simple instructions;*

16 *to write instructions, using a range of organizational devices;*

17 *to make clear notes;*

Sentence level

2 *the function of adjectives within sentences;*

3 *use the term adjective appropriately;*

Word level

24 *to explore opposites.*

Term 3

Text level

21 *to use IT to bring to a published form – discuss relevance of layout, font etc. to audience;*

25 *to revise and extend work on note-making from previous term;*

26 *to summarize in writing the content of a passage or text and the main point it is making.*

Using the Big Books/ICT Big Books: Shared reading

When you read a book, or sections from a book, always allow time for pupils to respond to the text and share their understanding and responses before moving on to analyse text and linguistic features.

Session 1

Text level

- Introduce the shared text, *A Bridge for Nearport* by Ray Swarbrick.

- Turn to page 2 (*Big Book 3b* page 16) and read the heading: *How do we cross a river?* Read the introductory paragraph underneath this heading and identify the opening statement that sets the scene for this discussion text.

- Read the subheadings, *Bridges*, *Boats* and *Tunnels* on pages 2, 4 and 6 (*Big Book 3b* pages 16, 18 and 20). Show how these subheadings are listed in the Contents on page 1 of the Core Reader, indented underneath the main heading: *How do we cross a river?* Read and discuss the information about bridges, boats and tunnels on pages 2 to 7 (*Big Book 3b* pages 16 to 21), including the captions.

Word/Sentence level

- Scan the text on pages 2 to 7 (*Big Book 3b* pages 16 to 21) for questions. What is the quickest way to identify questions when scanning text? (By looking for question marks, or by searching for words often used to begin questions, such as *who, when, why, what, how.*) Can the children answer any of the questions posed on pages 2 to 7?

- Help children to identify adjectives on pages 3 to 7 (*Big Book 3b* pages 17 to 21). Discuss and define what they have in common (i.e. they are words that qualify nouns). Pay particular attention to the adjectives on page 6 (*Big Book 3b* page 20): *big, expensive, long, huge, strong.* Which nouns do these adjectives qualify? Experiment with substituting some of the adjectives, noting the effects on meaning. Who can think of an opposite to each of these adjectives? Further examples of adjectives are highlighted in the Electronic Big Book.

Group/Independent task

- **AM** Activity Master 21 requires children to identify adjectives within a paragraph taken from page 6 (*Big Book 3b* page 20) before using some of the adjectives within sentences of their own. (Some children may need an adult to read the paragraph to them and help to identify the nouns for which adjectives are to be found.)

Plenary

- **AM** Check that children have completed the tasks on **Activity Master 21** and correctly identified five adjectives. Invite children to read aloud some of their own sentences incorporating the adjectives they identified within the text.

Session 2

Text level

- Check to see that the class can remember the three main ways of crossing rivers. Turn to pages 8 to 11 (*Big Book 3b* pages 22 to 25) and read about the fictional town of Nearport (see "faction" texts, page 17). How does the River Swift get its name? What do the people of Nearport currently have to do if they want to visit the south side of the River Swift? Why was the existing bridge built at Bridgetown?

- Read pages 12 and 13 (*Big Book 3b* pages 26 and 27). Discuss the different options for a new bridge at Nearport. Talk about the diagrams of the different types of bridges. In what ways are diagrams more effective than written descriptions in this instance?

- Turn to page 17 (*Big Book 3b* page 31) and read the instructions for making a model of an arch bridge. Identify the goal (statement of what is to be achieved) which, in this instance, is combined with the materials needed: *You could make a small model of an arch bridge using Plasticine and stiff paper or card.* Talk about the way in which the instructions are organized and the limitations of the text without the diagrams.

Word/Sentence level

- Focus on the use of imperatives for the instruction writing on page 17 (*Big Book 3b* page 31), e.g. *Make..., Use..., Place...*

- Help children to identify adjectives on pages 8 to 11 (*Big Book 3b* pages 22 to 25), e.g. *beautiful, heavy* (page 8), *busy, fresh* (page 9). Experiment with substituting some of the adjectives, noting the effects on meaning. Ensure that children do not confuse adverbs, e.g. *swiftly* (page 8) with adjectives.

Group/Independent task

- **AM** Using **Activity Master 22**, ask the children to sequence the instructions. When they have sequenced the instructions, they can attempt to follow them in pairs. Ask them to assess whether the instructions give sufficient detail or whether they need to be modified to make the task easier to complete. They

should note any alterations they want to make to the instructions.

Plenary

■ Discuss any modifications the children wish to make to the instructions and why.

Session 3

Text level

■ Look again at the four types of bridge on page 13 (*Big Book 3b* page 27): *suspension*, *arch*, *beam*, *cantilever*. Discuss the differences between the bridges.

■ Read and talk about the problems facing planners, outlined on pages 14 and 15 (*Big Book 3b* pages 28 and 29).

■ Read the remainder of the shared text on pages 16, 18, 20, 22 and 23 (*Big Book 3b* pages 30 and 32 to 35). Focus on instances where arguments for and against are outlined (examples are highlighted in the Electronic Big Book). What reasons are given to support them?

Word/Sentence level

■ Look for adjectives on pages 14 to 22 of the shared text. Experiment with substituting some of the adjectives, noting the effects on meaning.

■ Challenge children to think of opposites to some of the adjectives. Suitable words are highlighted within the Electronic Big Book.

Group/independent tasks

■ Ask children to plan an agenda for the public meeting in Nearport to discuss the advantages and disadvantages of the four types of bridge proposed. Suggest that they begin with an opening statement explaining the purpose of the meeting, list the four main types of bridge to be discussed, and briefly outline the problems facing the engineers.

■ Less able children could design a poster advertising the proposed meeting, detailing the purpose of the meeting, the date, time and venue. Offer the opportunity to incorporate the use of IT to as many children as possible. Discuss the relevance of layout, font, etc. to the proposed audience

Plenary

■ Stage a "public meeting" to discuss the advantages and disadvantages of the proposed bridge designs for Nearport using one of the children's agendas. How will the people of Nearport benefit from a new bridge? Talk about the different problems facing the engineers and try to think of ways for overcoming these. Which bridge is most appropriate for

Nearport? (Do not worry if the class are unable to reach a decision; another opportunity to debate this matter will be given during Session 4.)

Linking reading and writing: Shared writing

Session 4: focus 1 (Making notes)

Text level

■ Use the information about crossing rivers from *A Bridge for Nearport* to make notes by completing an information grid. Explain that the notes will be referred to during Session 5 to help write a simple discussion text. Make a blank grid of four rows and three columns. Write the column headings *Advantages* and *Disadvantages* across the top and *Bridges*, *Boats* and *Tunnels* down the left-hand side. Ask the class to help you complete the chart by filling in the relevant information.

■ Go on to make notes about the advantages and disadvantages of the four different types of bridge shown on page 13 (*Big Book 3b* page 27), referring to the information on pages 16 to 23 of the Core Reader. Discuss the most appropriate way to organize your notes. Explain that there may be gaps where advantages and disadvantages have not been cited by the author of *A Bridge for Nearport*. Include the children's own opinions and ideas in the notes.

Word/Sentence level

■ Write the words, *advantages* and *disadvantages* on the board. Discuss the function of the prefix *dis-*. (Definitions of these words are given in the Glossary on page 24 of the Core Reader.)

■ Investigate the effect of the prefix *dis-* on other words by generating antonyms from root words, e.g. *disability*, *disagree*, *disappear*, *dishonest*, *disobedient*. Surreptitiously include a word such as *dishwasher* to see if children are able to recognize when *dis-* at the start of a word is not an example of the prefix you are focusing on (i.e. *dishwasher* is a compound word).

Differentiated guided/independent writing tasks [lowest expectation first]

■ Ask children to make brief notes about the three main ways of crossing rivers under the main heading, *Crossing rivers*, and three subheadings: *Bridges*, *Boats* and *Tunnels*. The notes may be presented within a prepared grid showing the advantages and disadvantages of each, or in any other way that the children think appropriate.

AM Give each child a copy of **Activity Master 23**. Using the information on pages 13 to 23 of the Core Reader ask them to make notes about the advantages and disadvantages of each of the four different types of bridge outlined there.

AM Ask children to make notes about the advantages and disadvantages of the four different types of bridge outlined on pages 13 to 23 of the Core Reader. They may use the grid provided on **Activity Master 23**, or they may prefer to organize their notes in a different way.

Pointers for guided writing

■ Remind children that note-taking need not be a lengthy process. The most useful notes are often limited to key words and phrases.

■ Ensure that children are clear in their understanding of the antonyms *advantage* and *disadvantage*.

Plenary

■ Review the information summaries made during the shared writing session.

■ Take a class vote upon the most appropriate bridge for the people of Nearport. Once you have established the two most popular choices of bridge, separate the class into two and ask children to choose which side to take. Steer a debate about the two types of bridge, allowing children to swap sides if they hear something that leads them to change their minds.

Session 5: focus 2 (Discussion text)

Text level

AM **Activity Master 24** provides a writing frame for a discussion text. Use it as a basic format for modelling a discussion text about the different types of bridge proposed by the residents of Nearport. For example:

> *The people of Nearport need a bridge because there is a lot of traffic on the coast road. A bridge would be very useful for holidaymakers travelling along the coast and for market traders transporting their goods.*
>
> *There are a number of different options to be considered. Firstly, an arch bridge, made up of a row of small arches built on strong towers called piers, could be considered. Secondly, we could consider a suspension bridge. A suspension bridge can carry a road over a wide gap but they are very expensive to build. Another option worth considering is a beam bridge. This would have the advantage of being less costly to build because it could be made from a cheap material such as*

> *concrete. Finally, cantilever bridges can be built across very wide gaps but they are expensive to build and require a lot of maintenance.*
>
> *Some people would argue that ...*
>
> *However, I think ...*

Word/Sentence level

■ Identify the statement at the beginning of your writing that informs the reader of the matter under discussion. Focus on instances where arguments *for* and *against* are included. Have reasons been given to support them? Finally, look at the closing recommendation and conclusion.

Differentiated guided/independent writing tasks [lowest expectation first]

■ Ask children to write about their views on why a bridge is necessary for the town of Nearport.

■ Ask them to mention the two other ways of crossing a river (i.e. a tunnel or ferry crossing) and explain why a bridge is the preferred option. You may like to provide a simplified version of the writing frame on **Activity Master 24**, for example: *The people of Nearport need to be able to cross the River Swift because ...; There are a number of different ways to be considered ...; Another reason is ...; Some people may disagree with this view but ...*

AM Using the writing frame on **Activity Master 24**, ask children to write a discussion text about the different types of bridge proposed for Nearport.

AM Provide children with a copy of the writing frame on **Activity Master 24** to use as the basis for a discussion text about the different types of bridge proposed for Nearport. Ask them to evaluate the four main types of bridge and make clear their own views about which would be most appropriate for Nearport. Encourage them to adapt the sentence openers on the writing frame to suit their own purposes.

Pointers for guided writing

■ Show children how to use the sentence openers provided on **Activity Master 24** appropriately, making adjustments where necessary.

■ Ensure that an opening statement is made, informing the reader of the matter under discussion.

■ Check that children's discussion writing ends with a closing recommendation/conclusion.

Plenary

■ Invite children to read their discussion texts aloud to the class. Ask the rest of the class to listen out for instances where arguments *for* and *against* are included. Have reasons been given to support them?

21 Adjectives

A Bridge for Nearport

Read the following paragraph about tunnels. Then find and underline five adjectives.

You can cross under some rivers by tunnel. However, it is sometimes

difficult to build a tunnel because of big rocks in the way. Other

disadvantages of building tunnels are that they are expensive and

take a long time to build. This is because huge machines are needed

to dig the tunnel and to make the walls strong.

Use some of the adjectives you found in three sentences of your own.

1. _____

_____

2. _____

_____

3. _____

22 Building Bridges

A Bridge for Nearport

Cut out each instruction for building a simple arch bridge and arrange them in the correct order.

Begin by making some wedge-shaped blocks from a modelling material.

Test your design by placing small weights on top of the bridge.

Use sticky tape to fix a piece of card like this:

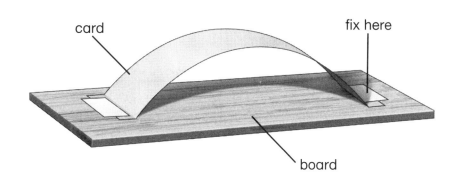

Make a small model of an arch bridge using a modelling material and card.

Place your blocks on top of the card like this:

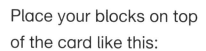
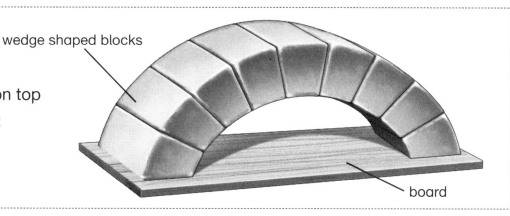

Now use your instructions to build the bridge!

23 For and Against

A Bridge for Nearport

Complete this information grid using pages 13 to 23 of *A Bridge for Nearport.*

| **Advantages** | | **Disadvantages** |

Arch bridge

Suspension bridge

Beam bridge

Cantilever bridge

24 Which Bridge?

A Bridge for Nearport

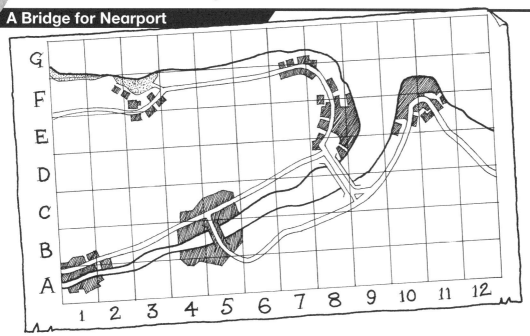

The people of Nearport need a bridge because _____

_____

There are a number of different options to be considered. Firstly, _____

_____

Secondly, _____

_____

Another option _____

_____

Finally, _____

_____

Some people would argue that _____

_____

However, I think _____

_____

The A–Z of Rocks and Minerals

David Orme and Helen Bird

nd Minerals
nd Helen Bird

etic

graphy

s of work

f materials

esources

ls featured in
copper, flint,
rble, rock salt,

g rocks and
ext, e.g. jewellery

dictionaries,
n books with

text

vords and

text
vices
ers
abetic order

NLS teaching objectives
Year 3

Depending on the term you choose to use this book, the following objectives would be the focus. Pupils should be taught:

Term 1

Text level

20 *to read information passages, and identify main points or gist of text;*

21 *to make a simple record of information;*

Sentence level

9 *to notice and investigate a range of other devices for presenting texts, e.g. enlarged or italicized print, captions and headings, inset text; to explore purposes and collect examples;*

Word level

13 *to collect new words from reading and work in other subjects and create ways of categorizing and logging them, e.g. personal dictionaries, glossaries;*

15 *to have a secure understanding of the purpose and organization of the dictionary.*

Term 2

Text level

17 *To make clear notes through identifying key words, phrases or sentences in reading;*

Word level

17 *to continue the collection of new words from reading and work in other subjects, and make use of them in reading and writing;*

19 *to use dictionaries to learn or check the spellings and definitions of words;*

20 *to write their own definitions of words, developing precision and accuracy in expression;*

21 *to use the term* definition;

23 *to organize words or information alphabetically, using the first two letters.*

Term 3

Text level

19 *to summarize orally in one sentence the content of a passage or text, and the main point it is making;*

24 *to make alphabetically ordered texts – use information with other subjects, own experience, or derived from other information books;*

Word level

8 *to identify short words within longer words as an aid to spelling;*

12 *to continue the collection of new words from reading and work in other subjects, and make use of them in reading and writing.*

Using the Big Books/ICT Big Books: Shared reading

When you read a book, or sections from a book, always allow time for pupils to respond to the text and share their understanding and responses before moving on to analyse text and linguistic features.

Session 1

Text level

■ Introduce the shared text to the class, focusing on the front cover of the Core Reader. Ask the children to read the title to you. Who are the authors? What does the front cover reveal about the contents and nature of the book? How will information about the rocks and minerals be listed? Show and talk about other books that organize information alphabetically (see Optional additional resources).

■ Read the introduction of the book together. Talk about the function of an introduction in a non-fiction text. What information do the authors consider that readers should know (a definition of a rock, mineral and metal) before they use the book?

■ Read through the headwords in the main body of the book: *amethyst, basalt, bauxite* etc. Establish which of these names are familiar to the children and which are new and unknown.

■ Read one or two of the entries for new and unknown examples and discuss.

Word/Sentence level

■ Study the Key on page 2 (*Big Book 3b* page 36) and practise using the features of the book that are described there. Find words in bold in the introduction, and locate them in the A–Z section of the book; then find words in italics and locate them in the Glossary. Discuss the usefulness of these organizational devices.

■ Explore other devices used for organizing the information, e.g. captions, headings. Are the illustrations purely for decoration? Text presentational devices are highlighted in the Electronic Big Book.

■ Talk about the function of the enlarged A–Z index letters along the edges of each page. Why are these necessary? Find similar examples in different dictionaries to demonstrate how they help readers locate alphabetically listed information more quickly.

Group/Independent task

■ Give each group a different topic, e.g. food or animals, and a dictionary. Challenge them to find something

beginning with every letter of the alphabet within their specific topic, and organize an alphabetic list.

Plenary

■ Give every group an opportunity to report on their success in compiling an alphabetic list. Ask the rest of the class to think of things for letters that children have not found a word for. Suggest compromises for "awkward" letters, such as settling for a word containing the letter, e.g. *fox* for the letter *x*.

Session 2

Text level

■ Find out which headwords the children can remember before reopening the book. Choose one of these and go directly to it, using the A–Z index letters to locate it. Read the definition together and cross-refer any emboldened or italicized words. Count the number of sentences within the definition. Why are there only a few? Explain that definitions need to be concise; words must be chosen carefully and arranged in the best order to aid understanding.

■ Choose other headwords, both familiar and unfamiliar, and read the definitions of each, ensuring that the children comprehend the information. Avoid reading the headwords in chronological order; invite children to locate specific words within the book and cross-refer to the Glossary.

Word/Sentence level

■ Turn to pages 6 and 7 (*Big Book 3b* pages 40 and 41) and focus on the way headwords are listed alphabetically, e.g. *bauxite* appears before *calcite*. Ask the class to demonstrate how they know that the words *calcite* and *chalk* are in alphabetical order by referring to the second letter and noting that *a* comes before *h* in the alphabet. (More able children may also be able to assert that *coal* and *copper* are in alphabetical order by pointing out the third letters.) Ask the children to check that other words beginning with the same letters are organized alphabetically, e.g. *flint* and *fossils* on page 9 (*Big Book 3b* page 43), *gold* and *granite* on page 10 (*Big Book 3b* page 44), *lead* and *limestone* on page 14 (*Big Book 3b* page 46). Letters determining alphabetical order are highlighted in the Electronic Big Book.

■ Invite eight children to the front of the class (at least two whose names begin with the same letter). Ask the class to arrange them in alphabetical order.

Group/Independent tasks

AM Distribute copies of **Activity Master 25**, featuring the headwords from **The A–Z of Rocks and Minerals**, to each child or pair and ask them to cut out the

words and organize them in alphabetical order. The less familiar and more challenging words are situated within the bottom two rows; these may be removed from the sheets given to less able children.

- Type a list of the words featured on **Activity Master 25** into a word processing document in random order. Give all the children an opportunity, in pairs, to reorganize the words into alphabetical order using the cut and paste tools. For less able children, provide a shorter list that does not include words beginning with the same letter.

Plenary

AM Enlarge a copy of **Activity Master 25** to A3 size and cut out the words. Give every child in the class one of the words. Work together to arrange the children and words in alphabetical order.

Session 3

Text level

- Find out what the children remember about the particular rocks and minerals they studied yesterday before returning to the book to reread the definitions. For each definition revisited, identify the extra information in the text that the children had not recalled.

- Read any remaining definitions that you have not yet studied together. Assess comprehension by asking children questions about uses, e.g. Which of the rocks and minerals we have read about are suitable for making jewellery? Which might you use to make a statue? Which was used in the Stone Age to make tools? Which might you use to make roof tiles?

Word/Sentence level

- Write the following list of words from the Core Reader on the board and invite children to find and underline or write out the smaller words within them: *limestone* (*lime, stone, me, ton, tone, one, on*), *pitchblende* (*pitch, itch, it, blend, lend*), *mineral* (*mine, in, miner*), *crystal* (*cry*). Discuss this activity as a strategy for spelling. Which of these words are compound words?

Group/Independent task

AM Using **Activity Master 26** ask the children to identify and write out smaller words within the longer words. Encourage them to compare their findings to see if children have identified different words.

- Alternatively, provide the children with a photocopied list of words from a current class topic and ask them to identify and write out smaller words within them. The lists may be differentiated for children of different abilities.

- Write some of the children's names on the board and encourage the class to look for smaller words within them. Remind children that this strategy is a useful aid to spelling.

Linking reading and writing: Shared writing

Session 4: focus 1 (Alphabetically-organized texts)

Text level

AM The writing frame on **Activity Master 27** is a template for a glossary using words featured in *The A–Z of Rocks and Minerals*. Alternatively, you may prefer to ask the class to think of key words relating to a current class topic, e.g. the Egyptians (*pharaoh, pyramid, River Nile, sphinx, Tutankhamen*) and organize them into an alphabetic list.

- Choose one of the words and compose a simple definition together, drawing contributions from as many children as possible. Review the definition and discuss ways to edit it to make it as clear as possible. Challenge children to summarize the definition orally in one sentence.

- Repeat for other words in your list and demonstrate how you are using the definitions to begin constructing a glossary.

Word/Sentence level

- Ask children to locate the words you have used in a dictionary. Use the dictionary to check spellings and compare the definitions with the ones you have composed together.

Differentiated guided/independent writing tasks (lowest expectation first)

- Ask the children, in small groups, to make an illustrated alphabet book or frieze for younger children (illustrations may be completed at a separate time). Agree a theme, such as food or animals, and ask the children to organize the words alphabetically. Provide dictionaries to help them find suitable words and decide upon a title, e.g. *Alphabet Picnic* or *Alphabet Zoo*.

- Provide children, in pairs, with a list of words particular to a current topic, e.g. weather (*forecast, ice, rain, temperature*). Ask them to organize the words alphabetically and write a simple definition for

each. Alternatively, you may prefer to provide copies of the writing frame on **Activity Master 27**, using words featured in *The A–Z of Rocks and Minerals*.

- Organize the children into small groups and ask them to compile a glossary for a current topic. Ask them to begin by making a list of specialist vocabulary particular to the chosen topic. They may then, with help from a range of information texts and dictionaries, write a definition for each word and arrange them alphabetically in a glossary for future class use.

Pointers for guided writing

- Remind those children making alphabet friezes or books of the age of their intended audience. Ideally, use IT to produce the friezes or books but, if this is not possible, ensure that letters and words are suitably clear and legible. Ask the children to check that the words are listed alphabetically using a simple dictionary or alphabet line.

- Review the definitions together to ensure that they are clear and concise. Ask the children to check with a partner that their definitions are in alphabetical order.

Plenary

- Encourage the children who have produced alphabet books or friezes for younger children to present them to the rest of the class. Discuss the appropriateness of each for their intended audience. If there are younger pupils in the school, arrange a time for the children to share their work with them.

- Invite children who have written definitions to read them aloud without using the headword (where headwords appear within a definition, ask the child to replace it with a nonsense word, e.g. *bloop*). Ask the rest of the class to listen carefully; who can work out what word is being defined?

Session 5 could be used to develop and complete work on alphabetically organized texts if necessary.

Session 5: focus 2 (Identifying main points)

Text level

- Choose a headword from the shared text, e.g. *coal*. Read the definition together and ask the class to think of a word or short phrase from the definition that describes it succinctly, e.g. *a rock*. Ask the class to extend the word or phrase by adding an adjective, e.g. *black*. Then ask the class to give one use for the material as concisely as possible, e.g. *to provide heat*. Using the words and phrases provided by the class,

write a complete sentence on the board, e.g. *Coal is a black rock used to provide heat*.

- Discuss how the class have extracted key words to write a more concise definition. Point out that this skill is a feature of making notes. (Key words and phrases are highlighted in the Electronic Big Book.) Explain that dictionary and glossary definitions tend to be very concise because only a small amount of information is needed. However, readers generally expect to find more detailed information within a non-fiction book on a specific topic. Revisit the definition in *The A–Z of Rocks and Minerals*, to extract the extra information.

Word/Sentence level

- Play a game whereby somebody gives a noun, an adjective and a use, e.g. *a white powder used to make bread and cakes*, and ask the rest of the class to guess what is defined (flour). List the words in a table on the board to reinforce the terms *noun* and *adjective*.

Differentiated guided/independent writing tasks (lowest expectation first)

- **AM** Give children a copy of **Activity Master 28** and explain that Ben needs a bit of help with his definition of gorillas. Ask them to assist by selecting the most important information (key words and phrases) and reorganizing it into a concise definition.

- Select an appropriate passage from an information book relating to a current topic. Ask children, alone or in pairs, to underline or highlight the key points and phrases.

- Provide the children with an appropriate passage from an information book relating to a current topic. Ask them to make notes from it, by listing or underlining key points and phrases, from which to write a summary of information.

Pointers for guided writing

- Remind the children that definitions should be entirely factual and should not include opinions, e.g. *I like gorillas*.

- Dissuade the children from writing out extended chunks of information by helping them to isolate key words and phrases.

- Look for opportunities in the children's writing to combine sentences to avoid repetition.

Plenary

- Enlarge a copy of Ben's definition (see **Activity Master 28**) to A3 size. Review it and discuss ways in which it could be improved. Discuss ways to combine sentences to avoid repetition. Talk about the inappropriateness of Ben's last sentence: *I like gorillas*.

25 Alphabetical Order

The A–Z of Rocks and Minerals

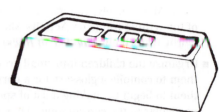

Cut out the words.

Arrange the words in alphabetical order.

granite	diamond	flint	jade	copper
chalk	meteorite	lava	silver	slate
iron	gold	talc	volcanic rock	limestone
emerald	ruby	coal	rock salt	fossil
opal	marble	oil	quartz	lead
basalt	silica	zircon	turquoise	calcite
hematite	bauxite	kimberlite	pitchblende	amethyst

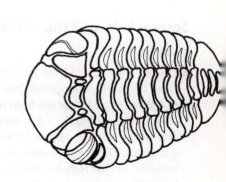

Identifying Words within Words

Name _____

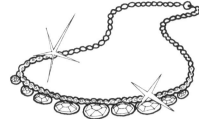

Find the smaller words within each word.

Write out the smaller words.

gemstone

_____

mineral

_____

granite

_____

diamond

_____

jewellery

_____

basalt

_____

crystal

_____

limestone

_____

pitchblende

_____

meteorite

_____

hematite

_____

Writing a Glossary

Name _____

	Definition
coal	
copper	
diamond	
fossil	
gold	
lava	
marble	
meteorite	
oil	
talc	

28 Writing a Definition

Ben has written a definition of gorillas. His teacher has asked him to improve it by selecting the most important bits of information.

Help Ben to do this by underlining the key words and phrases.

Gorillas are apes.

Gorillas are the largest

of all apes. They are very big. They have

thick, black fur and they are very strong.

Gorillas live in forests in a country called

Africa. Gorillas eat lots of food, such as

fruit and leaves. I like gorillas.

Use the words you have underlined to write a concise definition of gorillas.

Gorillas are _____

_____ .

Look Out!

David Orme and Helen Bird

NLS teaching objectives
Year 3

Depending on the term you choose to use this book, the following objectives would be the focus. Pupils should be taught:

Term 1

Text level

17 *to notice differences in the style and structure of non-fiction writing;*

22 *to write simple non-chronological reports from known information, e.g. from own experience or from texts read, using notes made to organize and present ideas. Write for a known audience, e.g. other pupils in class;*

Sentence level

3 *the function of verbs in sentences;*

5 *to use the term* verb *appropriately;*

9 *to notice and investigate a range of other devices for presenting texts, e.g. enlarged or italicized print, captions and headings, inset text. Explore purposes and collect examples;*

Word level

13 *to collect new words from reading.*

Term 2

Text level

12 *to identify the different purposes of instructional texts, e.g. rules;*

16 *to write instructions, using a range of organizational devices;*

17 *to make clear notes;*

Sentence level

8 *other uses of capitalization from reading, e.g. headings, special emphasis;*

Word level

11 *to use the terms* singular *and* plural *appropriately.*

Term 3

Text level

21 *to use IT to bring to a published form – discuss relevance of layout, font, etc. to audience;*

Word level

12 *to continue the collection of new words from reading.*

Using the Big Books/ICT Big Books: Shared reading

When you read a book, or sections from a book, always allow time for pupils to respond to the text and share their understanding and responses before moving on to analyse text and linguistic features.

Session 1

Text level

■ Introduce the shared text to the class, focusing on the front cover of the Core Reader. Ask the children to read the title to you. Who are the authors? What does the front cover reveal about the contents and nature of the book?

■ Read the *Safety First* introduction of the book on pages 3 and 4 (*Big Book 3b* pages 55 and 56). Take time to discuss the dangers that threaten children's safety. What measures can they take to avoid such dangers? For example, never play near railway lines; never fly kites near electricity pylons.

■ Read the warning on page 2 (*Big Book 3b* page 54) and talk about the other warning signs on pages 5 to 7 (*Big Book 3b* pages 57 to 59). Ensure children understand the meaning of unfamiliar vocabulary such as *ford*, *quayside*. (Refer to the glossary in the Core Reader for a definition of *quayside*.)

Word/Sentence level

■ There is a large number of plural nouns on pages 3 and 4 (*Big Book 3b* pages 55 and 56). How many can the children identify? For example, *storms*, *floods*, *earthquakes*, *volcanoes*. Which of these examples are regular (i.e. *s* or *es* has been added to make them plural)? Which are irregular, e.g. *people*? Further examples are highlighted in the Electronic Big Book.

■ Write the word *dangerous* on the board. Who can spot a smaller word within it (*anger*)? Look at the word *quayside* on page 5 (*Big Book 3b* page 57). Establish that *quay* is pronounced the same as *key*. Write both words side by side on the board.

■ Talk about the function of the signs on pages 2 and 5 to 7 (*Big Book 3b* pages 54 and 57 to 59). Identify specific words and phrases that are used to grab the reader's attention, e.g. *Warning! Beware.*

■ What features are used to ensure that the information on the signs does not go unnoticed? For example, use of the colour red; capital letters; larger font size, exclamation mark. Text presentational devices are highlighted in the Electronic Big Book. What are the advantages of using symbols rather than words alone

for road signs? Talk about the significance of the shape of different road signs, i.e. signs giving orders are mostly circular; warning signs are mostly triangular.

Group/Independent task

AM **Activity Master 29** requires children to match warning labels to corresponding signs.

Plenary

■ Look around the classroom for other signs that provide information or give warnings. List these on the board. If time permits, take the children to the nearest road or street and identify other signs and symbols, e.g. road names, shop names, Highway Code signs.

Session 2

Text level

■ Read the information on pages 8 and 9 (*Big Book 3b* pages 60 and 61). Talk about the use of colour coding to inform locals of the level of concern regarding the Sheveluch Volcano. Discuss the symbols used on page 9 (*Big Book 3b* page 61). Why are climbers of Mount St Helens required to sign in before and after their climb? What special equipment are they advised to take with them? Why is *BE PREPARED!* set in capital letters with an exclamation mark? What threat do human climbers pose to the volcano?

■ Read and talk about the warning signs and photographs on pages 10 to 12 in the Core Reader. What objects, chemicals and substances used in homes pose a danger to children and their families if misused? For example, *matches*, *medicines*, *cleaning solutions*, *bleach*. What is it about each of these household items that makes them dangerous? For example, *poisonous*, *flammable*.

Word/Sentence level

■ Study in greater detail the instructions on page 9 (*Big Book 3b* page 61). Who are they addressed to? (Note that instruction writing focuses on the generalized human agents, e.g. *climbers* rather than named individuals.) Further examples of instructions are highlighted in the Electronic Big Book.

■ Discuss the use of imperatives. For example, *Stay on established routes*; *avoid trampling plants*; *use the toilets provided.*

■ How many plural nouns can the children find on page 9 (*Big Book 3b* page 61)? Which of these examples are regular and which are irregular?

Group/Independent task

- Ask the children to make posters advising climbers of the rules, in bullet point form, to be adhered to when climbing Mount St Helens. They will need to refer to the information on page 9 (*Big Book 3b* page 61). Offer as many children as possible an opportunity to use IT; discuss the relevance of layout, font, etc. to the audience (in this instance, the climbers of Mount St Helens).

Plenary

- Pin completed posters (without identifying the authors of each) to a wall or lay them out on an appropriate surface for the class to view them. Ask the class to discuss which is the best poster, taking into consideration two main factors: firstly, the poster needs to contain all the relevant information; secondly, it needs to be presented in a way that effectively communicates that information to the reader.

Session 3

Text level

- Briefly review the different types of warnings shown on pages 5 to 9 (*Big Book 3b* pages 57 to 61) and pages 10 to 12 in the Core Reader. What have the children learned so far about the ways in which warnings are conveyed?

- Read and talk about the signs on page 13 (*Big Book 3b* page 62). How might old and precious items be damaged by too much handling and flash photography?

- Read and talk about the notices on page 14 (*Big Book 3b* page 63). What instructions are given to volunteer archaeologists? What dangers do archaeologists face in their work?

- Look at the warning sign on page 15 (*Big Book 3b* page 64). What is it warning visitors about? Focus on the presentational devices used to bring specific words to visitors' attention, e.g. different typefaces, capital letters, bold text. Why are some words larger than others? Do the children think the sign is effective? In what ways might it be improved?

Word/Sentence level

- Talk about the function of the notices on pages 13 to 15 (*Big Book 3b* pages 62 to 64). Identify specific words and phrases that are used to grab the reader's attention, e.g. *Please do not touch*; *Warning*. Why is *IMPORTANT NOTICE* set in capital letters?

- What features are used to ensure that the information on the signs does not go unnoticed? For example, use

of colour; capital letters; larger font size; emboldened lettering; variety of different typefaces. You may wish to draw the children's attention to such features on the warning signs and packaging that you have collected.

Group/Independent task

- **AM** **Activity Master 30** requires children to consider the best way to present a warning for visitors to a volcano. Offer as many children as possible an opportunity to use IT; discuss the relevance of layout, font, etc. to the audience.

Plenary

- Display the children's completed warning signs and discuss the different features of each.

Linking reading and writing: Shared writing

Session 4: focus 1 (Making notes for instruction writing)

Text level

- Ask the children to help you make notes about different suggestions for staying safe during Physical Education. Scribe for the class as they offer their ideas. For example:

  Always wear the correct clothes.
  Ensure long hair is tied back.
  Remove all jewellery.
  Tie your shoelaces securely if wearing trainers.
  Listen carefully to instructions.

  You may like to use bullet points to separate each idea. Keep the sentences to refer to during the Plenary session.

- Compare the list of rules with the Climbing Dos and Don'ts on page 9 (*Big Book 3b* page 61).

Word/Sentence level

- Challenge the children to locate the verbs within the sentences you have written. What tense have you used? Discuss the use of imperatives.

Differentiated guided/independent writing tasks [lowest expectation first]

- **AM** Give each child a copy of **Activity Master 31**. Ask them to complete the rules with a reason. For example: *Always tie shoelaces securely … because they may trip you up if left undone.*

- Set the task of writing a list of safety rules for Physical Education. Encourage children to elaborate on each rule, giving a reason for it.

- Ask children to type a list of safety rules for Physical Education using a computer. Ask them to elaborate on each rule, giving a reason for it. For example: *Always tie shoelaces securely as they may trip you up if left undone.* Once the task is complete, show children how to reorganize their list, putting the rules in order of importance, using the cut and paste tools. (Allow children to discuss their lists with one another to help sequence the rules in order of importance.)

Plenary

- Display the sentences you composed as a class during the shared writing session. Ask the class to identify the verbs within the sentences and ask specific children to write them for you on separate cards. Erase the verbs from each sentence and shuffle the word cards. Ask children to stick a verb in each space randomly so that the text no longer makes sense. For example:

   *Always **Remove** the correct clothes.*
   ***wear** all jewellery...*

- Talk about problems that have arisen aside from the fact that the text no longer makes sense, e.g. capital letters in the wrong place, verbs in the wrong tense.

- Invite children to sort the verbs into the correct spaces. Then ask children to change each verb to the past tense, e.g. *wore, removed.* How does this affect the sentences?

Session 5: focus 2 (Instruction writing)

Text level

AM Activity Master 32 offers a basic template for a poster warning of possible dangers during Physical Education and how to avoid them. Look at an enlarged copy of the template together. Talk about the illustrations and think of appropriate instructions to label them with, using the notes you made together during Session 4. For example, *Tie shoelaces securely to avoid tripping up.* Discuss how to write the instructions, e.g. in capital letters or a bright colour, such as red.

- The empty box on the template is for children to add an idea of their own. Take suggestions from different children and decide together on the most important or relevant idea for inclusion on the poster.

- Review the poster critically. How could the presentation be improved? Are the instructions clear and concise? Does the important information jump out at the reader effectively? How could the layout and presentation be improved? Treating the template as a preliminary plan, sketch out a new design to transfer the instructions and warnings on to.

Word/Sentence level

- Focus on the use of imperatives in the shared writing.

- Identify the connectives you have used where reasons for each rule have been given, e.g. *as, because, so that.*

Differentiated guided/independent writing tasks [lowest expectation first]

AM Activity Master 32 provides a template for a poster about safety rules during Physical Education. Ask children to write an instruction under each picture and add a fourth of their own.

- Ask children to design a poster for their peers instructing them on how to stay safe during Physical Education.

- Ask children to design a leaflet for their peers with instructions on how to stay safe during Physical Education.

Plenary

- Display the children's work (both finished and yet to be completed) and give them an opportunity to read and discuss one another's posters and leaflets. Ideally, once all the work has been completed, display it for other children in the school to refer to.

29 Reading the Signs!

Look Out!

Label each sign with the correct warning.

Quayside/Riverbank	Swing bridge	Height limit for a low bridge
Falling rocks	Crossing point for elderly	Wild animals
Road works	Children going to or from school	Slippery road

_____

_____

_____

_____

_____

_____

_____

_____

_____

30 Warning Signs!

Use the information in the box to design an eye-catching poster to inform visitors that the Sunset Crater Volcano is closed to climbers and hikers.

Sunset Crater Volcano   National monument

Flagstaff, Arizona   Important notice

To protect this fragile resource, Sunset Crater Volcano is closed to climbing and hiking

---

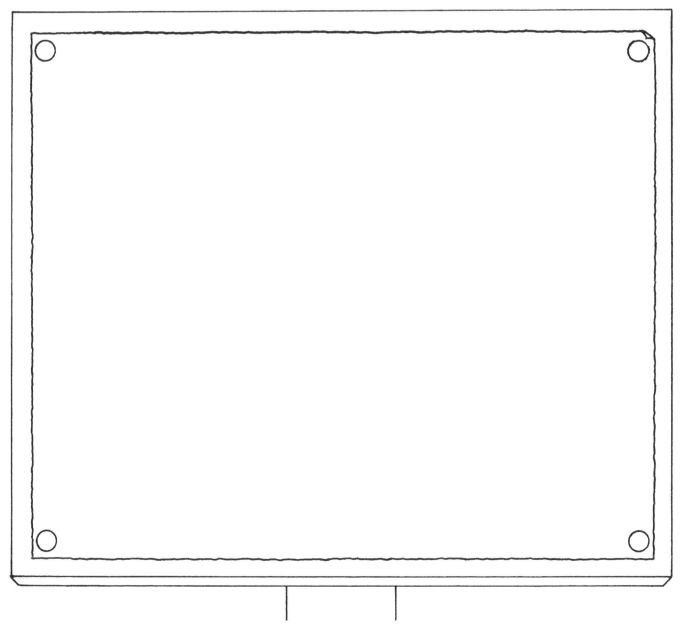

31 Reasons for Rules

Look Out!

Complete the following sentences by writing a reason for each rule.

Safety Rules

Tie the shoelaces of your trainers securely so that

_____

_____

Always wear the correct clothes for PE because _____

_____

_____

If you have long hair, tie it back _____

_____

_____

Remove all jewellery _____

_____

_____

Listen carefully to your teacher's instructions _____

_____

_____

Look Out!

Name _____

Stay Safe!

_____

_____

_____

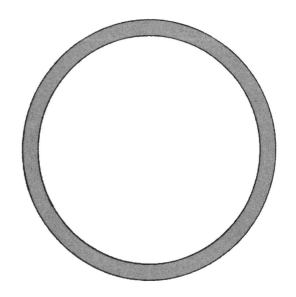

_____

Volcanoes

Gordon Askew

NLS teaching objectives
Year 3

Depending on the term you choose to use this CD-ROM text, the following objectives would be the focus. Pupils should be taught:

Term 1

Text level

20 *to read information passages and identify main points or gist of text;*

22 *to write simple non-chronological reports from known information, using notes made to organize and present ideas;*

Sentence level

9 *to notice and investigate a range of other devices for presenting texts, e.g. speech bubbles, enlarged or italicized print, captions and headings, inset text. Explore purposes and collect examples;*

Word level

13 *to collect new words from reading and work in other subjects and create ways of categorizing and logging them, e.g. personal dictionaries, glossaries.*

Term 2

Text level

15 *to read and follow simple instructions;*

16 *to write instructions, using a range of organizational devices;*

Word level

17 *to continue the collection of new words from reading and work in other subjects, and make use of them in reading and writing.*

Term 3

Text level

17 *to "scan" indexes, directories and IT sources, etc. to locate information quickly and accurately;*

21 *to use IT to bring to a published form — discuss relevance of layout, font, etc. to audience;*

Word level

12 *to recognize and generate compound words and to use this knowledge to support their spelling.*

Specific literacy learning intentions relating to the reading of interactive ICT texts:

- *to understand how to explore a multimedia ICT text, and discover what it has to offer;*
- *to learn to extract and orchestrate information from multimedia sources in an ICT text;*
- *to understand how to navigate a multimedia ICT text in order to locate and extract information.*

Key words for ICT texts start, quit, home, back, click, save, print, page, screen, CD-ROM

Key words for multimedia texts text, photograph, illustration, diagram, captions, animation, video, slideshow, commentary, sound bite

Key words for volcano topic erupt, eruption, magma, lava, crater, cone, vapour, vent, molten, active, dormant

Using the interactive ICT text instead of a Big Book

Shared reading

NB: To ensure visibility for whole class use the ICT output will need to be displayed on a large monitor, projected onto a screen or whiteboard, or networked around the machines in a computer suite so that the same text shows on each monitor. (Extensive advice on using ICT in whole class work, including hardware options, is available on the BECTA website, and on the NLS CD-ROM: "ICT in the Literacy Hour"). If no such facilities are available this ICT text can still be used for group work, using a standard monitor.

Session 1

Text level

- Tell the children that this week, instead of a Big Book, they are going to share an ICT text called **Volcanoes**. **Volcanoes** is a sort of CD-ROM. Explain what this is and how it can be used as a source of interest and information.

- The first encounter with **Volcanoes** needs to be a fairly free-ranging and open-ended exploration. As shared reading, explore and enjoy the ICT text together, with the teacher demonstrating the operation of the program. See what it does and find out what it has to offer. Encourage the children to join in the reading of the words on screen. Discuss the pictures, animations, video clips, etc. Use the mouse pointer to help follow the text, and to indicate things on screen.

- As you go along, practise and reinforce the key ICT and multimedia words (using word cards to reinforce if appropriate).

- Talk with the children about what the ICT text (program) is for. What is it doing and how? Examine fully the various options available on each screen. Discuss the choices that the user has to make and what effect they have on the outcome. Ask "What do you think will happen if we click here?"

- At some points where a decision has to be made, let the children talk in pairs or groups about what they would choose and why. What do they think the outcome of this choice will be?

- Discuss the way the user has to respond to show what choice has been made. After some teacher discussion and demonstration, let children come out to make the responses the class has chosen.

Word/Sentence level

- Use interactive games to practise reading and writing (on whiteboards if appropriate) the key ICT and multimedia words. Start to build up a class list of these words.

Group/Independent task

AM Explain to the children that in later lessons you are going to use this ICT text to find out more about volcanoes. As preparation for this, ask children, in groups, pairs or individually, to activate their prior knowledge about volcanoes, through brainstorming and/or concept mapping. Ask them to follow this up by generating a list of questions: things they would like to know about volcanoes. Provide differentiated support in doing this, as appropriate. **Activity Master 1** can be used to support this activity if required.

Plenary

- Take feedback on both what children already know about volcanoes and the things they would like to know (find out). Compile a collective list of *Our questions about volcanoes* and save these for the next day. Ask the children whether, from what they have already seen of the **Volcanoes** program, they think it will be able to provide answers to their questions. All or some?

Session 2

Text level

- Share and enjoy more fairly free-ranging "reading" of the text, reinforcing the previous session's learning, (especially reading/recognition key ICT and multimedia words) but this time especially exploring the different ways in which information is presented in this ICT text.

- Try to ensure that you explore and discuss information that is presented through written text, pictures and captions, photographs, diagrams, slide shows, animations, video clips and sound bites. (Examples of all of these are included in various parts of the program.) Also discuss the icons used to flag up each of these in the program.

Volcanoes

- On the basis of this, discuss how this ICT text is different from a book or other paper text. Spend some time talking about the advantages and disadvantages of the different information sources the ICT text can provide. What can you find out from a video clip, which you can't find from a written text? Is an animation more helpful than a written explanation? Etc.

Word/Sentence level

- From this reading and discussion, draw out different textual ways in which information is presented on screen. Draw attention to different textual devices (captions, labels, speech bubbles, etc.). Explore purposes and collect examples.

- While reading, collect examples of words specifically related to the volcano topic, which children may not know/understand (lava, magma, etc.). Show how you can use the "on screen glossary" to discover the meanings, discuss and start to build up a class dictionary of these words.

Group/Independent tasks

- In groups or pairs, ask the children to compile a list of the different ways the **Volcanoes** program provides information, i.e. the different media used as "information sources" – video, animation, photographs, sound bites etc. Various prompts such as word cards can be used to support this if required. This could be extended by asking the children to design/draw a little picture or icon for each one.

- **AM** For each information source, ask children to discuss and list some of the things they think they might be able to find out from this source, and some of the things they can't (i.e. exploring the advantages and disadvantages of each information source). **Activity Master 2** can be used to support this activity if required.

Plenary

- Take feedback and compile a collective list of the information sources (media) to be found in the **Volcanoes** ICT text. Discuss the advantages and disadvantages of each as a source of information.

- Look again at the list of questions generated the previous day. For each one discuss which information source might be most helpful in providing the answer: "Do you think we would find the answer to this by watching a video clip, by reading the written text, by watching an animation?" etc. Introduce the idea that we can sometimes draw information from a combination of media sources.

Linking shared reading and shared writing

Session 3

Text level

- Before returning to the ICT text, recap the questions generated in Session 1 and revisited in the plenary of Session 2. Select a question and use a further shared reading of the **Volcanoes** multimedia text to try to answer.

- Demonstrate how to navigate through the text to find the information required. At each stage of the reading ask questions like "Which do you think would be the best choice to make here, if we want to know (answer to the question)?"; "Where do you think we need to go next to find this?"; "Do you think we might be able to find some more about this somewhere else?"; "What do we need to click to get there?" Discuss fully the choices made, and their consequences, at every stage. Remember this is still shared reading so involve the children as interactively as possible, including their joining in the reading of the actual words on screen.

- When you have found the required information, backtrack to the beginning of the program, and confirm the best route through the program to reach it. Start to build up, through shared writing, a list of instructions for navigating the text to reach the information, e.g. *On the title page click* **skip introduction**. *When Popo appears click* **next**. *On the main menu click* **Volcanoes of the World**, etc. It will, of course, be an instruction or procedure text that you are creating.

- Once the instructions are written, ask a child to come out and "test" them, to see if they get you to the correct place in the program.

- If there is time, repeat this whole sequence with a different question, discovering and then writing and testing instructions for a different route through the text.

Word/Sentence level

- Practise some of the ICT/multimedia specific vocabulary using word cards, whiteboards etc. as you write the instructions. Continue to build up the class lists of these words.

- Provide prompts and reminders about appropriate language for instruction texts during the shared writing, possibly asking children to write some suggested words and phrases onto whiteboards at appropriate stages.

Volcanoes

- Continue to build up the class dictionary of volcano-specific words.

Group/Independent tasks

- If the necessary ICT facilities are available, e.g. in an ICT suite, ask pairs of children to use the *Volcanoes* program to try to locate the answers to specific questions. They should then write (on paper) instructions for navigating the text to get to the answer in exactly the way you modelled in the shared work. Finally they can "swap" instructions to test them.

- If ICT facilities are not available for paired or independent work, you will need to continue working in "whole class" mode for some of this session, demonstrating the route through the text on the big screen (following children's suggestions), but pausing at each stage for children to jot down their own instructions individually on paper or whiteboards. They could then spend further independent time putting these draft instructions into presentation format, adding drawings of appropriate icons, etc.

Plenary

- Feedback some of the instructions written, and test them out on the ICT text in the collective situation. (Perhaps with individual children or pairs coming out to operate the program.). Discuss the various routes suggested through the text, and whether there are in fact better ways of reaching the information required.

Linking reading and writing: Shared writing

Session 4

Text level incorporating some sentence and word level work

- Select from the list generated earlier (or devise) questions which will relate to one of the main sections of the *Volcanoes* ICT text (i.e. *Volcanoes of the World*, *Volcanic Eruptions* or *Volcanoes in History*).

- Start the shared work as in Session 3, demonstrating how to find the answer to a chosen question, but this time concentrating on the information you want, rather than on the route you need to take to find it. Choose questions that require information to be gleaned from multimedia sources, e.g. from one of the video clips, animations or sound bites, as well as from the written text. Again, remember this is still shared reading so involve the children as interactively as

possible, including their joining in the reading of the actual words on screen.

- As shared writing, demonstrate the composition of the "answer" to the chosen question, based on the information obtained from the multimedia sources of the ICT text. Include teaching of the sentence and word level objectives, and remember to model how the information is obtained, selected and sorted, as well as how it is actually written down. You may wish this to include the modelling of a note-making stage, as well as of a short prose "answer".

Group/Independent tasks

- If the necessary ICT facilities are available, e.g. in an ICT suite, ask pairs of children to use the *Volcanoes* program to try to locate the answers to specific questions. They should then write (on paper) appropriate notes and "answers", in exactly the way you modelled in the shared work.

- **AM** If ICT facilities are not available for paired/independent work, you will need to continue working in "whole class" mode for some of this session, demonstrating the location of the required information on the big screen (following children's suggestions), but pausing for children to jot down their own notes on the information obtained on paper or whiteboards. They could then spend further independent time putting these draft notes into the required written format, "answering" the selected question, as you demonstrated earlier. **Activity Master 3** can be used to support this activity if required.

Plenary

- Discuss some of the children's "answers". Ask the writers to describe how they found the information, and from what source, and then ask other children to evaluate the writers' use of the information available. (Did they find/use all the available sources, etc?)

Session 5

- Repeat Session 4, but using questions relating to a different section of the *Volcanoes* ICT text. In actuality, this will make for quite a different session, as the nature of the information provided, and therefore both the location and nature of the "answers" will be quite different.

In this, or the earlier session, the activity can be enlivened by using the character Popo from the ICT text, e.g. phrasing the questions as *We asked Popo why volcanoes* . . . and the answers as *Popo told us that* . . . or *Popo showed us a video of* . . . *which helped us understand that* . . .

Scottish 5–14 Guidelines matching objectives chart for Year 3 (Scottish Level C)

5–14 Strands	Digging for Dinosaurs	Finding Out about Volcanoes	Art for Everyone	How to Make a Rain Gauge	The Shadow of Vesuvius	A Bridge for Nearport	The A–Z of Rocks and Minerals	Look Out!
Talking about experiences, feelings and opinions	✓	✓	✓	✓	✓	✓	✓	✓
Talking about texts	✓	✓	✓	✓	✓	✓	✓	✓

Opportunities should still be taken to encourage pupils to discuss the different texts either as a whole class or in small groups. There is a need at this stage to consider the process of organizing the research and obtaining the necessary information. Pupils should be encouraged to take account of each others' views and be supported in going beyond the simple statement to identify and express reasons and opinions.

5–14 Strands	Digging for Dinosaurs	Finding Out about Volcanoes	Art for Everyone	How to Make a Rain Gauge	The Shadow of Vesuvius	A Bridge for Nearport	The A–Z of Rocks and Minerals	Look Out!
Reading for information	✓	✓	✓	✓	✓	✓	✓	✓
Awareness of genre	✓	✓	✓	✓	✓	✓	✓	✓
Knowledge about language	✓	✓	✓	✓	✓	✓	✓	✓

At this stage, pupils will be helped to identify the sequence of information and experiment with ways of recording. The teacher should continue to support pupils in questioning the nature of the text and how information is likely to be organized. The reading tasks provide varied opportunities for pupils to locate specific information, words and meanings of words, to develop vocabulary and to organize words or information alphabetically. They should understand the main ideas and be able to identify the key points. Pupils will become familiar with the terms and features of non-fiction text as they explore and discuss the different types of text and IT sources.

5–14 Strands	Digging for Dinosaurs	Finding Out about Volcanoes	Art for Everyone	How to Make a Rain Gauge	The Shadow of Vesuvius	A Bridge for Nearport	The A–Z of Rocks and Minerals	Look Out!
Functional writing	✓	✓	✓	✓	✓	✓	✓	✓
Punctuation and structure	✓	✓	✓	✓	✓	✓	✓	✓
Spelling	✓	✓	✓	✓	✓	✓	✓	✓
Handwriting and presentation	✓	✓	✓	✓	✓	✓	✓	✓
Knowledge of language	✓	✓	✓	✓	✓	✓	✓	✓

At this stage, the purpose and audience for the writing are clearly established for each activity, particularly at the planning stages. Teachers should help pupils to make notes, to analyse the text, identify important data and subsequently write reports, letters etc. Conventions such as the simple use of comma and question mark will be discussed and used by pupils in their writing. An awareness of paragraphing will be introduced. Pupils will be encouraged to explore a range of devices for presenting texts and continue to take responsibility for clear handwriting and correct spelling.

High frequency words

Use these lists as an aide-memoire to help check that the "sight recognition" and spelling work has been covered and to ensure all the words are revisited and reviewed if necessary.

Reception year

a
all
am
and
are
at
away
big
can
cat
come
dad
day
dog
for
get
go
going
he
I
in
is
it
like
look
me
mum
my
no
of
on
play
said
see
she
the
they
this
to
up
was
we
went
yes
you

Years 1 to 2

about	just	then
after	last	there
again	laugh	these
an	little	three
another	live(d)	time
as	love	too
back	made	took
ball	make	tree
be	man	two
because	many	us
bed	may	very
been	more	want
boy	much	water
brother	must	way
but	name	were
by	new	what
call(ed)	next	when
came	night	where
can't	not	who
could	now	will
did	off	with
do	old	would
don't	once	your
dig	one	
door	or	■ days of the week
down	our	■ months of the year
first	out	■ numbers to twenty
from	over	■ common colour words
girl	people	■ pupil's name and address
good	push	■ name and address of school
got	pull	
had	put	
half	ran	
has	saw	
have	school	
help	seen	
her	should	
here	sister	
him	so	
his	some	
home	take	
house	than	
how	that	
if	their	
jump	them	

Spotlight on Fact permissions and acknowledgements

Every effort has been made to trace copyright holders and to obtain their permission for the use of copyright material. The author and publishers will gladly receive any information enabling them to rectify any error or omission in subsequent editions.

Digging for Dinosaurs/Big Book 3a (Big Book page numbers in bold)

llustrations: John Batten (cartoon illustrations) pp.6-16 (**6-16**); © HarperCollins*Publishers* pp.1, 3, 4-5, 8BR, 9T, (**1,3,4-5,8,9**) 20BL, 20-21C; Susi Martin pp.2T (**2**)

Photographs: Steve Lumb Photography pp.1, 6, 7, 10, 11TR, 12, 13 (**1,6-7,10-13**)

The publishers wish to thank the following for permission to use photographs:
The Dinosaur Farm Museum for all photographs except Corbis (Kevin Shafer) p4 (**4**), (Richard Cummins) 15T (**15**); Oxford Scientific Films pp.9T,14 (**9,14**),17C,19 ; Mike Everhart, Oceans of Kansas Paleontology p.15B (**15**); AntBits Illustration/Richard Tibbitts p.21

The publishers would like to thank the following for their invaluable help:
The Dinosaur Farm, Military Road, near Brighstone, Isle of Wight PO 30 4PG.
Tel: 01983 740844.
Website: www.wightonline.co.uk/dinosaurfarm

Finding Out about Volcanoes/Big Book 3a

Illustrations: Peter Stevenson (Linden Artists) cartoon character pp.1-23 (**17-32**); HarperCollins*Publishers* p.3,5 (**19,21**) (on screen), 9 (**25**) (on screen), 11B, 14-15, 20BR (**29**) (on screen); Susi Martin p.17 (**26**); Chris Taylor p.20C/BL (**30**), 23; Georgina Meek p.22 (**32**).

Photographs: Steve Lumb Photography pp.2, 4, 5, 6, 7, 8, 9, 10, 16, 18, 19 (**18-24,25,27-28**).

The publishers wish to thank the following for permission to use photographs:
Corbis p.12 (Christie's Images), 13T (Kevin Shafer), 13B (Roger Ressmeyer), 16BL (**25**), 21 (**30**) (Michael S. Yamashita).

Art for Everyone/Big Book 3a

Illustrations: Roger Payne (Linden Artists) p6-7, 8, 14 (**36-38,42**).

The publishers would like to thank the following for permission to use photographs:
Ancient Art & Architecture Collection p.1, 3BL, BR (**33**), 13 main; Ancient Egypt Picture Library p.2T, BR (**32**), 4, 5, 17T (**34-35,45**); Sylvia Cordaiy p.2BL (**32**); The Art Archive p.3T, 10 (**33,40**) (Musée des Arts Africains et Océaniens/ Dagli Orti), p16T/B (**44**) (Museo del Oro, Lima/Dagli Orti), 20-21 (**48-49**) (Musée des Antiquités, St. Germain en Laye/Dagli Orti); Werner Forman Archive pp.5, 11T, 12, 15R, 17B (**35,41,43,45**) (Wallace Collection, London), 19R/L (**47**) (Provincial Museum, Victoria, British Columbia); Still Pictures p9 (**39**) (© Gilles Martin), 11B (**41**) (© Perkins/UNEP), 13 inset (© John Cancalosi); The Hutchison Library p15L/18 (**43,46**) (© Michael MacIntyre); Gianfranco Gorgoni/Courtesy Dia Center for the Arts, New York © The Estate of Robert Smithson/VAGA, New York/DACS, London 2001 p22-23 (**50-51**); Courtney Milne, from The Sacred Earth/www.CourtneyMilne.com p23 (**51**).

How to Make a Rain Gauge/Big Book 3a

Illustrations: John Batten p.11

Photographs: Steve Lumb Photography pp.1, 6, 7, 10, 11R, 12, 13 (**56,57,60-63**)

The publishers would like to thank the following for permission to use photographs:
Corbis pp.2T (Charles & Josette Lenars), 2B (**52**) (Carl & Ann Purcell); PA Photos/Toby Melville p.3 (**53**); Mr. & Mrs. John Short, Winulta, South Australia p.4 (**54**); NASA p.5 (**55**); Wind & Weather, Fort Bragg, California www.windandweather.com p.11T (**61**); Frank Lane Picture Agency pp. 14T (Michael Hollins), C (Ray Bird), BL (Jurgen & Christine Sohns), BR (Chris Demetrion)

The Shadow of Vesuvius/Big book 3b

Illustrations: Peter Bull Art Studio p.2 (maps) (**2**)

The publishers would like to thank the following for permission to use photographs:
Corbis p.1 (Sean Sexton Collection),3,4/5T/B/6BR/7B (**3-7**) (Mimmo Jodice), 8T/10B (**8,10**) (Roger Ressmeyer), 8B,9T/B (**8-9**) (Bettmann), 10T (**10**) (James A. Sugar), 15T (**15**); The Art Archive/Galleria Borghese/Dagli Orti (A) p.6T (**6**); The Art Archive/Bibliothèque des Arts Décoratifs, Paris/Dagli Orti (A) p.6BL (**6**); The Art Archive/ Archaeological Museum, Naples/Dagli Orti (A) p.7T, C (**7**); USGS/Austin Post p.11T (**11**); Private Collection p.11B (**11**); The Art Archive/Hermitage Museum, St. Petersburg/Dagli Orti (A) p.13 (**13**); NASA pp.14,15L (**14,15**).

A Bridge for Nearport/Big Book 3a

Illustrations: Peter Bull Art Studio p.1,8T,12-13,17,19T, 21,23 (**22,26-27,31,35**); Roger Payne (Linden Artists) p2-3,4 (**16-18**).

The publishers would like to thank the following for permission to use photographs:
Collections p.3T/16/18/19B (**17,30,32**) (Brian Shuel), 8 (**22**) (Ashley Cooper), 11 (**25**) (Gordon Hill); Corbis p.5T (**19**) (Nik Wheeler), 7 (**21**) (Macduff Everton), 9 (**23**) (Julian Calder), 13 (**27**) (Marc Garanger), 15T (**29**) (Paul A. Souders), 15C (**29**) (Carl & Ann Purcell), 20 (**33**) (Ecoscene/ Mark Caney), 22 (**34**) (Angelo Hornak); Ray Swarbrick p5B (**19**), Rex Features p6 (**20**) (SIPA Press/Fievez), 10 (**24**) (J. Sutton Hibbert), 15B (**29**) (Peter Price)

The A–Z of Rocks and Minerals/Big Book 3b

Illustrations: Dave Burroughs

Photographs: Steve Lumb Photography p1,3T,3M, 4T,4B, 5M,6T,6M,7T,7B,8T,9T,9B,11B,14T,16B,17M,17B,18T, 18M,19,20M,20B,21B,22,24B (**37-43;46,48,49-52,53**)

The publishers wish to thank the following for permission to use photographs:
Robert Harding p2BL,5B,6B,10T,10B,14B,15T,16T,18B (**36,39,40,44,46-48**); Geo Science Features p2BR,8BL,12B, 21T (**36,42**); Telegraph Colour Library p3B (**37**); Trip Photos p8BR,11T,13,15B,17T,20T,20B,23,24 (**42,45,47, 50,53**); Ancient Art and Architecture Collection p9C,12T (**43**); Collections p20T(**50**).

Look Out!/Big Book 3b

Illustration: Peter Bull Art Studio p15 (**64**)

The publishers wish to thank the following for permission to use photographs and text extracts:
Robert Harding Picture Library (International Stock/© Warren Faidley) p3T (**55**), (© Ian Griffiths) 4C (**56**); Trip Photos p4T (**56**) (H.Rogers), 4B (**56**) (Phototake © Richard T.Nowitz), 8T (**60**) (Australian Picture Library) 9,15 (**61, 64**) (M.Barlow); © BBC Weather Centre p.5 (**57**); Alaska Volcano Observatory, a cooperative program of the United States Geological Survey, the University of Alaska Fairbanks Geophysical Institute, and the Alaska Division Geological and Geophysical Surveys p8B (**60**); Science Photo Library (Astrid & Hanns-Frieder Michler) p10; The Art Archive (Musee des Antiquites, St Germain en Laye/ Dagli Orti) p11T (Museo Nazionale, Taranto/Dagli Orti).